STRATEGIES FOR
IMPROVING
VISUAL LEARNING

STRATEGIES FOR IMPROVING VISUAL LEARNING

A Handbook for the Effective Selection Design, and Use of Visualized Materials

FRANCIS M. DWYER
Senior Research Associate of Education and Coordinator, Office of Instructional Evaluations, University Division of Instructional Services, The Pennsylvania State University, University Park, Pennsylvania.

LEARNING SERVICES
Box 784
STATE COLLEGE, PENNSYLVANIA

ADDITIONAL INSTRUCTIONAL MATERIALS

- **Student's Manual**

- **Instructors's Manual**

- **The Experimental Package**

  The experimental package includes nine visual sequences in filmstrip format, the instructional script, a sample visual sequence—to facilitate audiotaping/synchronization of the script with the visualization, four criterion measures and answers. These materials were employed by the author in the Systematic Program of Evaluation.

Information regarding the above materials is available from Learning Services, P.O. Box 784, State College, Pennsylvania 16801.

CONTENTS

LIST OF TABLES

LIST OF FIGURES

PREFACE

The use of visualized materials (drawings, photographs, film, television, transparencies, charts, computer assisted instruction, programmed instruction, etc.) to complement regular classroom instruction has become a common instructional technique at all levels of education—extending from pre-school activities through graduate school and also into in-service training and development programs. The primary purpose of this text is to emphasize the interrelatedness of variables associated with the effective use of visual materials and to attempt to draw general trends from prior research for the effective design and use of visual media.

The book is intended for those professions whose members actively use or produce visual materials for instructional and/or training purposes. In this respect, it presents the concept of visualized instruction, not as an isolated phenomenon, but as an interrelated constituent process operating at varying levels of complexity—the elements of which acquire significance only in the context in which they are used. In an attempt to provide an integrated and comprehensive treatment of the variables associated with visualized instruction, more than 650 articles have been cited representing the research results and insights of more than 625 researchers from numerous scientific disciplines.

The conclusions obtained from studies in this book indicate that the present methods of selecting and using visual materials for instructional purposes are grossly ineffective and wasteful and that, in many cases, for specific educational objectives visualization of content material is no more effective than the same instruction without visualization. Specifically, the results indicate that the use of visual materials to complement oral/print instruction is not equally effective in all instructional environments. Effectiveness is primarily dependent upon (a) the amount of realistic detail contained in the visualization used; (b) the method by which the visualized instruction is presented to students (externally paced vs. self-paced); (c) student characteristics, i.e., intelligence, prior knowledge in the content area, reading and/or oral comprehension level, etc; (d) the type or level of educational objective to be achieved by the students; (e) the technique used to focus student attention on the essential learning characteristics in the visualized materials, e.g., cues such as questions, arrows, motion, verbal/visual feedback, overt/covert responses, etc.; and (f) the type of test format employed to assess student information acquisition, e.g., for certain types of educational objectives visual tests have been found to provide more valid assessments of the amount of information students acquire by means of visualized instruction.

The book consists of *thirteen* chapters. The first chapter describes the potentials and limitations of visualized instruction with emphasis on the need for practical research. *Chapter 2* presents a general overview of multiple and single channel research and theory as it relates to visualized instruction. *Chapter 3* presents the author's strategy for the experimental evaluation of visualized instruction. In this approach control was exercised over content, presentation format, different types of visualization, criterion measures, objectives, experimental design, and procedures for reporting results. *Chapter 4* summarizes the results of studies investigating the relative effectiveness of three different methods of presenting visualized instruction—slide-audiotape, television, and programmed instruction. *Chapter 5* summarizes studies evaluating externally paced (slide/audiotape and televised) visualized instruction with emphasis on objectives, variables investigated, presentation format, instructional treatments, and results. A summary and the conclusions derived relative to the studies is also presented. *Chapter 6* follows the same format as *Chapter 5*; however, studies evaluating self-paced visualized instruction (programmed instruction and textbook-like materials) are presented and discussed. *Chapter 7* provides a general orientation to the use of color as a variable in visualized instruction. Included in the discussion are the physiological effects of color on learners, color coding, color cueing, information processing, student preferences, and the instructional effects of color. *Chapter 8* describes the general parameters and research results related to cueing as an instructional strategy in visualized instruction; *Chapter 9* presents the results of studies investigating the relative effectiveness with which different cueing strategies facilitated student achievement in a program of systematic evaluation. In *Chapter 10* the importance of the relationship which exists between the results of aptitude-by-treatment interaction (ATI) research and the effective design and use of visualized instruction is emphasized; types of interactions and representative ATI studies are discussed. *Chapter 11* presents empirical results of studies investigating individual difference variables and their affect on students' ability to profit from visualized instruction. *Chapter 12* provides a theoretical justification for visual testing along with a synopsis of the research findings related to visual testing. *Chapter 13* suggests a procedure to be followed for the empirical validation of visual materials for instructional purposes—a procedure that will provide a reasonable basis for selecting the types of visual materials possessing the most beneficial cost-effectiveness relationship in terms of facilitating student achievement of predetermined educational objectives.

1

Potentials and Limitations of Visualized Instruction

LEARNING OBJECTIVES

Upon completion of this chapter the student will be able to:

1. *Explain in writing why oral and printed instruction are not always the most effective techniques for transmitting information.*
2. *Describe what is meant when a visual illustration is considered to be 100 percent realistic to a designated object.*
3. *List six researchers whose writings and research have contributed to the "Realism Theories."*
4. *Construct a visual realism continuum (b&w and color) for visual illustrations in accordance with the "Realism Theories".*
5. *Construct a list containing the major reasons commonly cited as to why visualization should be used to complement oral/print instruction.*
6. *Explain what is meant by "the limitations of visualized instruction."*
7. *Identify and describe the major categories of independent variables inherent in the visual learning environment.*
8. *Describe the kind of practical research that should be conducted on visualized materials.*
9. *State what is meant by variations in the amount of realism in visual materials.*

LECTURE METHOD

The optimal development of man is dependent on his ability to learn and to communicate. Although the most common form of communication is the spoken word, misinterpretations are constantly being encountered when attempts are made by one individual to communicate specific ideas to another individual. The fact that words often fail to communicate precisely the intended messages substantiates the contention that the process of using verbal symbols in the instructional/ communication process is a complicated and often unreliable method of transmitting information—unreliable in the sense that since individuals as entities do not share common experiences, they cannot possess identical meanings for symbolic referents.

The lecture continues to be the primary vehicle for information transmission in education today. For the teacher who has a comprehensive command of the content to be conveyed, a realistic understanding of the types of students in the class, and an exceptional facility with language which would permit a complete transmission of the intended information, the lecture method may be the most efficient technique for facilitating optimum student achievement. However, for most educators the basic lecture is not the most effective technique for transmitting information to students. This fact has been verified repeatedly in experimental situations where students, immediately after receiving an identical lecture, are given a quiz on the information presented. The wide variation of scores achieved on the quiz shows quite conclusively that there are significant differences in the amount of information that is acquired by individuals exposed to identical oral instruction. Figure 1-1 represents a typical classroom and attempts to illustrate what happens when students are exposed to oral instruction.

In Figure 1-1, I_0 represents the information that the teacher wishes to transmit to the students and the symbol $\wedge\!\!\wedge$ is used to represent the oral bits of information (ideas, facts, concepts, etc.) prerequisite to adequate comprehension of I_0. Although all students in the class are receiving identical instruction designed to convey I_0, only a small percentage of the students actually receive the original message with the meaning intended by the teacher. Students receiving the same information acquired a variety of different kinds of messages, I_1, I_2, I_3.

There are a number of different types of variables which can function to impair the effectiveness of oral instruction. For example, each individual who enters into the instructional situation represents a totality of individual differences, i.e., physical, mental, social, etc., and consequently reacts to words, as symbols, in unpredictable ways based on his own experiences, aspirations, and attitudes. Since information presented orally is not always salient or easily interpreted, its effectiveness as a communication medium is primarily dependent on the comprehension level of the learner, that is, his ability to successfully interact with and manipulate the audible symbols which constitute the message.

Figure 1-1. Verbal presentation.

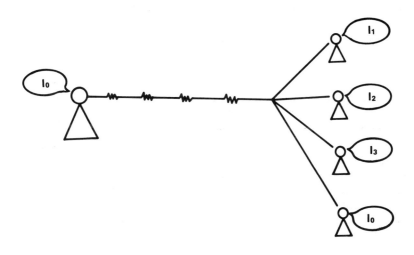

Under these circumstances the clarity and understandability of the audible message depends on the learner possessing an adequate repertoire of concrete symbols in the message area so that he will be able to internalize the audible information within the range of his own past experience. In this sense the quality of what is learned from an oral presentation is dependent on the kinds of responses elicited within the learner by the use of audible symbols. The degree to which an individual has acquired the prerequisite kinds of background knowledge (e.g., terminology, definitions, facts, concepts) in the content area in which he is receiving the instruction determines the relative ease with which he will be able to interact with the audible symbols presented and to profit from the instruction.

In this sense, learning proceeds from the concrete to the abstract. Oral symbols employed by participants in a conversation or in printed communication are not likely to have identical referent associations for the different participants in the conversation. The closeness of the experience referred to by the oral symbols determines the completeness of the communication between two people. For example, if two people have shared the same experience, when they describe it in oral symbols, one will usually understand the other. Consequently, if children and naive learners are to successfully acquire new content material in depth, they must first experience personal interaction and involvement with a rich store of concrete sensory experiences which will serve as background for subsequent understanding and learning. Once these experiences can be related to specific symbols, learners then will be able to talk or communicate effectively with others about such experiences.

THE USE OF VISUAL MATERIALS

The basic question in instruction is how to proceed in order to facilitate the acquisition of essential background information by individuals who have not had the opportunity to benefit from first-hand experience. There is no easy solution to this problem since there are many objects, situations, and processes which are not easily accessible to the student in the classroom. The strategy most commonly practiced to alleviate the need for concrete personal experience and to facilitate student learning has been to integrate visual materials, illustrating relevant content information, into the teaching-learning process to complement both oral and printed instruction.

However, the success by which the visualization of content will facilitate learner acquisition of information is related to the individual's present level of perceptual and associative learning in the content area in which the new learning is to occur. The individual has to have sufficient experience and maturity to realize that the use of visualization is merely an attempt to vicariously represent reality and is an alternate way by which he might expand his understanding of his environment through indirect experiences derived from symbols.

If all visuals were equally effective in facilitating student achievement of all kinds of educational objectives, there would be virtually no problem associated with visualizing instruction. However, this is not the case since there are many different types of visuals, differing in the amount of realistic detail they contain. For example, at the present time educators, when faced with a choice of selecting one type of visualization from an array of available materials, have no way of knowing whether one type of visual is any more effective than another in transmitting certain types of information, nor do they know whether instruction without visuals would be any more effective than the same instruction with visuals. The significance of this dilemma is brought into focus when one becomes cognizant of the tremendous volume of visualized materials currently being produced both privately and commercially. Obviously, this indiscriminate proliferation of visual material is not in itself a guarantee that educational needs will be satisfied. As might be expected, the types of visual materials used for instructional purposes are the ones which have become most readily available. The accessibility of many different kinds of visual materials is increasing instructors' opportunities for making choices, but guidelines for making these choices are not available. At present there is very little evidence for instructors to use when selecting specific types of visuals that will be most effective and efficient in facilitating student achievement of designated learning objectives.

Initially, it would seem that the availability of many different types of visualization is confusing and only makes the selection of *the* most effective visualization impossible. However, it may be possible to identify and select the kinds of visuals which will be most effective in assisting us to communicate identical kinds of messages to populations of students possessing different characteristics. What is urgently needed at the present time is systematic research efforts focused on three basic areas designed to provide data on: (a) what specific individual difference variables in learners actually make a difference in student achievement in the teaching-learning process, (b) which of these individual difference variables interact significantly with different kinds of visualization used to complement oral/printed instruction, and (c) what is the extent of the range within specific individual difference variables that are accommodated by the use of specific types of visualization.

REALISM IN VISUALS

Realism in visual illustrations may be described as the amount of stimuli available to convey information to the student. A visual considered to be one-hundred percent realistic with respect to a designated object could not be differentiated from the object itself because it would possess exactly the same qualities possessed by the object.

The kinds of stimuli characteristics inherent in and presented by different types of visuals differ in kind, amount, and degree of realism. These differences have been found to have differential effects on the achievement level of students (Dwyer, 1972a). The primary problem associated with the relationship which exists between differences in the amounts of realistic stimuli contained in the different types of visual illustrations and the level of student achievement is that the relationship is not linear but curvelinear. Increases in realism, that is, density of instructional stimuli in visualization, and the level of student achievement do not appear to be a straight line function. In other words, at the extremes, illustrations containing too much or too little instructional stimuli affect student achievement adversely. Highly realistic illustrations may contain so many stimuli that the student will experience difficulty in identifying those essential learning cues with which he should interact, and also since there is a great deal of stimuli in the visual he may experience difficulty attending to and interacting with the essential learning cues for the amount of time necessary to achieve understanding of the information being presented. In this case the students' behavior might be described as depicting the scanning syndrome—a constant surveillance of the entire perceptual field while not focusing or interacting with any specific stimuli. At the other extreme are the simple line illustrations containing very little instructional stimuli. Students receiving these illustrations are at a disadvantage since the visuals are limited in the amount of information they are capable of transmitting to the students regardless of how long the students are permitted to view and interact with the illustrations.

THEORETICAL ORIENTATIONS

Man throughout the ages has relied upon different forms of visualization in an attempt to improve his communication. Consequently, it is not unexpected that many educators employ the visual medium in an attempt to improve the teaching-learning process. The use of slides, filmstrips, transparencies, diagrams, photographs, and so forth is becoming an integral part of instructional strategies and course development activities at all levels of instruction. Even textbooks and workbooks contain more illustrative materials than ever before. Of significant importance is the fact that considerably more of the learning content is being contained in the pictorial rather than in the oral or printed element of the instructional materials.

An explanation for the current widespread use of visualization can be traced back to the 1940's and 1950's (Figure 1-2) when a number of theoretical orientations were identified—specifically, the iconicity theory identified by Morris (1946), Dale's (1946) cone of experience, and the sign similarity orientation developed by Carpenter (1953). For convenience these orientations and others are referred to collectively as the realism theories. The basic assumption held by each proponent of the cited realism theories is that learning will be more complete as the number of cues in the learning situation increases. They suggest that an increase in realism in the existing cues in a learning situation increases the probability that learning will be facilitated. (See Chapter 2 for detail on the realism theories.)

According to the writing of Finn (1953), the basic concept around which these realism theories and others have been oriented is the concrete-to-abstract dimension of learning. Finn (1953) and Dale (1946) have recommended that for instructional purposes the more

Figure 1-2. Theoretical orientations referred to collectively as the realism theories.

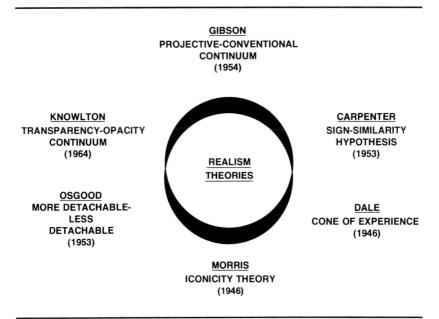

realistic or lifelike the stimulus is, the greater the probability it has for facilitating learning. The writings of several other authors appear to substantiate this basic concept presented by Finn and Dale; for example, Gibson's (1954) projective-conventional continuum, Osgood's (1953) more detachable-less detachable continuum, and Knowlton's (1964) transparency-opacity continuum.

An inspection of the different types of available visual illustrations reveals that they possess recognizable structural characteristics, that is, line drawings, detailed shaded drawings, photographs of three-dimensional models, realistic photographs, and so forth. However, it seems reasonable to assume that for instructional purposes, visual illustrations varying in the amount of realistic detail they contain are not multipurpose in character—some may be more effective than others in facilitating student achievement of different types of educational objectives. For example, Lordahl (1961) and Walker & Bourne (1961) found that as additional irrelevant detail is increased in a visual, student performance decreases.

There is a considerable amount of literature available that contends that an increase in the amount of information presented in a visual will not add proportionally to the amount of learning achieved by the student. Unless there is experimental evidence about how learners will react to variations in the amount of stimuli contained within the many types of visual illustrations, their use may be impeding rather than facilitating the learning process. It may be that for the promotion of specific educational objectives, visuals possessing realistic detail beyond a certain point add very little or actually decrease student learning.

A REALISM CONTINUUM FOR VISUAL ILLUSTRATIONS

Based on the realism theories a realism continuum for instructional materials would extend from the object or situation itself to a very simplified line representation of the object or situation, whereas a realism continuum for still visuals would extend from a realistic photograph of the object or situation to a very simplified black and white line representation (Figure 1-3).

In Figure 1-3, Plate 1 illustrates the different points on such a continuum in accordance with the realism theories. If this continuum is separated into its basic components there would be two realism continuums: one for black and white illustrations (Plate 2) and one for colored illustrations (Plate 3). In each continuum all visuals listed simulate reality at a level closer to direct experience than would abstract symbolism represented by the spoken or printed word; oral and printed symbols possess low degrees of realism because they in no way physically represent the denota. A basic contention implicit in the cited continuums, which have been constructed in compliance with the realism theories, is that different types of visuals function differentially in facilitating student achievement—as the amount of realistic detail in a visual increases so should its potential to improve student achievement.

POPULARITY OF VISUALIZATION

In addition to the theoretical orientation provided by the realism theories which justify the use of visualization for instructional purposes, hundreds of articles and research studies (e.g., Day & Beach, 1950; Allen, 1960; Wendt & Butts, 1962; Chu & Schramm, 1967; Briggs, 1968b; Levie & Dickie, 1973) have also contributed to the popularization of using visualization in the instructional process. In addition, Figure 1-4 presents data distributed by the Socony-Vacuum Oil Company which illustrates the importance attributed to the visual medium in the learning process (Treichler, 1967, p. 15).

Figure 1-3. Points on the visual realism continuum in accordance with the "realism theories."

Simple Line Representations (b & w)	Simple Line Representations (color)	Drawings (detailed and shaded) (b & w)	Drawings (detailed and shaded) (color)	Photographs of a Model (b & w)	Photographs of a Model (color)	Realistic Photographs (b & w)	Realistic Photographs (color)

Low   Efficiency in Facilitating Learning   High

Plate 1. Realism continuum for black and white and colored illustrations.

Simple Line Representations (b & w)	Drawings (detailed and shaded) (b & w)	Photographs of a Model (b & w)	Realistic Photographs (b & w)

Low   Efficiency in Facilitating Learning   High

Plate 2. Realism continuum for black and white illustrations.

Simple Line Representations (color)	Drawings (detailed and shaded) (color)	Photographs of a Model (color)	Realistic Photographs (color)

Low   Efficiency in Facilitating Learning   High

Plate 3. Realism continuum for colored illustrations.

In Figure 1-4, Plate 1 presents a summary of how much information is learned through the various senses. In general, one would agree that we learn more through vision than through hearing and more through hearing than smelling, etc., but seemingly it would be difficult to determine experimentally the percentages of learning attributed to each of the senses. Similarly, with Plate 2, the percentages indicating the amount of information people remember as a result of interacting in different mediums appears logical; however, no supportive evidence has been provided so that the reader can judiciously interpret these percentages. The same holds true for the information provided in Plate 3.

The naive individual glancing at these percentages might be left with the impression that merely integrating visualization into his lectures will automatically facilitate increased learning and retention on the part of the students. In this sense, the reported percentages are misleading. By looking at the data reported there is no way of knowing:

1. How the data was obtained—by survey techniques or experimentation?
2. What kind of learners (men, women, or children) were involved in the derivation of the percentages?
3. How was the instruction presented to the learners—self-paced or externally paced instruction?
4. What kind of learning tasks (educational objectives) were to be achieved by the learners?
5. What kinds of evaluation instruments were employed?
6. What kind of content was presented?

As a result of widespread claims emphasizing the advantages to be obtained through the use of visual media in the teaching-learning process, educators on all levels have been incorporating visualization in their classes in an attempt to improve the reliability of their oral/printed communication and to facilitate increased information acquisition and retention on the part of the learner. Unfortunately, however, in many instances it appears that the visual media are being employed rather indiscriminately with the expectation that since visualization is being used in the classroom, the quality of instruction is being improved, and the students are automatically acquiring more information.

VISUALIZATION RATIONALIZED

Visual illustrations can be used to impart information in almost

Figure 1-4. The effectiveness of visualization.

```
WE LEARN:

 1%    THROUGH TASTE
1½%    THROUGH TOUCH
3½%    THROUGH SMELL
 11%   THROUGH HEARING
 83%   THROUGH SIGHT
```

Plate 1. Learning through the senses.

```
PEOPLE GENERALLY REMEMBER

10%    OF WHAT THEY READ
20%    OF WHAT THEY HEAR
30%    OF WHAT THEY SEE
50%    OF WHAT THEY SEE AND HEAR
70%    OF WHAT THEY SAY AS THEY TALK
90%    OF WHAT THEY SAY AS THEY DO A THING!
```

Plate 2. How we remember.

METHODS OF INSTRUCTION		RECALL 3 HOURS LATER	RECALL 3 DAYS LATER
A	TELLING WHEN USED ALONE	70%	10%
B	SHOWING WHEN USED ALONE	72%	20%
C	WHEN A BLEND OF TELLING AND SHOWING IS USED	85%	65%

Plate 3. Effect of visualization on delayed recall.

---

any subject area, to compress information, and to illustrate the salient parts of an instructional presentation. Users of the visual medium, when asked why they use visualization in their classes, respond with a variety of reasons. Following is a list of some of the characteristics commonly attributed to visuals in explaining their potential value in improving instructional presentations:

1. Increase learner interest, motivation, curiosity, and concentration;
2. Provide important instructional feedback;
3. Provide remedial instruction;
4. Present to the learner the opportunity to perceive an object, process, or situation from a variety of vantage points;
5. Facilitate the retention of information acquisition;
6. Span linguistic barriers;
7. Foster generalizations of responses to new situations;
8. Stimulate discussion and raise questions;
9. Increase reliability of communication, making learning more precise and complete;
10. Bring into the classroom inaccessible processes, events, situations, materials, and phase changes in either space or time;
11. Provide greater flexibility and variety in the organization of instruction;
12. Illustrate, clarify, and reinforce oral and printed communication—quantitative relationships, specific details, abstract concepts, spatial relationships;
13. Summarize the important points in a lesson;
14. Isolate specific instructional characteristics
15. Sharpen powers of observation
16. Guide learners to think carefully and make conclusions;
17. Present relationships, locations of parts, etc.;
18. Facilitate discrimination and identification of relevant cues;
19. Overcome time and distance;
20. Introduce, organize, and present new information;
21. Emphasize and reinforce aural and printed instruction;
22. Function to integrate facts, skills, and judgements.

Bretz (1971, pp. 31-33), in addressing himself to the issue of determining whether or not visualization should be used at all, has identified four criteria which may serve as an aid in determining whether there is a primary need for visualization in a presentation:

1. Is visual recognition and identification of objects, signs, or symbols other than language symbols an objective of the lesson or required for job performance?

2. Is the recognition or recall of a procedure, the physical actions or positions of which are unfamiliar to the learner, one of the objectives of the lesson?
3. Is the understanding of two-dimensional physical or spatial relationships an objective?
4. Is the recall or recognition of the three-dimensional structure of some physical system or object required?

LIMITATIONS OF VISUALIZATION

Since the visualization of instruction has gained popularity, many educators are using visual materials to complement their regular classroom instruction. However, considerable difficulty is being experienced in the identification, selection, and organization of visual materials in order to promote effective classroom instruction. This fact is evidenced by the large number of experimental studies (reviewed by Stickell, 1963; Chu & Schramm, 1967; MacLennan & Reid, 1967) which indicate that the use of visually mediated instruction results in no significant differences in student learning when compared with conventional types of instruction. This seems to indicate that although educators are increasing their use of visualization to complement their instruction many students are still failing to acquire the intended information. One explanation for this hypothesis might be that even though visualization is being integrated into the teaching-learning process, it does not accurately illustrate and/or clarify the content material being presented.

In Figure 1-5 the teacher is using visuals $\boxed{\text{V}}$ to complement the in-

Figure 1-5. Ineffective use of visualization.

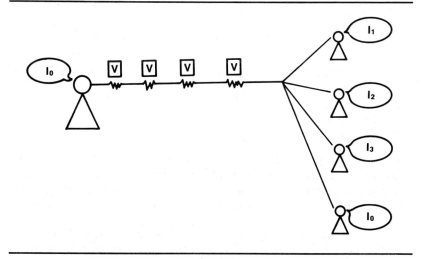

formation being presented to students. However, since many students are receiving messages (I_1, I_2, I_3) different from the one intended by the teacher (I_0), the visuals being used may be nonfunctional in terms of facilitating increased information acquisition on the part of the student. In fact, the percentage of learners acquiring the intended message from the teacher may not be as high as the percentage of students gaining information from the verbal presentation without visuals. Under these circumstances it is reasonable to assume that there is very little correlation between the information the learner is receiving through the oral channel and the information being received through the visual channel. Furthermore, it is also possible that in some instances where efforts to visualize instruction results in the integrations of the wrong type of visualization into the instruction, the visualization itself may interfere with the students' learning causing the presentation with the visualization to be instructionally less effective than the instruction without visualization.

Even when appropriate visualization has been carefully selected to complement oral instruction, insignificant differences in student achievement may still occur because the visualization selected may contain either too little or too much information. Visuals containing small amounts of information may not be adequate to challenge the student and quickly cause him to become disinterested or bored. Visuals containing too much information may tend to overwhelm the student and cause him to withdraw from rather than engage in the necessary kind of interaction with the visualization which will enhance the learning experience. For example, there are a number of options open to a student who is presented with the visualization containing excessive amounts of information. He may survey the stimuli and then deal with them one at a time. Or, he may respond randomly to whatever stimulus happens to present itself into his perceptual field. He may group stimuli into broad categories and respond to categories rather than to individual stimuli themselves. He may also cease activity and simply wait for the stimulus field to dissipate or pass from his awareness. If the student for some reason terminates interaction with the information being presented visually and that information is prerequisite for subsequent learning, visualization tends to impede rather than facilitate learning.

Ideally, the goal to be achieved through research is one which would provide guidelines for the effective use of different types of visuals which in turn would enable educators to design and/or select specific kinds of visualization which would possess the highest degree of predictability for ensuring that a majority of the students, for which the instructional module was designed, would receive the

Figure 1-6. Effective use of visualization.

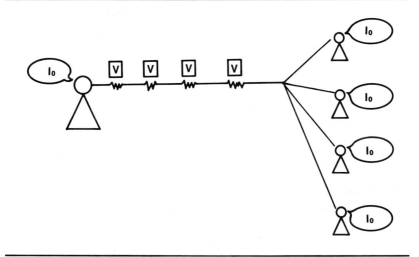

intended message (Figure 1-6). This goal, however, is not easily attainable since there are many different kinds of visual illustrations, i.e., line drawings, detailed, shaded line drawings, drawings of models, realistic photographs (both in b&w and color). And presumably all these different types of visuals are not equally effective in facilitating student achievement of different kinds of educational objectives. Consequently, visuals designed to complement oral and/or verbal instruction not only need to have a high correlation with the message they are attempting to support, but specific types of visuals may need to be designed to provide the learning environment with the prerequisite types of stimuli needed by particular types of students to achieve specific kinds of educational objectives.

COMPLEXITIES ASSOCIATED WITH VISUALIZED INSTRUCTION

There appears to be an infinite number of variables associated with the effective and efficient use of visual media in the teaching-learning process. Gagné (1963), for example, contends that each type of educational objective or type of learning has its own characteristic problems, needs, and peculiarities which must be attended to in order to facilitate maximum learning. In addition to the variables infused into the visual environment by the educational objective dimension, there are several other primary types of variables which need to be considered: (1) differences in the types of visualization which can be used to facilitate student achievement of different types of educational objectives; (2) student individual difference variables, e.g., physical, mental, social, etc.; (3) differences in the type of cueing or attention-gaining techniques employed, and (4) the type of presentation strategy employed in transmitting the information to students, i.e., self-paced or externally paced instruction.

In self-paced instruction the student can proceed through the instructional sequence taking as much time to interact with the instructional content and accompanying visualization as is necessary to achieve adequate comprehension of the content material before proceeding further. However, in the externally paced instruction strategy the student is receiving group type instruction, i.e., film, television, visualized lecture, and has no control over the rate by which the information is transmitted. Under the conditions of externally paced instruction it is assumed that all students see the same thing in a visualized presentation at the same time; it is also assumed that all the students are able to learn at the same rate. Table 1-1 provides a more detailed summary of some of the types of variables influencing student information acquisition from visualized instruction.

DISCUSSION

Currently, a greater concern than ever before is being focused on the proper use of visualized material in the instructional process. Despite the widespread acceptance and use of visual materials for instructional purposes, surprisingly little is known relative to the instructional effectiveness of different types of visual materials, both from the standpoint of how learners react to variations in the amount and kinds of stimulation contained within the various types of visual media and how visuals differing in amounts of realistic detail influence learner achievement of different educational objectives. Usually the production of visual illustrations (media) is based on subjective feelings of the designer about what is best, the accessibility of raw information, the availability of materials, the cost, the attractiveness of the finished product, and the availability of a ready market. Production is based on the assumption that when students view visual illustrations they will all see the same thing and learn in the same way and at the same rate. To date, very little research effort has been devoted to the isolation, identification, classification, and measurement of those essential stimuli characteristics, used both singly and in various combinations in visual illustrations, which are instrumental in significantly increasing student learning.

Hoban (1961, p. 2), in commenting on the instructional use of visualization, has stated, "For approximately forty years, research has

Table 1-1. Types of independent variables in the visual learning environment.

INSTRUCTIONAL VARIABLES: *Behavioral or Content*	STUDENT CHARACTERISTICS: *Educational, Psychological or Physical*	METHOD OF PRESENTATION: *Externally Paced or Self-Paced*	TYPES OF TESTING FORMATS
A. Cueing Techniques	Academic Ability	Audio Recordings	Classification
Color	Age	Charts	Fill-in
Arrows	Aggressiveness	Computer Assisted	Identification
Inserted Questions	Capacity	Instruction	Matching
Oral Instructions	Character traits	Demonstration	Multiple-
B. Mode of Instruction	Creativeness	Drawing	Choice
Inductive	Creativity	Film	Single-Answer
Deductive	Cultural Factors	Oral Presentation	Situation-Type
C. Content Organization	Educational Set	Photographs	True-False
Level (Elementary/	General Aptitude (I.Q.)	Printed Textbooks	Visual Testing
Intermediate/Advanced)	Grade Level	Programmed Booklets	(verbal and
Length	Hearing	Slides	visual)
Difficulty	Interest	Television	
Sequence/Hierarchical	Learner Aptitude and	Textbooks	
Logical Continuity	Abilities	Transparencies	
Meaningfulness	Level of Aspiration	Workbooks	
D. Instructor	Motivation	3-D Objects	
Personality	Motivation to Learn		
Educational	Perception		
Background	Perseverence		
Teaching Experience	Personality Characteristics		
Maturity	Prior Experience and Knowledge		
E. Educational Objectives	Readiness		
Behavioral Learning	Self Concept		
Perceptual Skills	Sex		
Motor Skills	Tolerance for Ambiguity		
Cognitive Learning	Verbal and Conceptual Ability		
Factual Information			
Visual Identification			
Terminology			
Comprehension/Problem			
Solving			
Total Understanding			
Affective Learning			
Values			
Emotions			
Appreciations			
Attitudes			
Understandings			
F. Feedback			
Practice (Overt/			
Covert)			
Reinforcement			
(Verbal/Visual)			
Response Mode			
(Overt/Covert)			
Frequency			
(Variable/Fixed			
Ratio)			
Time (Immediate/			
Delayed)			
G. Type of Visualization			
(B&W/Color)			
Line Drawings			
Detailed Drawings			
Model Photographs			
Realistic Photo-			
graphs			

produced empirical evidence to support the popular truism that children, adolescents, and adults do learn from motion pictures, and other forms of pictorial representation." Although it has been established that visual aids specifically designed to explain, clarify, and reinforce the important concepts in an instructional presentation do facilitate student learning, this fact should not be generalized liberally and interpreted to imply that merely visualizing instruction will automatically improve student achievement. One of the fundamental problems concerning the use of visual illustrations for instructional purposes is the obvious deficiency of information describing the effects of stimuli emitted by various types of visual illustrations. Allen (1960), Hoban (1960), and Dwyer (1972a) have stated that extensive research needs to be conducted on the physical characteristics inherent within pictorial illustrations which lead to increased student learning and to the attainment of specific educational objectives.

Consequently, it seems evident that instructional media which depend primarily upon the visual medium to transmit their messages would profit immeasurably from programmatic research designed to investigate and define the characteristics and variables inherent in the various types of visual illustrations and how they might best be utilized to mediate, at an optimal level, the functions of instruction and learning. Once this research has been completed, justification for the use of various types of visual illustrations in the teaching-learning process will be dependent on their distinctive contributions to specific types of learning.

SUMMARY: MAIN IDEAS

The spoken and written word alone has been found to be an unreliable medium for optimum communication between and among individuals who have had limited opportunities for sharing identical concrete experiences.

Visuals differ in the amount and kind of realistic detail (information and stimuli they may contain).

All types of visual illustrations are not equally effective in facilitating student achievement of all kinds of educational objectives.

The basic assumption held by each proponent of a realism theory is that learning will be more complete as the number of cues in the learning situation increases.

A realism continuum for still visuals based on the realism theories would extend from a realistic photograph (in color) of the object or situation to be depicted to a very simplified black and white line representation.

There are a variety of different reasons commonly cited in justifying the use of visual media in the teaching-learning process.

There appears to be an infinite number of variables associated with the effective and efficient use of visual materials in the educational process.

Visual materials have certain limitations in facilitating student achievement.

Justification for the use of the various types of visual illustrations needs to be based on their distinctive contributions to specific types of learning.

At present there is very little evidence for instructors to use in selecting specific types of visuals which would be both efficient and effective in facilitating student achievement of designated educational objectives.

REVIEW ACTIVITIES

1. List the limitations of oral and printed instruction.
2. Summarize the implications of the realism theories for instructional development activities.
3. List the reasons commonly cited for using visualization in instruction.
4. Identify the theories collectively referred to as the realism theories.
5. Construct a realism continuum for visual illustrations in accordance with the realism theories.
6. Critically analyze the information contained in Figure 1-4 relating to the effectiveness of visualization.
7. Summarize the limitations associated with visualized instruction.
8. List the major categories of independent variables associated with visualized instruction
9. Identify three areas related to visualized instruction which could profit from a program of systematic investigation.

RECOMMENDED READINGS

Carpenter, C. R. 1953. A theoretical orientation for instructional film research. *AV Commun. Rev. 1:* 38-52.

Gibson, J. J. 1954. A theory of pictorial perception. *AV Commun. Rev. 2:* 3-23.
Knowlton, J. Q. 1966. On the definition of "picture." *AV Commun. Rev. 14:* 157-183.

2

Multiple and Single Channel Communication

LEARNING OBJECTIVES

Upon completion of this chapter the student will be able to:

1. *Explain what is meant by channel capacity.*
2. *List the reasons why multiple channel communication is important in visualized instruction.*
3. *Explain the differences between single and multiple channel communication.*
4. *Cite those researchers whose research and writing have made important contributions in support of multiple channel communication.*
5. *Explain in writing what is meant by the sign similarity hypothesis, iconicity theory, and cue summation theory.*
6. *Summarize the major instructional implications resulting from research conducted on the single and multiple channel communication orientations.*
7. *Discuss in writing the contradictory research results as it relates to the instructional effectiveness of single and multiple channel communication.*
8. *Explain how the apparent inconsistency of research results between single and multiple channel communication may, in fact, be actually complementary.*

CHANNEL CAPACITY

Two basic questions generic to the use of visual media in the classroom are: (*a*) does man function as a multiple or single information processing system, and (*b*) is it economically justifiable, in terms of increased student learning, to incur the additional expenses associated with visualizing content material. Although the human learner has shown himself to be highly adaptable in that he can learn from a variety of media techniques and instructional strategies, it is generally agreed that humans are restricted in that they possess a limited information processing capacity, and merely increasing the amount of information presented to learners in an instructional situation will not automatically increase their learning of the content material. This appears to hold true when additional superfluous stimuli is added to one channel or when excessive information inputs are received from two or more channels simultaneously. Apparently, the arbitrary addition of visual stimuli makes it more difficult for learners to identify the essential learning cues from among the more realistic background stimuli. Existing data (Lumsdaine & Gladstone, 1958; Dwyer, 1972a) support the contention that for specific types of educational tasks, increases in student achievement are directly related to increases in instructional stimuli up to a point beyond which if additional stimuli is added the achievement level of the learners either remains constant or deteriorates.

Multiple channel communication is generally considered to involve a continuous simultaneous presentation of information over two or more channnels. The basic idea behind this mode of presentation is that the additional information input through different sensory channels (i.e., sight, sound, touch, etc.) will provide additional stimuli reinforcement which in turn will assist learners in organizing and structuring incoming information, thereby ensuring that more complete learning will occur.

In general, sight and hearing are considered to be the primary senses for information acquisition; consequently, the use of visual materials designed to complement oral/print instruction plays an important role in the teaching process. An example of such an instructional presentation would be one in which the instructor, in discussing the structure and location of the various valves within the human heart, used a series of line drawings to illustrate their structure and their relative location to one another as this same information was being presented orally. In this example, the visual channel is presenting identical or redundant information in an attempt to clarify and reinforce the information being presented via the oral channel.

Speaking on the importance of one channel reinforcing information contained in a different channel, Hsia (1968c, p. 326) has stated that ". . . in dual or multiple channel information processing, dimensionality of information generally increases, and one channel provides cues and clues for the other, provided that the amount of information to be presented has not reached the capacity limit, thereby eliminating probable interference or information jamming. Increase in dimensionality usually results in the increase of information processing.'' The implication of Hsia's statement is that the presentation of information through multiple channels increases the number of available cues for students' interaction. Since the learner has the opportunity to interact with any combination of the available cues to achieve his learning task, the probability increases that he will interact with the appropriate cues prerequisite to achieving the designated learning.

MULTIPLE CHANNEL RESEARCH

Hartman's study (1961a, p. 42) indicates that "redundant information simultaneously presented by the audio and print channels is more effective in producing learning than is the same information in either channel alone." Miller et al. (1957) have discussed the use of multiple channel communication at length and Hartman (1961a), pp. 28-29) has very succinctly expressed their conclusions:

> If one stimulus complex is to be distinguished from another, the subject may use any of a number of cues or stimuli in which the complexes differ to make a discrimination between them, although a single cue is obviously sufficient. Increasing the number of cues increases the likelihood of a single subject's making the correct discrimination over a period of time, and of a higher percentage of subjects making the discrimination simultaneously. The more handles there are, the easier it is to find one particularly suited to a given individual.

Justification for the argument that the presentation of information simultaneously through two or more channels improves student acquisition of information more so than a single channel presentation of the same information alone is evidenced by the literature reviews of Day & Beach (1950) and Hoban & Van Ormer (1950a). The Day & Beach review focused on studies comparing the audio and print channels, while the Hoban & Van Ormer review concentrated on studies primarily related to audio and pictorial comparisons. Hartman (1961a), in reviewing studies in which related material (information) was presented both through single and multiple channels, indicated that the multi-channel format was generally more effective. Table 2-1 provides a sampling of the researchers whose findings may be interpreted as being supportive of the multiple channel orientation.

Table 2-1. Literature supporting the multiple channel communication orientation.

Wise, 1939	Bourne & Haygood, 1959; 1961
McCowan, 1940	Wesley & Barrow, 1959
Goodman, 1942	Fonesca & Kearl, 1960
Dale, 1946	McLuhan, 1960
Morris, 1946	Murray, 1960
Vernon, 1946	Hartman, 1960; 1961a,b; 1963
Hoban, 1949	Adams & Chambers, 1962
Nelson, 1949	Garner, 1962
Day & Beach, 1950	Gropper, 1962; 1963; 1966
Gagné & Baker, 1950	Ketcham & Heath, 1962
Hoban & Van Ormer, 1950	Wittich & Schuller, 1962
Nelson & Moll, 1950	Knowlton, 1964
Arnoult, 1953	Twyford et al., 1964
Carpenter, 1953	Lumsdaine & May, 1965
Finn, 1953	Conway, 1967
Kale & Grosslight 1955	Rohwer et al., 1967
Kopstein & Roshal, 1954	Severin, 1967a, b, c, d
Osgood, 1953	Shepard, 1967
Mowbray, 1953; 1954	Cole et al., 1968
Gibson, 1954	Hsia, 1968a, b
Bricker, 1955	Perrin, 1969
Nelson & VanderMeer, 1955	Baker, 1970
Webb & Walton, 1956	Galfo, 1970
McCormick, 1957	Loveless, Brebner & Hamilton, 1970
Bousfield et al., 1957	Travers & Alverado, 1970
Rappaport, 1957	Menne & Menne, 1972
Williams, Paul & Ogilvie, 1957	Strang, 1973
May & Lumsdaine, 1958	Donahue, 1976

Hoban (1949, p. 9), in summarizing the instructional value of increasing the number of learning cues and/or the amount of realistic detail contained in a visualized presentation, stated:

> . . . it becomes increasingly clear that the power of any medium of communication to provoke audience reaction is determined by the richness of the symbols, or perceptual and conceptual cues employed in the medium. The more cues to meaning that are included, i.e., the greater the variety of relatedness of the symbols used, the greater the response of the audience to the medium, other things being equal.

The implication which may be derived from these citations may be interpreted as meaning that in multiple channel communication redundancy or repetition of the message content is a very viable factor in improving the quality of the communicative act. Garner's research (1962, p. 135) substantiates the value of having the opportunity to be able to receive increased dimensionality of information through two or more channels and indicates that in many instances for adequate learning to occur "a simple channel capacity concept is clearly inappropriate. . . ."

MULTIPLE CHANNEL COMMUNICATION THEORY

A number of theoretical orientations have evolved in support of the multiple channel communication theory. Dale's book (1946. p. 37) presents what he refers to as the cone of experience which represents experience ordered from the most abstract to the most concrete, the implication being that the more realistic or lifelike the stimulus is, the greater probability it has for facilitating learning. Wittich and Schuller (1962, p. 22) have also said, "Ideally, learners should have available combinations of audiovisual experiences which reinforce one another if we are to provide the most efficient paths possible for the mastery of understandings and concepts." Similarly, Carpenter (1953, p. 41) has presented what he called the sign similarity hypothesis which states that:

> . . . films whose signals, signs, and symbols have high degrees of similarity ("iconicity") to the objects and situation which they represent will be more effective for most instructional purposes than films whose signals, signs, and symbols have low degrees of "iconicity."

Carpenter's sign similarity hypothesis probably is based on the iconicity theory identified by Morris (1946) in which he defines iconicity as the degree of similarity a symbol has to the object or situation it denotes. For example, a motion picture of a specific event may be described as being highly iconic, whereas a pencil sketch of the same event may be described as being of low iconicity. Closely associated with the iconicity theory is the stimulus generalization theory (McGeogh & Irion, 1952; Hartman, 1961a), the primary contention of which is that increases in learning will occur as the testing mode approximates the mode in which the information was presented to the learner. That is, the effectiveness of instruction presented to students by means of both the oral and visual channels might most appropriately be measured by employing criterion measures assessing the contributions of both the oral and visual modes of instruction. For example, instruction presented via a film (visual modality) and evaluated via the conventional technique (print—pencil and paper) would probably not provide an accurate representation of the total amount of learning that has occurred—at least it would not provide a valid assessment of the contribution of the total amount of learning achieved through the visual medium. A number of educational researchers (Lefkowith, 1955a,b; Hartman, 1961b; Miller et al., 1957) have indicated that a more valid assessment of the amount of learning that has been achieved by the students would be obtained if researchers would design and employ criterion tests constructed to measure learning in the format (channel) in which it was initially presented to students.

Closely related to these cited orientations is the cue summation theory which predicts that the learning of discriminations is increased as the number of available cues or stimuli is increased in the learning situation. For convenience in categorization, the above cited theoretical orientations, along with the contributions of Knowlton (1964, transparency-opacity continuum) and Gibson (1954, projective-conventional continuum) are referred to collectively by the author as the realism theories.

SINGLE CHANNEL COMMUNICATION

There are limits to the amount of information a learner can process. Therefore, it is necessary that the information to be transmitted is appropriately limited prior to transmission in order to reduce the processing demands made upon the learner. It is generally agreed that learners entering an instructional situation in which they encounter novel content material have limited discriminative capacities (Frick, 1953; Miller, 1956) which seriously restrict their information processing rates. Consequently, as the number of stimuli characteristics are increased in a learning situation, severe limitations may be imposed on the information processing capabilities of the learners and also on their ability to isolate relevant learning attributes in the instructional presentation. Walker & Bourne (1961), Hunt (1962), and Dwyer (1972a) found that as the number of irrelevant stimuli dimensions increase in the learning situation, the number of errors committed by the learners also increase.

Simplification or precompression of information prior to presentation to learners increases their achievement of the content material (Dwyer, 1972a). Since all incoming stimuli must be coded prior to being received by the central nervous system, it would seem reasonable for educators to reduce both irrelevant and superfluous information contained in both verbal and visual stimuli prior to their presentation to students. By reducing unnecessary information from reaching the student, the first step in the coding process is implemented and the learner is spared from having to discriminate the relevant from the irrelevant. Since the essential learning cues would be presented to learners in a readily identifiable coded format, optimum information processing would be facilitated. The advantages of this strategy can quickly be appreciated. However, Gagné (1970a) has indicated that the use of reality-oriented visualization can be important if the learner will eventually be required to generalize from his instructional presentation to a reality-oriented situation. His implication is that information can be precompressed or simplified to the point where a stimulus deprived visual is the result, and learners will not be able to transfer their subsequent learning to realistic situations, and, in addition, the learners' generalizability of the information may be significantly impaired. An example of this type of situation can be illustrated in the studies conducted by the author (Dwyer, 1972a) in which students who received their instruction on the human heart complemented via line drawings were rather unsuccessful in recalling this information when the testing situation involved their interaction with a more realistic detailed, shaded drawing of the human heart.

SINGLE CHANNEL THEORY AND RESEARCH

There exist both theory and research which suggest that the basic assumptions underlying the realism theories—that the bimodal presentation of information and/or the systematic procedure of increasing the amount of realistic detail in existing cues in a single channel presentation will increase learner acquisition of information—while plausible, do not adequately fit theoretical models proposed by other researchers also concerned with improving the effectiveness of the communication process. The fact that the perceptual system generally functions as a single channel system and that the central nervous system has a limited information processing capacity has been well documented. Research has provided evidence that when audio and visual/print information is presented to students simultaneously the audio channel suffers more from the stimuli competition than either the pictorial or print channels (Mowbray, 1952, 1953, 1954; Klemmer, 1956, 1958; Bulgarella & Archer, 1962; Lockhard & Sidowski, 1961; Williams & Derks, 1963; Hinz, 1969; Koen, 1969).

Hsia (1971, p. 58) has stated, "The information processing capacity for any organism is limited mainly by physiological factors. Of fundamental importance in communication is the limited capacity of the central nervous system and the auditory and visual information processing modalities." For example, the channel capacity of both the auditory and optic nerves for transmitting information far exceeds the capacity of the central nervous system to process the information.

Carpenter (1953, p. 43) in addressing the channel capacity issue has indicated that:

> . . . there are definable limits to the amount of content which can be channeled through a sound motion picture, i.e., through the visual and auditory modalities of perception; and there are limits to the capacities of individuals for reacting to, imprinting, and retaining the information or content.

Hartman (1961b, p. 255) has also expressed concern about the process of merely increasing the number of cues in a learning situation and/or the number of channels through which information is presented to learners in the hope that greater learning will occur. He indicated that:

> A common practice among multiple channel communicators has been to fill the channels, especially the pictorial, with as much information as possible. The obvious expectation is for additional communication to result from the additional information. However, the probability of interference resulting from the additional cues is very high. The hoped-for enhanced communication resulting from a summation of cues occurs only under special conditions. Most of the added cues in the mass media possess a large number of extraneous cognitive associations. The possibility that these associations will interfere with one another is probably greater than that they will facilitate learning.

Miller et al. (1957), in discussing the implications of the realism theories for educational practice, have indicated that it would be a mistake to assume that merely adding one cue to another or merely increasing the realistic appearance of existing cues would increase learning by a linear increment. Jacobson (1950, 1951) and Quastler & Wulff (1955) support this point of view and state that the brain is capable of receiving and processing only minute proportions of the available information, considerably less than its hypothesized theoretical capacity. Livingstone's research (1958, 1959, 1962) supports the contention that receptor sensitivity to stimuli may be reduced or inhibited by processess of the central nervous system. This concept—that the brain only is allowed to receive a portion of the information originally perceived—has significant implications for both producers and users of instructional materials who intend that their utilization of technology in the teaching-learning process will improve learner acquisition of information.

Broadbent (1958, 1965) has explained that the reduction of learning which occurs when bimodal presentations of information are utilized in the teaching-learning process is a direct result of a filtering process occurring in the central nervous sytem. Apparently, while the central nervous system is transmitting information received from the senses to the brain, there also is a filtering process occurring simultaneously which functions to edit and reduce the realistic and/or superfluous qualities of stimuli, thereby permitting only the essential or basic characteristics to attain active reception in the brain. Similarly, research conducted by Hernandez-Peon and his associates (1956; 1961) has led to the hypothesis known as the Hernandez-Peon Effect which contends that information being received and processed via one sensory modality results in a partial block to the reception of instructional stimuli being transmitted through other sensory modalities. Consequently, regardless of the amount of information the senses are capable of receiving and transmitting to the central nervous system, only limited amounts are ever received in the brain.

Broadbent (1958) also contends that the perceptual system holds at any given time information being received from only one sensory modality, i.e., information from only one source may gain access to the processing centers of the brain at any given time, and additional stimulus inputs are temporarily stored. If after this momentary storage period, the stimuli do not gain access to the infromation processing center, their information is not retained. If this is the case, in a multi-channel presentation the learner is confronted with the problem of switching from one channel to the other; thus, his learning is dependent upon how successfully he can alternate between channels. Support for the existence of a "hypothesized filter" which monitors the information flow from the senses to the central nervous system can be derived directly or interpreted indirectly from the data and writings provided by a number of prominent researchers (Shannon & Weaver, 1949; Pollack, 1953; Cherry, 1953; Spaulding, 1956; Broadbent, 1956, 1957b, 1958, 1965).

In addition to the research cited in the previous section, there is extensive literature and experimental data which can be cited as either providing direct support for or results which can be interpreted as supporting the position that single channel communication can be as effective as multiple channel communication. Table 2-2 provides a sampling of the researchers whose findings may be interpreted as being supportive of the single channel information processing orientation.

An interpretation of the data provided by the proponents of the single channel communication system would seem to support the contention that additional cues—provided by the use of two or more information channels simultaneously—or excessively realistic cues within a single channel may be distracting or even evoke responses

Table 2-2.   Literature supporting the single channel communication orientation.

Shannon & Weaver, 1949	Hernandez-Peon et al., 1956
Jacobson, 1950; 1951	Hernandez-Peon, 1961
VanderMeer, 1950a	Walker & Bourne, 1961
Frick, 1953	Hunt, 1962
Pollack, 1953	Feigenbaum & Simon, 1963
Attneave, 1954; 1959	Van Mondfrans & Travers, 1964
Cherry, 1953	Evans, 1964
Grosslight & McIntyre, 1955	Travers, 1964, 1967, 1970
Quastler & Wulff, 1955	Travers et al., 1964; 1965; 1966
Broadbent, 1956; 1957a,b; 1958; 1965	Herman, 1965
Miller, 1956	Hebb, 1966
Spaulding, 1956	Welford, 1968
Davis, 1957	Anderson, 1970
Rappaport, 1957	Clark, 1969
Livingstone, 1958; 1959; 1962	Corballis & Raeburn, 1970
Beach, 1960	Chan, Travers & Van Mondfrans, 1970
Glasgow, 1961	

in opposition to the desired types of learning. Consequently, under some circumstances multiple channel information input may be detrimental to student information acqusition. Furthermore, information presented via two or more channels simultaneously requires that the learner alternate his attention from one channel to the other and back again, and this fluctuation of attention is detrimental to optimum student learning. Travers et al. (1964, p. 1.19) have stated that, "Merely confronting a person with stimuli identical to those emitted by the real environment is no guarantee that useful information will be retained."

In further commentary regarding the use of the realism theories as a guide in the use and production of instructional materials, Travers (1964, p. 380) concluded:

> . . . the emphasis on "realism" found in books on the design and use of audiovisual materials is the worship of a false god. The nervous system is not effective in dealing with the environment in all its wealth of detail. It handles it by simplifying it, and it is through such simplified inputs and the resulting perceptions and conceptualizations that man learns to cope with a very complex universe. Through providing simplified presentations of the environment in learning situations, the teacher can be sure that the compression process is effective. When this is done, the separation of the important elements in the message from the less important elements and the noise in the message is not up to the learner who may fail to separate them. The separation is made for him.

Travers et al. (1964, p. 1.18) feel that the presentation of much instructional material provides unnecessary detail, and that the real objective of instruction is ". . . not so much to bring the pupil into close touch with reality, but to help the learner become more effective in dealing with reality." This they contend can be done very effectively via the use of symbols. In summarizing their position Travers et al. (1964, p. 2.110) contend ". . . the evidence points to the conclusion that simplification results in improved learning. This seems to be generally true regardless of the nature of the presentation—whether it is pictorial or verbal." Attneave (1954) had conducted research guided by the hypothesis that one function of the perceptual machinery was to reduce redundant stimulation and to encode incoming information so that only the essentials travel through the central nervous system to the brain. In support of his hypothesis, he indicates that lines bordering objects provide the essence of the information to be conveyed by accentuating boundaries and regions of high contrast. This, he feels accounts for the effectiveness of cartoons and stick drawings as conveyors of information. This implies that those visuals closely representing line drawings and containing the essential information to be transmitted would be more efficient in facilitating learning than more detailed types of illustrations, which would have to be coded initially by the central nervous system before being transmitted. Studies by Ryan & Schwartz, (1956), Hockberg, (1962) and Guckin (1966) may be cited in support of this position.

In essence, when information is edited into a cartoon format or into any symbolic representation less realistic than reality, we may say that information compression has occurred. Generally this can be taken to mean that superfluous or redundant detail has been eliminated, and only the essentials of the intended communication remain. Presumably, compression of information facilitates more efficient and more complete processing of the remaining information in the central nervous system. Travers (1964, p. 380) discusses information compression in the following manner:

> Information compression is a natural process which permits a limited capacity nervous system to handle a very complex environment. Without the compression of inputs of information, the nervous system would be overwhelmed. The effective transmission of information in educational situations involves the use of communications which are readily and effectively compressed by the receiver. How can one be sure that a particular communication can be readily compressed? One can never be sure about this, so the safest procedure for effective communication appears to be to compress the material before it is transmitted. Most teachers generally do this without recognizing what it involves. Every classroom provides illustrations of pre-compressed information being transmitted to the learners. One of the most familiar of these is the line drawing on the blackboard which appears to derive its effectiveness from the fact that it presents those aspects of a visual display which carry the most information and suppresses other aspects.

Although information compression appears to be a reliable instructional consideration in the design of instructional messages, it also has limitations which should be acknowledged. In many cases information may be edited (compressed) far below the information processing capacity of the central nervous system. Under these circumstances the learner would be exposed to less information than he is capable of handling. It is also possible to edit information to the point where the learner is capable of acquiring the essentials of the transmission but because of the lack of additional or supportive detail difficulty will be experienced in generalizing to reality from the edited symbolic information.

The following citations by Travers and his colleagues summarizing the results of empirical research, relating to the learning of redundant and non-redundant material presented through sensory modalities, seemingly captures the feelings of the proponents of the single channel communication orientation regarding the instructional effectiveness of the multi-model presentation strategies.

1. . . . no advantage is achieved by transmitting redundant information simultaneously through both the auditory and the visual modality, except where unusually high speeds of transmission are involved (Travers, 1964, p. 378).
2. Studies conducted at the University of Utah which have attempted to repeat earlier work [which provided data showing that the simultaneous transmission of information through more than one sensory modality improves learning] with the introduction of proper controls have failed to demonstrate any particular advantage for the transmission of redundant information through more than one sensory channel (Travers et al., 1964, p. 6.26).
3. These studies indicate, clearly and unequivocally, that the transmission of information through more than one sense modality provides no advantage . . . (Travers et al., 1966, p. 264).
4. No advantage was found in providing redundant information through visual and auditory modalities as compared with the transmission of information through the visual modality alone (Travers et al., 1966, p. 53).

DISCUSSION

A note of caution must be expressed in generalizing these research findings associated with the single channel communication orientation to practical teaching-learning situations. A considerable amount of the data has been generated utilizing non-meaningful learning tasks in which two different messages were being presented simultaneously to students. Hartman (1961b, pp. 249-250) has pointed out that Broadbent's hypothesis regarding the existence of a "filter" in the central nervous system is based on research data obtained from presenting unrelated content material to learners simultaneously through two or more modalities. Travers et al. (1964, pp. 7.39-7.40), in commenting on the experimental research conducted by Broadbent, contends that the data:

> . . . interpret most clearly those phenomena in which nonredundant information is transmitted through two sensory channels simultaneously for a period of a few seconds. From such data one can infer to only a limited extent what will happen when information is transmitted through multiple sensory channels over a more extended period.

Teachers in their classes when using visual materials to complement their regular instruction are doing so in an attempt to facilitate increased student achievement of the information being presented. The visualization employed is usually redundant or closely related so that it will have the maximum opportunity of conveying clearly the intended message. It would certainly seem to be ineffective to transmit unrelated or contradictory information to students simultaneously through two or more channels. A teacher in discussing geometric theorems orally in class would not at the same time be showing slides illustrating the process of photosynthesis in plants. It is understandable that under these circumstances the individual would attend primarily to one or the other of the messages while disregarding the other.

In essence, there is a considerable amount of data supporting the single channel communication hypothesis; however, a great deal of this evidence has been obtained from studies where unrelated or contradictory stimuli was presented to learners and where the type of learning measured did not resemble that which students in a conventional classroom are expected to achieve. Consequently, the question which remains to be more systematically explored is whether or not man functions as a single channel communication system when redundant and/or related information is presented simultaneously through two or more channels. Also needed is systematic research in which the type of learning to be measured is typical of what is usually expected in conventional instruction.

SUMMARY: MAIN IDEAS

The arbitrary addition of stimuli in visuals makes it difficult for learners to identify the essential learning cues from among the more realistic background stimuli.

Multiple channel communication is generally considered to involve a continuous simultaneous presentation of information through two or more channels.

The channel capacity of both the auditory and optic nerves for transmitting information far exceeds the capacity of the central nervous system to process the information.

There is substantial research and literature supporting both the multiple and single channel communication orientations.

There are both instructional advantages and disadvantages associated with information compression.

Caution must be expressed in generalizing the research findings associated with the single channel communication orientation to practical teaching-learning situations.

The basic assumption held by each proponent of the realism theories is that learning will be more complete as the number of cues in the learning situation increases.

For visualization to have maximum effectiveness in complementing oral/print instruction, it should be specifically designed to improve learning and should be presented simultaneously with the information it has been designed to illustrate and clarify.

REVIEW ACTIVITIES

1. Discuss the relationship that exists between channel capacity and the amount of instructional stimuli that can exist in different types of visual illustrations.
2. Summarize the basic research findings which tend to support the multiple channel communication orientation.
3. Identify the theoretical orientations commonly cited as being supportive of the multiple channel communication orientation.
4. Describe the basic differences among the proponents of the multiple and single channel communication orientations.
5. Summarize the basic research findings which tend to support the single channel communication orientation.
6. Discuss the instructional advantages and disadvantages related to information compression.

SMALL GROUP OR INDIVIDUAL OPTIONAL ACTIVITIES

1. From the original articles cited in Table 2-1 construct an annotated bibliography of the research articles and literature supporting the multiple channel communication orientation. Use the following criteria in summarizing each research study: (*a*) a state-

ment identifying the primary objective(s) of the study; (*b*) number and grade level of students involved in the study; (*c*) variables investigated in the study; (*d*) the instructional format used to present the content to the students; (*e*) the kinds of visualized materials employed in each study; (*f*) type of experimental design and/or statistical procedures employed, and (*g*) general conclusions of the study. List the generalizations which can be made as a result of this review.

2. From the original articles cited in Table 2-2 construct an annotated bibliography of the research articles and literature supporting the single channel communication orientation. Follow the same procedure outlined in the activity cited above.

RECOMMENDED READINGS

Hartman, F. R. 1961. Recognition learning under multiple channel presentation and testing conditions. *AV Commun. Rev. 9:* 24-43.

Hsia, H. J. 1971. The information processing capacity of modality and channel performance. *AV Commun. Rev. 19:* 51-75.

Severin, W. 1967. The effectiveness of relevant pictures in multiple channel communication. *AV Commun. Rev. 15:* 386-401.

3

A Strategy for Experimental Evaluation

LEARNING OBJECTIVES

Upon completion of this chapter the student will be able to:

1. *Explain why some media related research studies provide significant results while others investigating similar problems produce insignificant results.*
2. *List the major questions which need to be answered relative to the use of visual materials in the classroom.*
3. *Summarize how it might be possible to reduce and/or control the identified deficiencies in media research.*
4. *Explain why it is necessary for educators to be aware of the concept of sequencing educational tasks implied in a hierarchy of educational objectives.*
5. *Draw a diagram explaining the "phases" inherent in a learning hierarchy.*
6. *Explain the differences among redundant, related, unrelated, and contradictory information.*
7. *Describe the kinds of educational tasks measured by the terminology, identification, drawing, comprehension, and total criterion tests used by the author and his associates.*
8. *Arrange the educational tasks measured by the terminology, identification, drawing, and comprehension tests into a learning hierarchy and explain the rationale for such an arrangement.*
9. *List the eight types of visualization employed in the program of systematic evaluation conducted by the author and his associates.*

MEDIA RELATED RESEARCH

There exist experimental research and plausible theory justifying both the single and multiple channel communication orientations as usable instructional strategies for increasing student learning. However, the positions seem to be contradictory. While it appears that the multi-modal approach to presenting information plays an important role in achieving a wide range of educational goals in the teaching-learning process, it also appears that this approach has certain limitations which under specific circumstances makes its instructional impact no more effective than instruction presented in a single channel presentation format. With the existence of such contradictory theoretical orientations it is understandable why much of the data generated by media researchers is inconclusive and/or uninterpretable. It also provides a partial explanation for the fact that when significant differences were obtained in empirical studies, these results were seldom in agreement with other research findings investigating similar problems (Hoban & Van Ormer, 1950a,b; Silverman, 1958; Davis, 1962; Wendt & Butts, 1962; Stickell, 1963; Briggs, 1968; Edling, 1968). Therefore, it is understandable why producers and users of visualized instructional materials are more concerned with the aesthetic and artistic characteristics of the media than they are with their concern for promoting more effective communication.

EXPERIMENTAL ORIENTATION

It has been stated rather convincingly in previous sections that the use of visualization to complement regular classroom instruction can achieve a multitude of purposes and that this effectiveness of visualization to complement oral/print instruction is intimately and directly related to a variety of different types of variables. If a sound understanding relative to the effective and efficient use of visual materials for instructional purposes is to result, answers to specific questions need to be resolved. In order to initiate such an investigation, the author developed a list of questions which provided a general orientation for a program of systematic evaluation of variables associated with the effective and practical use of visualization in the teaching-learning process. These questions are:

1. Are all types of visual materials (illustrations) equally effective in facilitating student achievement of all types of educational objectives?

2. Are identical types of visual illustrations equally effective in complementing both oral and printed instruction?
3. Is the realism continuum for visual illustrations an appropriate and reliable predictor of instructional effectiveness when it is used to complement oral and printed instruction, or are there points on the realism continuum at which further increases of realism in visual illustrations fail to produce significant differences in student achievement of specific educational objectives?
4. Will the use of visual illustrations that are specifically designed to complement oral and printed instruction automatically improve student achievement?
5. Is color in visuals an important instructional variable in facilitating student achievement of specific objectives?
6. Will the use of visuals to complement oral/print instruction affect delayed retention of the content material?
7. Are student perceptions of the value of different types of visual illustrations a valid assessment of the instructional effectiveness of the visuals?
8. Does the method in which visuals are presented to students, e.g., slides/audiotape, television, programmed instruction, etc., affect the ability of the visuals to facilitate achievement of different educational objectives?
9. Does the amount of time students are permitted to interact with visualized instruction affect their level of achievement of different educational objectives?
10. Are identical types of visual illustrations equally effective for all education levels, or do the different types of visual illustrations possess differing degrees of instructional effectiveness for students at different educational levels and for different educational objectives?
11. Are different cueing techniques (motion, inserted questions, knowledge of specific learning objectives, etc.) equally effective in complementing visualized instruction?
12. Can oral and printed questions be used to improve the instructional effectiveness of visualized instruction?
13. Do boys and girls in the same grade level (high school) learn equally well from the same types of visual illustrations on tests designed to measure achievement of different educational objectives?
14. Is there only one visual learning continuum representing instructional effectiveness of visuals for complementing both oral and printed instruction?

15. Can student achievement of different educational objectives be improved by increasing the size of the visual illustrations that are used to complement oral instruction?
16. How does a student's entering behavior (prior knowledge in a content area) influence his ability to profit from visualized instruction?
17. What effect do specific individual difference variables (intelligence, reading comprehension, educational level, etc.) have on students' ability to profit from different types of visualization?
18. What kinds of visual illustrations—in what patterns, combinations, and sequences—provide the best stimulus conditions for maximum achievement of specific kinds of educational objectives?
19. How does the type of reinforcement (printed vs. visual) that students receive in progressing through an instructional module affect their level of achievement of different kinds of educational objectives?
20. What specific individual difference variables interact disordinally with different types of visual illustrations for specific educational objectives?

CRITICISMS OF MEDIA RELATED RESEARCH

Along with the complications introduced in media research by the apparent contradictory nature of the single and multiple channel communication orientations, a number of other criticisms have been identified which also tend to further complicate data interpretation and frustrate any attempts to derive broad generalizations useful to practitioners in their classroom use of visual media. Following is a list of some of the most common criticisms associated with media research.

1. Many studies have obvious weaknesses in experimental design, i.e., lack of randomization of students, vagaries in sampling, inadequate numbers of students in treatment groups, lack of tests of significance and probability statements, absence of any control factors.
2. A considerable number of media related studies which have been reported are without any hypotheses or predictions based on theory.
3. The content material being presented experimentally in media related studies has been restricted in that it is far removed from that which is currently being taught in schools (nonsense

syllables, digits, letters, etc.); consequently, the results have had little practical significance to educators involved in applications in the classroom.

4. The difficulty and meaningfulness of the content material (in terms of the kinds of educational tasks to be achieved by the students) used in the experimental treatments has not been specified precisely.

5. In many media related studies content to be taught has not been pretested to determine where visualization of the content is appropriate; in other words, a considerable amount of visualization used in media related experiments has not been specifically designed to complement the content material to be presented.

6. In media related research the relationship that exists between the content information in each channel (visual, oral, print) to the information in the other channel(s) needs to be specified precisely.

7. The method of presenting the visualization has not been described precisely, and in many cases the content material which was presented by one method (for example, slide/audiotape vs. film) has not been equivalent to the content material presented by a second method.

8. The precise purposes of visualization in many mediated studies has not been stated.

9. The amount of realistic detail (line drawings, detailed, line drawings, photographs) contained in visualization designed to complement oral/print instruction in media research has not been described precisely so that data from different studies can be compared.

10. Mediated instruction normally is evaluated via printed criterion items. To properly assess the instructional contribution of visualization, a significant proportion of the evaluation battery should reflect all the channels (visual, print, oral, etc.) used by the learner to acquire the information.

11. Many of the criterion tests currently being used to measure achievement are global in nature attempting to measure the students' total learning, rather than being designed to measure media's contribution to students' achievement of specific kinds of educational objectives. In using the global criterion test to measure student achievement of different types of objectives, the variances are pooled (for the different objectives) thereby concealing any effects that media may have in

facilitating student achievement of specific educational objectives.

12. Many of the criterion measures used to assess student information acquisition may be invalid or unreliable—reliability and validity coefficients are very infrequently reported in media related research.

13. The type of test items used to measure student information acquisition has not been adequately specified. This is important because item format can influence the student's level of achievement; i.e., a fill-in type test in which the student is required to provide the correct word is more difficult than a recognition type multiple-choice type test in which the student is required to select the correct response from an array of possible alternatives.

14. Researchers have failed to specify the time-span (seconds, minutes, hours, etc.) between the presentation of the information to the students and the testing.

15. The amount of time students have been permitted to view and interact with the instructional presentations has not been adequately controlled and/or reported.

16. Media researchers in preparing their research for publication have omitted essential characteristics of their studies which prevents exact replication, i.e., time of treatment, age or grade level of students, mean intelligence of students, prior knowledge in the content area, etc.

17. Very few of the media related studies have been replicated to establish confidence in the results.

18. The diversity of interests and a lack of a common usable terminology used by media researchers has compounded the misinterpretation of many media related studies and restricted their generalizability.

19. To a certain extent the results of experiments have been determined by the statistical techniques used—a liberal test providing one interpretation of the results, a conservative statistic another.

REDUCING EXPERIMENTAL CRITICISMS

Acknowledging that a number of valid criticisms have been leveled at media research, the author initiated a number of appropriate measures to reduce and control, as much as possible, deficiencies identified in prior media research. For example, specific types of educational objectives to be achieved were identified; a specific content area which permitted meaningful learning to occur was selected; four individual criterion tests measuring student achievement of different types of educational objectives were constructed; eight complete visualized experimental treatments were assembled—each containing visualization possessing varying amounts of realistic detail, and a stable experimental procedure was identified.

LEARNING HIERARCHY

One of the basic criticisms leveled at media related research is the contention that researchers do not adequately specify the type of learning tasks students are expected to achieve. This in turn prevents researchers from generalizing results obtained from individual studies and probably explains why some studies using media achieve significant results while others obtain insignificant results. One possible explanation for these contradictory findings may be that specific types of visualization may function very well in facilitating student achievement of specific types of educational objectives while for other types of educational objectives visualization may not be necessary or may actually function to inhibit learning. Implicit in this orientation is that there are many different kinds of learning, an idea which is not new. A number of prominent researchers have emphasized the importance of recognizing the existence of different kinds of learning and of the different conditions prerequisite to achieving the different levels of learning (Bloom et al., 1956; Skinner, 1957; Woodworth, 1958; Mowrer, 1960; Ausubel, 1962, 1968a,b; Mager, 1962; Krathwohl et al., 1964; Tyler, 1964; Gagné, 1965; Merrill, 1973). Briggs (1968a, p. 3) has described the present state of a taxonomy of learning tasks and its relative importance in interpreting empirical research in the following manner.

> One difficulty encountered in attempting to draw conclusions from the experiments . . . is the lack of a taxonomy of learning tasks which is acceptable to all experimenters. While nearly all authors of research reports . . . would concede that the importance of sequencing and the specific factors involved in optimal sequencing would vary with the type of tasks (type of learning), there is not anything approaching universal agreement on how many kinds of learning there are, and furthermore many reports do not classify the specific task in terms of the type of learning the author thinks it represents. While it is true that there is some disagreement on the basic hypothesis that there are several kinds of learning, even those subscribing to the hypothesis have not reached consensus on the number and identity of such learning types.

The basic contention among learning theorists appears to be that there is a hierarchy consisting of different types of learning tasks extending from the most simple to the most difficult. White and Gagné (1974, p. 19) have described hierarchies of learning as:

> . . . patterns of learning tasks which lead to a terminal skill: each subordinate task would be a prerequisite for the task above it, and would mediate transfer for that task. The basic premise underlying learning hierarchies is that failure to learn a particular skill is principally due to lack of essential subordinate skills, and conversely, that learning should be easy to induce if all relevant subordinate skills are possessed by the learner.

An awareness of the fact that there are different kinds of educational objectives each requiring specific prerequisites is crucial to educators who aspire to employ the visual media effectively. Basically, the organization of learning activities into a hierarchy will enable educators to approach the teaching of complex learning activities in a systematic manner, beginning with the simple and progressing to the more complex. For example, for students to successfully engage in problem solving they need to be able to handle the basic terms, definitions, and facts of the discipline. They also need to be able to combine facts into concepts, concepts into generalizations, and so forth. Asch (1971, p. 13) in reviewing the research relating to the sequencing of experiences and stimuli found that:

> The evidence is clear that correctness between experiences is dependent upon the way in which they are related. The same experiences when differentially related produce different grades of coherence, observable at the level of memory and by inference at the point of original experience. Further, the particular relations that bind experiences produces effects distinctive to them.

This finding coincides with an earlier observation presented by Bruner (1960, p. 24) when he contends, "Perhaps the most basic thing that can be said about human memory, after a century of intensive research, is that unless detail is placed into a structured pattern it is rapidly forgotten." Smith (1964) also has indicated that the proper structuring of content can significantly affect learning by facilitating increased information acquisition, retention and transfer of learning. Simply stated, the message being offered is that content material which has natural and sequential organization is easier to receive, store and recall than material which has no apparent organization. The implication to be derived from the concept of a learning hierarchy is that since there are different kinds of educational objectives there also are different kinds of learning, each requiring students to perform different kinds of activities and each possessing unique conditions for optimum learning to occur.

CONTENT PREPARATION

Since one of the objectives of the systematic program of evaluation by the author and his associates was to develop a more comprehensive awareness of the instructional effects that different types of visualization have on student achievement of different types of educational objectives, it was necessary to determine the kinds of tasks students are typically expected to perform in the classroom. This was achieved by interviewing a number of high school teachers and college professors to determine the kinds of performances normally expected of their students and the kinds of tests commonly used to measure student performances. The survey indicated that, over a wide variety of disciplines, students were expected to: (a) learn terminology and facts basic to the course content, (b) identify locations and/or positions, (c) construct and/or understand relationships, and (d) engage in problem solving activities.

In order to be able to assess student achievement of these types of educational objectives involving meaningful learning, a 2,000 word instructional unit was developed on the human heart, its parts, and the internal processes which occur during the systolic and diastolic phases. This content material was selected specifically because it provided a hierarchy of several types of educational objectives extending from the learning of basic facts to complex problem solving, success on each subsequent objective being dependent on satisfactory acquisition of specific prerequisites. For example, if the instruction began by discussing the diastolic and systolic phases of the heart without providing students with the opportunity to learn the different parts of the heart, their locations, and their interrelationships, the ensuing instruction would be too difficult and the students would learn a disproportionately small amount of information compared to the amount of time spent in interacting with the content. Students need to possess competency in prerequisite skills or basic learning levels before they can be successfully introduced to ideas which are comparatively complex or abstract or which extend beyond the learner's existing range of experiences.

The 2,000 word instructional script constituted the subject content for the systematic evaluation program and was presented to all students participating in the individual studies; in some instances the content was presented orally via a tape recorder, and in others it was presented in a printed format, e.g., programmed and textbook-like booklets. After the script was developed, extensive effort was expended in developing criterion instruments which would measure student achievement of different educational objectives. Four such criterion measures were designed.

CRITERION MEASURES

The educational objectives employed throughout the program of systematic evaluation represented the hierarchy of learning tasks of the instruction extending from the simple (terminology) to the complex (comprehension). First the student learned the basic terminology associated with the content; he then learned to identify the basic structures, position them in their respective locations, and comprehend their interrelated simultaneous functions which occur both during the systolic and diastolic phases of the heart.

The following description of the kinds of performances measured by the criterion tests illustrates that the kinds of educational objectives that were assessed transcend specific discipline boundaries.

Terminology Test. This test consisted of 20 multiple-choice items designed to measure the student's knowledge of specific facts, terms, and definitions. The objectives measured by this type of test are appropriate to all content areas which have as a prerequisite to the more complicated types of learning a comprehensive understanding of the basic elements (terminology, facts, and definitions) indigeneous to the discipline.

Identification Test. The objective of the identification test was to evaluate student ability to identify parts or positions of an object. This multiple-choice test (N=20 items) required students to identify the numbered parts on a detailed drawing of a heart. Each part of the heart which had been discussed in the presentation was numbered on the drawing and appeared in a list on the answer sheet. The objective of this test was to measure the student's ability to use visual cues to discriminate one structure of the heart from another and to associate specific parts of the heart with their proper name. Tests similar to the identification test could be used in any course in which the student is required to be able to locate and identify the various parts of objects (for example, in an automotive repair course to identify the parts of a car engine, or in a botany course to locate and name the parts of different types of plants).

Drawing Test. The objective of the drawing test was to evaluate student ability to construct and/or reproduce items in their appropriate context. For example, the drawing test (N=18 items) provided the students with a numbered list of terms, e.g., (1) superior vena cava, (2) aorta, (3) tricuspid valve, (4) pulmonary vein, etc., corresponding to the parts of the heart discussed in the instructional presentation. The students were required to draw a representative diagram of the heart (a symbol like a valentine sufficed; the quality of the drawing did not enter into the scoring) and place the number of the listed parts in their respective positions. For this test the emphasis was on the correct positioning of the verbal symbols with respect to one another and in respect to their concrete referents. The educational objectives measured by this type of test could very easily be applied to a social studies class in which the relative location of the fifty states, with respect to one another, was being taught, or to an automotive course in which students were being taught the relative locations of the various parts of a carburetor.

Comprehension Test. The comprehension test consisted of 20 multiple-choice items. Given the location of certain parts of the heart at a particular moment of its functioning, the student then was asked to locate the position of other specified parts of the heart at the same point in time. This test required that the students have a thorough understanding of the heart, its parts, its internal functioning, and the simultaneous processes occurring during the systolic and diastolic phases. The comprehension test was designed to measure a type of understanding that occurs when the individual understands what is being communicated and can use the information being received to explain some other phenomenon occurring simultaneously. Tests similar to the comprehension test can be used in any discipline area in which the objective is to measure the student's understanding of complex procedures and processes. The following sample is a typical multiple-choice type question taken from the comprehension test:

During the systolic phase, in what position is the aortic valve?
    a. fully open   c. partially closed
    b. partially open   d. fully closed

In examining the distractors for this particular item, it becomes apparent that the alternatives b and c—partially open and partially closed—may be interpreted as meaning the same thing; i.e., a door may be described as being partially closed by one person and the same door described as being partially open by another person. Consequently, for students to consistently select the correct alternative on this type of question they must first be familiar with the terminology used to describe the heart; they must be able to recollect the location of the various parts of the heart and be able to position the individual parts of the heart in their "minds eye" as they relate to one another. Furthermore, they must also be able to mentally simulate the functions and movements of the various parts of the heart as they would occur during both the systolic and diastolic phases of the heart. Only when the students have acquired a comprehensive understanding of the content material—the description and location of the various parts of the heart and their individual functions during both the systolic and diastolic phases of the heart—can they consistently respond correctly to the type of questions contained in the comprehension test.

Total Criterion Test. The items contained in the four individual criterion tests were combined into a 78-item total criterion test. The purpose of this test was to measure the student's total understanding of all the content material presented in the instructional unit.

Students received the drawing test first, then the identification and terminology tests, the comprehension test being administered last. Each student was permitted to take as much time as he required to complete one criterion measure before proceeding to the next. Scores achieved on the four individual criterion tests were combined into a composite 78-item total criterion test score. The Kuder-Richardson Formula 20 Reliability coefficient for the five criterion measures was computed for each study. An average reliability coefficient for each criterion test has been computed from a random sampling of the studies; they are: .83—terminology test, .81—identification test, .83—drawing test, .77—comprehension test, and .92—total criterion test.

Figure 3-1 provides a summary of the objectives measured by each of the criterion measures.

Figure 3-1. Criterion measures.

TERMINOLOGY TEST
- Botany
- Physics
- Physiology
- Chemistry
- Geography
- History

Plate 1. Evaluate student knowledge of specific facts and definitions.

IDENTIFICATION TEST

- Organs in the human body
- Parts of a plant
- Locations of states on a map of the United States
- Parts of a carburetor

Figure 3-1. (Continued)

Plate 2. Evaluate student ability to identify parts or position(s) of an object.

DRAWING TEST

DRAW & LABEL
- States on a map of the United States
- Parts of a carburetor
- Parts of a plant
- Major parts of the body, a camera, film projector

Plate 3. Evaluate student ability to reproduce items in their appropriate context.

COMPREHENSION TEST

- Function of organs of the body
- Relationship of parts of a camera or film projector
- How a carburetor works
- How a car engine works to make the wheels turn

Plate 4. Evaluate student understanding of complex procedures and/or processes.

TOTAL CRITERION TEST

- Drawing
- Identification
- Terminology
- Comprehension

Plate 5. To measure the total amount of information acquired by students.

GENERALIZABILITY OF EDUCATIONAL OBJECTIVES

It is important to emphasize the fact that the different types of educational objectives used in the program of systematic evaluation have generalizability across different disciplines since the conditions prerequisite to successful attainment of identical learning tasks are identical regardless of differences in content area. Students learning basic terminology and facts in psychology or history would engage in the same type of learning processes if they were learning terminology and facts in biology or geography. Whatever the discipline, the process is the same. Figure 3-2 represents the sequential learning process involved in mastering the heart content, and this same process can be generalized to any discipline area in which similar types of objectives are to be achieved. As naive students interact with unfamiliar content they first have to learn the basic terminology and

Figure 3-2. Phases in a learning hierarchy.

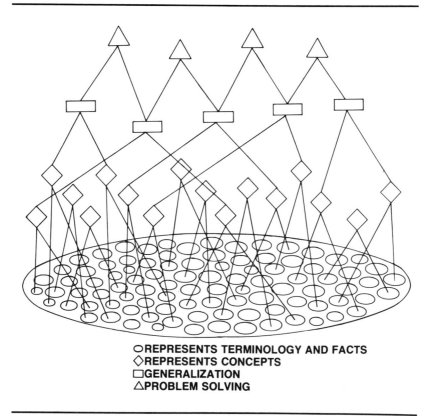

○REPRESENTS TERMINOLOGY AND FACTS
◇REPRESENTS CONCEPTS
□GENERALIZATION
△PROBLEM SOLVING

facts which make up the basic components of the language of the discipline. The more terms, facts, and definitions, etc. (○) that a person is familiar with in a content area, the better prepared he is to relate and combine these units of information to form concepts (◇). The more concepts (◇) a person possesses, the easier it is for him to form generalizations, rules (□) and so forth. Based on this kind of orientation to learning, ease of subsequent learning is directly related to the quality and quantity of the prerequisite learning.

VISUALIZING CONTENT MATERIAL

Another of the criticisms leveled at media related research is that the relationship between information contained in the visual and the oral/print channels has not been precisely described. Hartman (1961b, p. 242), in discussing the relationship existing between the information in each channel in multiple channel communication, has stated that there are four possibilities:

1. Two channels may present *redundant* information such as the same word, printed and spoken.
2. Two channels may present *related* information such as a pictorial representation of an object and verbal description of the object.
3. Channel information—such as a picture of a tree in the pictorial channel and the word *nine* in the audio may be *unrelated.*
4. The information presented may be *contradictory* as in the simultaneous presentation of the printed word, *woman,* and the spoken word, *man.*

Hsia (1968a, p. 246) in commenting on this same problem has indicated that:

> The simultaneous AV channel inherits the advantages and disadvantages of both A and V channels, and presumably has advantages over the A and V only if, for example, its A and V stimuli are closely identical . . . such that one channel provides cues and clues for the other channel when the number of clues is no more than optimum, or when the sum of information is not in excess of the capacity of the central nervous system, as additional cues might cause distraction and conflicting responses.

Hartman (1961b, pp. 249-250), in commenting on between channel interference which occurs when unrelated information is simultaneously presented through two channels, has concluded:

> . . . interference occurs when unrelated information is simultaneously presented and attention cannot be successfully alternated, and that it reduces the learning in both channels; that increasing the difficulty of the presented information results in increasing losses through interference; that when the information presented in the channels is of unequal difficulty, the less difficult information suffers the greater loss . . . . Interference may also be generated by adverse cognitive relationships in information.

Similarly Coppen (1972) has indicated that when information is received simultaneously through two or more channels, the difficulty of the learning task will be influenced by the relationships which are created by the two (or more) information sources. They may combine forming one thought, idea, or concept, or they may offer more or less competing messages. It was the intent of the author's program of evaluation to employ visualization in such a way that it would complement oral/printed instruction so as to provide the one thought concept—correctly received.

Inherent in the criticism that the relationship between the information contained in the visual/print channels in multiple channel are two critical questions related to the effective and efficient use of visualization in the teaching-learning act: (a) when is it most desirable to incorporate visualization in the instructional presentation, and (b) after the decision has been made to utilize visualization, what kind of visualization should be used?

Since the primary objective of the program of systematic investigation was to identify strategies for systematically employing visualization to increase student achievement of specific educational objectives, it seemed most logical to incorporate visualization in areas of the instruction where the students experienced difficulty acquiring the oral/print information. Consequently, the visualization to be integrated into the oral/print instruction was redundant in that it was designed to illustrate, as accurately as possible, the information that students were having trouble comprehending from the oral/print instruction alone. The justification for using redundant information in both channels was to provide the student with the opportunity to receive information alternately from either channel and not experience information loss as a result of channel switching.

Once the instructional script had been prepared and the four individual criterion tests developed the next step in the procedure was to identify where in the instructional script visualization should be incorporated in order to facilitate maximum student achievement. This was achieved by presenting the content material to students orally (Figure 3-3; Plate 1), and then immediately after the students received the instruction each responded to the four criterion measures which provided an indication of how much information they

Figure 3-3. Strategy for visual integration.

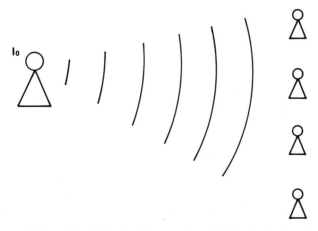

Plate 1. Content material presented orally to students.

Figure 3-3. (Continued)

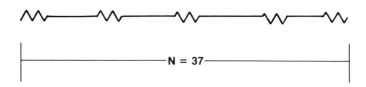

Plate 2. ∿ Represents areas in the instruction where students experienced difficulty in acquiring the information.

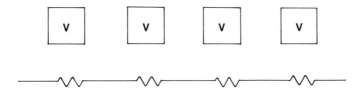

Plate 3. Illustrations were designed specifically to illustrate, as accurately as possible, the information students were experiencing difficulty acquiring.

had acquired from the presentation. Student performance on the individual criterion tests was then item-analyzed to determine where
students experienced difficulty in answering the criterion items.
Thirty-seven such areas were identified (Plate 2). These difficulty
areas were then traced back to the instructional script where the information necessary to achieve on these items was originally
presented. Once these difficulty areas had been identified, visuals
were designed specifically to illustrate the information in each of the
thirty-seven critical areas. In this sense the visuals used to complement the oral/print instruction in this program of systematic evaluation can be considered to be *redundant* (Plate 3).

TYPES OF VISUALIZATION

Since one of the objectives of the program was to determine the
relative effectiveness with which different types of illustrations facilitated student achievement of different types of educational objectives, eight different visual treatments of the heart content were produced. The realistic photographic treatment of the heart was the first

visual treatment produced. A veterinary surgeon performed cuttings on pork hearts so that photographs depicting the designated concepts could be obtained. From the original sequence of realistic photographs, professionally produced, a graphic artist produced the line presentations and the detailed, shaded drawing presentations, both the black and white and colored versions. The heart model photographs in black and white and color were included in the evaluation program because they represented the type of visual illustrations currently being included in many modern textbooks. They also possessed more realistic detail than the detailed, shaded drawing presentations. The eight complete visual sequences were designed and reproduced as 2 x 2-inch slides; four sequences were in black and white, and four were in color. Each instructional sequence contained thirty-seven slides. Printed symbols were used in each illustration to facilitate the correct spelling of the terminology being presented and to enable students to differentiate between those parts of the heart in which pronunciation and spelling are almost identical. The same set of printed symbols was used in all experimental treatments, and they were positioned in identical locations in each illustration. The types of visualization used to complement the oral/print instruction remained constant throughout all the studies.

Arrows were used in the visual illustrations to focus students' attention on the particular part or location of the heart being emphasized in the instruction. The shape, length, and position of the arrows in similar illustrations for the various visualized treatments were identical. Both black and white arrows were used in the illustrations; white arrows were used in those slides on which black arrows would have blended into the background.

EXPERIMENTAL VISUALIZED TREATMENTS

The eight visualized sequences were considered to be the experimental treatments; the students receiving slides or illustrations on which appeared only printed symbols of the terms being discussed in the instructional presentation were considered to be the control group. The amount of realistic detail possessed by the visual illustrations varied for each of the visualized treatments; however, all treatment groups received identical instructional content. The intent or objective of using different types of illustrations was to determine the relative effectiveness of the four different types of black and white and colored illustrations in facilitating student achievement of different kinds of educational objectives. For purposes of this evaluation program, each black and white and colored visual sequence was considered to be a separate type; consequently, the discussions throughout will focus on the following eight types of visual illustrations:

1. simple line drawings (b&w)
2. simple line drawings (color)
3. detailed, shaded drawings (b&w)
4. detailed, shaded drawings (color)
5. heart model photographs (b&w)
6. heart model photographs (color)
7. realistic heart photographs (b&w)
8. realistic heart photographs (color)

A sample of each type of visual used in the eight instructional treatments is presented in Figure 3-4. The instructional treatments were:

Oral/Print Presentation. Students receiving the oral/print presentations received no visuals of the heart but viewed displays containing the names of the parts and/or processes of the heart as they were discussed in the instructional presentation (Plate 1).

Simple Line Drawing Presentation (b&w). Students receiving the simple line drawing presentation (b&w) viewed simple line illustrations depicting the form and the relative locations of the parts of the heart as they were mentioned in the instruction. The line drawings used in this presentation were similar to instructional drawings used in many current science textbooks (Plate 2).

Simple Line Drawing Presentation (color). Students receiving this treatment viewed simple line illustrations in color to complement their instruction. The colors used in this treatment, blue lines on a pink background, were selected solely to provide color contrast and were not designed in any way to provide additional learning cues for the students (Plate 6). The color used in the three additional colored treatments did not intentionally provide more information than did their complements, the black and white treatments. However, the use of color in some instances may have facilitated more rapid identification of specific parts and related systems of the heart.

Detailed, Shaded Drawing Presentation (b&w). Students receiving this treatment viewed detailed, shaded drawings (b&w)

to complement their instruction. These drawings were more complex than the simple line drawings, and they represented the heart and its related parts more realistically, rather than merely identifying and locating them as in the simple line drawing presentations (Plate 3).

Detailed, Shaded Drawing Presentation (color). Students receiving the detailed, shaded drawing presentation (color) viewed illustrations similar to those in the previous group, except that they were colored (Plate 7).

Heart Model Presentation (b&w). Students receiving this treatment viewed photographs of a heart model (b&w) while the heart and its related parts were being described in the instruction (Plate 4).

Heart Model Presentation (color). Students receiving this treatment viewed colored photographs of a heart model (Plate 8).

Realistic Photographic Presentation (b&w). Students receiving this treatment viewed realistic photographs (b&w) of the heart (Plate 5.).

Realistic Photographic Presentation (color). Students in this treatment group received realistic photographs of the heart which were in color (Plate 9).

PROCEDURES FOR REPORTING RESULTS

Efficiency and effectiveness as they relate to visualized instruction mean using that type of visual which will be most effective in facilitating student achievement of specifically designated educational objectives. It is reasonable to assume that if two or more types of visuals are equally effective in increasing student achievement of the same educational objective then the least expensive type of visual should be used since it is not justifiable to produce expensive visualization when less costly material has proven to be equally effective. Consequently, all analyses resulting from this program of systematic evaluation are made in terms of instructional effectiveness, financial economy, and simplicity of production; that is, the type of visualization reported as being most effective in facilitating student achievement on the different criterion measures in each of the individual studies is the one possessing the most favorable overall relationship of instructional benefit (capacity to increase most ef-

Figure 3-4. Sample visuals used to complement the nine instructional treatments.

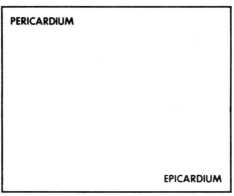

PERICARDIUM

EPICARDIUM

PLATE 1.
Oral/print presentation.

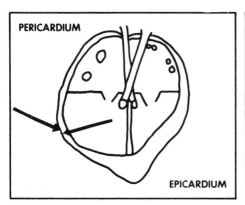

PERICARDIUM

EPICARDIUM

PLATE 2.
Sample line drawing presentation (b & w)

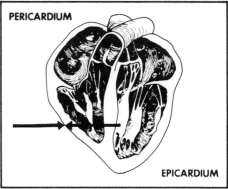

PERICARDIUM

EPICARDIUM

PLATE 3.
Detailed, shaded drawing presentation (b&w)

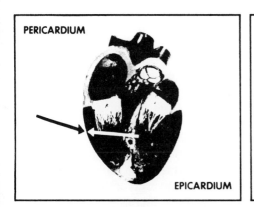

PERICARDIUM

EPICARDIUM

PLATE 4.
Heart model presentation (b & w)

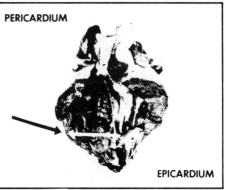

PERICARDIUM

EPICARDIUM

PLATE 5.
Realistic photographic presentation (b & w)

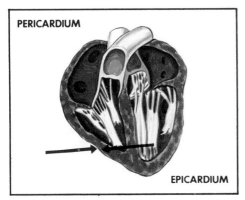

PLATE 6.
Simple line drawing presentation (color)

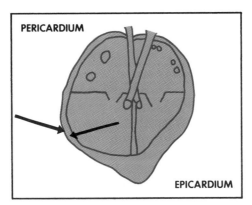

PLATE 7.
Detailed, shaded drawing presentation (color)

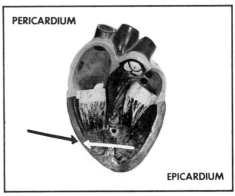

PLATE 8.
Heart model presentation (color)

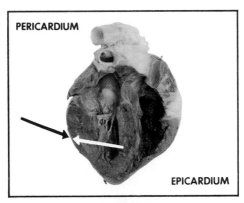

PLATE 9.
Realistic photographic presentation (color)

ficiently student achievement of specific educational objectives) to cost. For example, if in an experiment three visualized treatments—the line drawing presentation (b&w), the detailed, shaded drawing presentation (b&w), and the heart model presentation (color)—were all found to be significantly more effective than the presentation without visuals of the heart on a specific criterion measure and equally effective among themselves, the recommendation would be to use the simple line presentation since this type of visual can be produced most economically. If the results of the study indicated that the oral or print instruction without visuals of the heart was as effective at the visualized treatments for a specific educational objective, the oral or printed instruction alone would be recommended as the most efficient procedure for transmitting that specific type of information to the student.

DISCUSSION

To date over one hundred separate studies have been conducted by the author and his associates in this systematic program of evaluation. The sample population involved in the studies represents over 3,000 high school students (ninth, tenth, eleventh, and twelfth grades) and over 20,000 college level students. In each study the same instructional unit, criterion tests, and visualized treatments have been employed. However, each study was designed to investigate one or more specific instructional variables such as: (a) effect of method of presentation (i.e., externally paced—television, slide/ audiotape vs. self paced—programmed and textbook-like materials; (b) effect that different amounts of realistic detail in visualization, designed to complement oral/print instruction, has on facilitating student achievement of different educational objectives; (c) color versus black and white as an instructional variable in visualized instruction, (d) effectiveness of different cueing techniques (arrows, motion, inserted questions, knowledge of objectives, overt responses, etc.) in improving the effectiveness of different types of visuals; (e) effect of students' individual difference variables (prior knowledge in the content area, I.Q., reading comprehension, educational level, etc.) on their subsequent level of achievement from different types of visualization.

In each study, each student received a pretest, participated in his respective instructional treatment, and received four individual criterion tests. Three different pretests were used at different times throughout the series of studies. They were: (1) a physiology pretest, used to measure the student's prior knowledge in the specific content area, (2) the Otis Quick-Scoring Mental Ability Test (Form Fm), which provided a "rough" I.Q. score and (3) the reading section (only) of the Iowa Silent Reading Test (Form E) provided a reading comprehension score. Although randomization of students to treatment groups was effected in the majority of the studies, it was not possible to implement this technique in all studies (that is, the studies using high school students). However, all students, including those randomly assigned to treatment groups, received a pretest. Scores achieved on the pretest measures were analyzed, and when significant differences occurred among the treatment groups, these scores were used as a covariate to partial out their effect. Analysis of variance and covariance (where significant differences occurred on the pretest measures) were used throughout the cited studies. Where significant differences among groups were obtained via the analysis of variance or covariance techniques, Dunn's "C" Procedure (initial studies only) or Tukey's W-Procedure were employed to analyze differences between pairs of means.

SUMMARY: MAIN IDEAS

If a sound understanding relative to the effective and efficient use of visual materials for instructional purposes is to result, answers to specific questions need to be resolved.

A significant number of criticisms related to media research have complicated data interpretation and frustrated any attempts to derive broad generalizations useful to practitioners in their classroom use of media.

One of the basic criticisms leveled at media related research is the contention that researchers do not adequately specify the type of learning tasks students are expected to achieve.

The organization of learning activities into a hierarchy of educational objectives will enable educators to approach the teaching of complex learning activities in a systematic manner, beginning with the simple and progressing to the more complex.

Visualization used to complement oral or printed instruction may be redundant, related, unrelated or contradictory.

The types of educational objectives (terminology, identification, drawing, comprehension) used in the program of systematic evaluation by the author have generalizability across different disciplines since the conditions prerequisite to successful attainment of identical learning tasks are the same regardless of differences in content area.

Visuals were positioned in the instructional script as a result of pretesting and item analysis. This enabled visuals to be placed precisely where students experienced difficulty in acquiring the content being presented.

Eight types of visuals were used in the program of systematic evaluation (line drawings, b&w, color; detailed, shaded drawings, b&w, color; photographs of a model, b&w, color; realistic photographs, b&w, color).

REVIEW ACTIVITIES

1. List several questions which need to be answered in order for educators to be able to make effective and practical use of visualization in the teaching-learning process.
2. Identify the major criticisms which have been leveled at media related research.
3. State several procedural strategies which if implemented would tend to reduce some of the criticisms currently attributed to media research.
4. Explain why the heart content was selected as the content material to be used in the program of systematic evaluation by the author.
5. Describe the kinds of learning measured by the terminology, identification, drawing, comprehension, and total criterion tests.
6. Using the kinds of learning measured in the program of systematic evaluation, draw and label a hierarchy of educational objectives for the heart content.
7. Summarize the major characteristics of a learning hierarchy.
8. Define and give an example of what is meant by redundant, related, unrelated, and contradictory information.
9. Explain the rationale for integrating the visualization into the instructional script used in the program of systematic evaluation.
10. List the specific types of visualization used in the program of systematic evaluation.
11. Discuss, in writing, the procedure for reporting results of studies conducted in the program of systematic evaluation.

RECOMMENDED READINGS

Hsia, H. J. 1968. On channel effectiveness. *AV Commun. Rev. 16:* 245-267.

Okey, J. R. 1973. Developing and validating learning hierarchies. *AV Commun. Rev. 21:* 87-108.

Merrill, M. D. 1973. Content and instructional analysis for cognitive transfer tasks. *AV Commun. Rev. 21:* 109-125.

4

Effect of Method of Presenting Visualized Instruction

LEARNING OBJECTIVES

Upon completion of this chapter the student will be able to:

1. *Describe the differences between externally paced and self-paced visualized instruction.*
2. *Identify the types of visualization found to be most effective in externally paced and self-paced visualized instruction.*
3. *Discuss the hypothesis that the amount of time students are permitted to interact with visualization dictates to a certain extent the amount of information they will be able to absorb.*
4. *Explain why the type of visualization to be used to complement instruction is dependent on the method of instructional presentation and the type of educational objective to be achieved.*
5. *List three examples of externally paced and self-paced instruction.*
6. *List the conditions under which simple line illustrations are most effective in facilitating student achievement; list the conditions under which the more realistic types of illustrations are effective in increasing student achievement.*

ORIENTATION

It has been documented that properly designed visual materials can significantly improve student achievement (VanderMeer, 1950b; Kopstein & Roshal, 1954; Treichler, 1957; Gropper, 1962; Dwyer, 1972a). One basic problem yet to be investigated is one which tends to focus on whether or not one method of presenting visualized instruction is more effective than another in facilitating student achievement of specific educational objectives when identical visuals are used across methods.

RESEARCH LITERATURE

A considerable amount of research evidence currently exists regarding the comparative instructional effectiveness of two or more media, i.e., sound motion pictures, silent motion pictures, and still pictures. Many of these studies (e.g., McClusky & McClusky, 1924; Vernon, 1946; Heiderken, 1948; VanderMeer, 1950a; Torkelson, 1954; Murnin et al., 1954; Kale & Grosslight, 1955) have found no significant differences in effectiveness between two or more media (such as films vs. filmstrips) in increasing student achievement. However, other studies (Carson, 1947; Hovland, Lumsdaine & Sheffield, 1949; Slattery, 1953; Ortigiesen, 1954; Vris, 1955) have shown the superiority of filmstrips over films, while others (e.g., Goodman, 1942; Craig, 1956) have demonstrated the superiority of silent motion pictures over sound motion pictures. There have also been a number of studies (e.g., VanderMeer, 1950a; Cogswell, 1952, 1953; Bathurst, 1954; Fullerton, 1956) which made comparisons along other dimensions. However, in many of these studies the illustrative material displayed through the various media has seldom been equivalent. Even when the slides have been made from frames of a film, they are out of context and consequently do not convey exactly the same content as the film. These studies seem to indicate that no valid comparisons can be made unless material equivalent in content appears in all the media being compared. Caution is therefore needed in attempting to generalize or to establish trends based on the research previously cited.

EXTERNALLY PACED AND SELF-PACED INSTRUCTION

Each instructional medium has unique characteristics which should be employed to achieve specific educational objectives. Films may be used when motion is required to convey information regarding manipulative tasks or processes. Still pictures may be effective in place of films under conditions in which the film would proceed too fast or shift scenes too quickly to adequately stress or highlight important content information. Slides and filmstrips enable the instructor to increase the time students may view and interact with the illustrative materials, to answer their questions, and to make comments.

Essentially there are two basis strategies for presenting visualized materials for instructional purposes. The first may be characterized as being externally paced—a situation in which students as a group receive instruction via film, television, transparencies, etc. The determining characteristic of the externally paced strategy is that the content material is linearly programmed in that it is presented sequentially, and that it is usually difficult for the student to slow down the rate of information presentation, to ask questions, or to review the content material during or after the presentation. In this method of information presentation all students receive the same instruction for the same amount of time. The implied assumptions associated with this method of presentation is that: (a) all students receiving the presentation are at the same level of content sophistication, (b) all students view the same thing (in a visual) at the same time, and (c) all students learn at the same rate regardless of the complexity of the content material being presented.

The second instructional strategy is called self-paced and is defined as a learning situation in which each individual student controls the rate at which he proceeds through the instructional materials (e.g., textbooks, workbooks, computer-assisted instruction, individualized slide presentations, videotape cassettes, and so forth). In receiving instruction in this format, students are able to interact with the oral/print instruction and also interact with their respective visuals for as long as they feel necessary in order to comprehend the information being presented.

Many studies attempt to compare the effectiveness of the different media in presenting the same information, but do not give adequate consideration to the inherent capabilities and limitations of the different types of media or to the conditions prerequisite in establishing adequate experimental procedures. In some instances, it would seem inappropriate to compare the effectiveness of a motion picture and a series of slides abstracted from a film in presenting the same information. Each medium should be evaluated in terms of the learning objectives for which it is best designed. Furthermore, many of the studies which have made comparisons between the different media have not properly reported the type of content used, the kinds of educational objectives to be achieved, the types of visualization used in each medium, level of students participating in the study, type of experimental design, etc. These kinds of comparison studies produce results which are non-generalizable and pragmatically uninterpretable.

Acknowledging the nature of the problems associated with any attempt to investigate the relative effectiveness of different methods of presenting visualized instruction, an attempt was made by the author to reduce the weaknesses identified in prior studies. The decision to undertake an in-depth comparison of media was justified since it appears that many decisions regarding the selection of methods to present visualized instruction (television, textbooks, programmed instruction booklets, slides, and so forth) and the types of visualization that will be presented to students are currently being based on factors other than sound research results (availability of existing equipment, familiarity with a particular method or medium, etc.). In the following sections three studies which compare methods of presentation and which were conducted by the author are reported in detail.

TELEVISION vs. SLIDE/AUDIOTAPE vs. PROGRAMMED INSTRUCTION

The purpose of this study (Dwyer, 1973b, p. 438) was to evaluate the effectiveness of three methods of presenting visualized instruction. Specifically, this study was designed to:

1. Measure the relative effectiveness of three methods of presenting visuals (television, slide/audiotape, programmed instruction) used to complement oral and printed instruction;
2. Determine whether the same types of visuals viewed via the three presentation formats are equally effective in improving student achievement;
3. Measure the degree of effectiveness by which illustrative material presented via television slide/audiotape, and programmed instruction facilitates student achievement of different educational objectives.

Four hundred sixty-five students participated in this study. Students were randomly assigned to one of three methods of presentation and then to one of the five treatment groups within each presentation format: Group 1—oral/print presentation without visuals of the heart; Group 2—simple line drawing presentation; Group 3—detailed, shaded drawing presentation; Group 4—heart model presentation, and Group 5—realistic photographic presentation. All visual sequences employed in this study were black and white. Students in each treatment group received a pretest, participated in their respective instructional presentation, and then received four individual criterion tests. Following is a description of the three presentation methods evaluated in this study.

Method 1: Television. Students receiving the televised presentation viewed their respective instructional treatments on conventional 22-inch monitors. The oral instruction—tape recorded and presented to students via television receivers—

was identical for all treatments. During the oral instruction an audio signal on the tape cued the changing of the slides, thereby synchronizing the oral and visual presentations so that the appropriate visuals appeared simultaneously with the oral instruction they were designed to complement. The instructional period for students receiving the televised method of presentation was the same for each treatment group—32 minutes.

Method 2: Slides. Students participating in the slide method of presentation received the same oral and visual sequences as did students who received the television method. The slides were presented by means of an electrically synchronized 2x2-inch slide projector and audiotape recorder. The projected slides were viewed by students as 3x4-foot projected images. The slide method differed from the televised method in that students viewed larger illustrations and were permitted to interact with them for a longer period of time—40 minutes.

Method 3: Programmed Instruction. Students receiving programmed instruction received the same instructional script as did students receiving the other methods of instruction; however, their content material was linearly programmed into 37 paragraph-type frames and typed on 8½ x 5½-inch sheets. Each frame contained a 2⅛ x 3¼-inch visual illustration made from the slides used in Methods 1 and 2; in addition, each frame contained from one to six questions which students were to answer mentally by reading the written presentation and by inspecting the visual illustration located on the same frame. Immediate feedback as to the accuracy of the mental response was provided by the appearance of the correct response on the subsequent frame. The students receiving the programmed method of instruction spent an average of 26 minutes interacting with their instructional units.

Table 4-1 presents a summary of the relative effectiveness of the three methods of presenting visualized instruction employed in this study. The blank areas indicate that significant differences in achievement did not occur among the three methods of presentation; i.e., in some comparisons all three methods were found to be equivalent in terms of transmitting information to students. For example, no significant differences in achievement were found to exist among methods on the criterion tests when students in the respective treatment groups received oral/print instruction without accompanying visualization—apparently, it does not matter whether students listen to or read the content material.

Table 4-1. Analysis of the effectiveness of three methods of instructional presentation: TV, slides, PI (Dwyer, 1973b, p. 447).

			Instructional Treatments		
Criterion Measures	*Oral/ Print* I	*Simple Line* II	*Detailed Drawing* III	*Heart Model* IV	*Photographic* V
Terminology			PI > TV**	PI > TV*	PI > TV** PI > Slides**
Identification				PI > Slides*	TV > Slides* PI > TV** PI > Slides**
Drawing		TV > PI** Slides > PI**	Slides > TV*	PI > TV** PI > Slides**	PI > TV** PI > Slides**
Comprehension			PI > Slides*		PI > TV** PI > Slides**
Total Criterion			Slides > TV* PI > TV*	PI > TV** PI > Slides**	PI > TV** PI > Slides**

$*p < .05; ** p < .01$

A closer look at Table 4-1 indicates that for students receiving the simple line drawing or detailed, shaded drawing presentations, there is no one specific method for presenting the content material that is most effective in terms of facilitating student achievement on all five criterion measures. For students receiving the heart model treatment, the programmed method of presentation was found to be significantly more effective than both the slide and televised methods on the drawing and total criterion tests. There were also several comparisons for which the programmed method was most effective on both the identification and terminology tests. For the realistic photographic treatment students receiving the programmed method achieved significantly higher than did students who received the slide and televised methods on all five of the criterion measures.

It is also interesting to note that students who received the programmed method of instruction required less time (students averaged 26 minutes) than did students receiving the slide method (40 minutes) and televised method (32 minutes). With one exception (the drawing test for the simple line presentation) students receiving the programmed instruction method achieved as well as or better than students did who received instruction via the other two methods of presentation.

An explanation for the results obtained in this study was provided in the original article (Dwyer, 1973b, pp. 448-449):

> . . . since the slide and televised methods were externally paced, students did not have appropriate time intervals to interact with the projected visuals. This particular possibility coincides with the hypothesis that in a group learning situation all viewers do not see the same thing at the same time, and all students do not learn at the same rate. Expanding this notion we can account for the lack of a most effective method of presentation for the oral/print, simple line, and detailed, shaded treatments. Since the types of illustrations used in these treatments were limited in the amount of information they contained, students were able to obtain a restricted amount of information in interacting with them. Although the more realistic illustrations contained more information, they were at a disadvantage in facilitating achievement since students did not have sufficient time to study and absorb the additional information. Furthermore, students receiving the externally paced methods of presentation did not have the opportunity to review material or to spend additional time on certain parts of the instruction where they experienced difficulty in comprehending the information. Apparently, the effectiveness of the externally paced methods in presenting the less realistic visualized treatments resides in the fact that the information they contained could be perceived and absorbed in the time allocated for viewing them. Another possible explanation may also be suggested to account for the failure of the more realistic illustrations in improving students' achievement: the initial impact of the realistic detail in the visuals may have had the net effect of distracting students from the essential learning cues.
>
> The effectiveness of the programmed method may be explained according to a similar rationale. Since the more realistic illustrations contained more inherent information, they had more to offer students who were reacting to them. Since the instruction was presented via programmed booklets, the students were able to spend as much time as they wished in interacting with the realistic detail in the illustrations and absorbing as much information as necessary to complete their understanding of the concepts being presented. This flexibility enabled the students to interact for longer periods of time with those aspects of the instruction that they considered to be more difficult to comprehend. This opportunity to interact with the more realistic illustrations for a longer period of time may have provided the students with additional information making them more capable of making those discriminations necessary for achievement on the criterion measures. The illustrations in the detailed, shaded drawing treatment, the simple line treatment, and the oral treatment possessed decreasing amounts of realistic detail and were therefore limited as to the amount of information that they would be able to transmit to the students regardless of how long the students were permitted to view and study their respective illustrations. This may be the reason why no one method of presentation was found to be consistently more effective than the others on the five criterion measures.

SLIDE/AUDIOTAPE vs. PROGRAMMED INSTRUCTION

In a more elaborate study (Dwyer, 1973c), also investigating the effectiveness of externally paced versus self-paced instruction (slide/audiotape vs. programmed instruction), eight visualized treatments of the heart content (four black and white and four colored treatments) were employed. Table 4-2 shows where significant differences in achievement occurred between students receiving the two different methods of presentation.

Table 4-2. Method of presentation most effective in facilitating achievement on each criterion measure (Dwyer, 1973, p. 299).

		Instructional Treatments							
Criterion Measures	*Oral/Print*	*Simple Line Drawing*		*Detailed Drawing*		*Heart Model*		*Realistic Photographs*	
		B&W	Color	B&W	Color	B&W	Color	B&W	Color
Terminology						P > S			P > S
Identification		P > S			S > P				P > S
Drawing			S > P					P > S	
Comprehension							P > S		P > S
Total criterion							P > S		P > S

Note: P = Programmed instruction; S = Slide/Audiotaped Instruction; B & W = black and white.

By comparing the results from Table 4-2 with those of Table 4-1 it can be seen that when oral/print instruction without visualization is presented to students no one method of instruction is consistently more effective than the other. Also, where visuals are found to be effective in the externally paced method of instruction the more simple types of illustrations are the ones most effective. It is interesting to note that the two instances where the externally paced instruction was more effective than the self-paced instruction the illustrations were in color. As in Table 4-1 the results obtained in this study indicated that the programmed instruction treatment presenting realistic photographs of the heart was significantly more effective than the externally paced method of presentation on the five criterion measures. In addition, it is interesting to note that on four of the five criterion measures it was the colored version of the realistic photographic presentation (programmed instruction) which was most effective in facilitating student achievement.

COMPARISON OF THREE METHODS OF INSTRUCTIONAL PRESENTATION

A comparison of three methods of presenting visualized instruction was made using the results obtained from three studies involving slides (Dwyer, 1967a), television, (Dwyer, 1968c) and programmed instruction (Dwyer, 1967b). These studies were conducted using college level students who received three different types of black and white visuals—simple line drawings, detailed, shaded drawings, and realistic photographs. Instruction received by students in the control group was identical to that received in the experimental groups; however, they did not receive visuals complementing the oral/print instruction.

Table 4-3 presents a summary and comparison of the results obtained from the slide, television, and programmed instruction studies. The following explanation of these results is from a publication by the author (Dwyer, 1970b, pp. 240-241):

Table 4-3. Instructional presentations found most effective (Dwyer, 1970b, p. 241).

			Criterion Tests			
Instructional Method	*Terminology Test*	*Identification Test*	*Drawing Test*	*Comprehension Test*	*Total Criterion*	*Time*
Slides (Dwyer, 1967a)	Oral	Simple Line Presentation	Simple Line Presentation	Oral	Simple Line Presentation	40 min.
Television (Dwyer, 1968c)	Oral	Oral	Simple Line Presentation	Oral	Oral	17 min.
Programmed Instruction (Dwyer, 1967b)	Programmed Instruction	Realistic Photographs	Realistic Photographs	Programmed Instruction	Realistic Photographs	Average 22 min.

In the three studies students received the same instructional content but through different methods of presentation. If we compare the results obtained from the slide study with the results obtained from the programmed instruction study we find that the same objectives, as measured by the drawing, identification, and total criterion tests, were facilitated by the use of visuals, but by different types of visuals for each study. In the slide study, the simple line illustrations were found to be most effective in facilitating student achievement. However, in the programmed instruction experiment the presentation containing the realistic photographs was found to be most effective in facilitating student achievement. It is interesting to note that in each of the three studies the treatment without visuals was found to be as effective as the visualized treatments in facilitating student achievement of those objectives measured by the terminology and comprehension tests.

In comparing the results of the slide study with the television study we will notice that the instructional period has been reduced from 40 to 17 minutes, greater than a 100 percent reduction. This reduction in the amount of time students were permitted to interact with the visualized presentation in the televised study also reduced the effectiveness with which visuals facilitated achievement on two criterion tests—the identification and total criterion tests.

Students viewing the externally paced instruction (slide/audiotape) interacted with their respective treatments for forty minutes. When students were allowed to interact for this length of time, the simple line drawing illustrations were found to be the kind of visuals most effective in facilitating achievement on the drawing, identification, and total criterion tests. When these same instructional treatments were presented via television and the amount of time available for interaction was reduced to seventeen minutes, the effectiveness of the visualization in improving student achievement was erased on the identification and total criterion tests. Apparently, the amount of time that students were permitted to interact with the visualization was below that which was necessary for them to acquire the information needed to achieve on these two criterion tests. When the amount of time available for interacting with the visuals was reduced by more than 100 percent students were interacting with visuals at twice the rate—as compared to students who were permitted to interact with their respective instructional presentation for forty minutes. Under similar circumstances when it is found that visualization used to complement instruction does not improve achievement it may be a worthwhile strategy to increase the amount of time students are permitted to interact with the instructional unit—to see if altering the time variable will have a positive effect on the level of achievement obtained.

The fact that on both the terminology and comprehension tests the oral/print presentation without any visualization was as effective as the visualized treatments may be explained by the fact that since most of the instruction which students receive is in the oral/print modes, they have out of necessity developed an ability to learn from this type of instruction. There is also the possibility that students have not been taught how to look at and learn from visuals, their prior exposure serving mainly to acquaint them with reality. It is also possible that the educational objectives measured by these two criterion tests did not require students to effectively utilize the information contained in the visuals. For example, the kind of knowledge measured by the terminology test was of the kind that could be obtained by definition alone—it may not be necessary to visualize the fact that the apex is the area at the bottom of the heart. Similarly, many students high in verbal fluency and having some prior knowledge in the content area might be able to achieve the more complex learning objectives via oral instruction alone. However, for the most part a majority of the students exposed to a content area for the first time acquire concepts by observation quite readily, and the research indicates that visualization can significantly improve their achievement of the more complex educational tasks.

This explanation of the effectiveness of the oral presentation on the terminology test seems plausible, but how do we explain its effectiveness on the comprehension test—a test measuring a more complex educational objective. In general, a major portion of the instruction that students receive is of a non-visual nature; consequently, they are quite familiar with and are relatively comfortable in receiving instruction by means of the oral/print modes. Out of necessity students have developed the capability to learn from oral/print instruction. They realize that sentences are linear in format each having a subject, verb, etc., and that if they attend conscientiously to the instruction they generally will be able to acquire the information being presented. However, when complex content material is presented, it usually requires that students make a number of mental manipulations in order to achieve comprehension. When visualization is used to complement complicated content material, two sources of stimuli are in competition for the students' attention. Even through the visualization is illustrating and reinforcing the information presented in the oral/print channel, it may functionally be impairing rather than facilitating student achievement. Visualization is not in itself linear; its message is immediate and total. To acquire the intended information students have to attend to and systematically scan the visual in search of essential learning cues. If students do not have time to switch from one channel to the other, the situation becomes very frustrating. Students exposed to such circumstances may tend to block out or ignore the less familiar communication channel (visual) and concentrate more intently on the information channel which is most familiar (oral/print). For example, Travers and Jester (1965) found that when students received an audiovisual presentation they tended to block one channel by closing their eyes or covering their ears. Under these kinds of competing circumstances visualization of the content material would have little, if any, effect in improving student performance on criterion tests designed to measure student achievement of complex educational objectives.

DISCUSSION

Realistic visuals of an object or situation contain more instructional stimuli than do simple line drawings of the same object which in turn represent an edited version of reality. Since students need a certain amount of time to perceive, explore, interact, assimilate and consolidate information obtained from instructional cues in visuals, the amount of time students are permitted to interact with the visualization becomes a very important instructional variable. If time is fixed so that students can interact with the visuals for only specific amounts of time (e.g., in externally paced situations where students receive instruction via film or television), the research indicates that there are optimal levels beyond which adding realistic detail to visuals produces no further increases in learning and may even function to reduce learning.

The results of the cited studies indicate that the amount of time students are permitted to view and interact with their respective presentations determines the kind of visualization which is most efficient in facilitating student achievement of specific kinds of educational objectives. These findings are in agreement with information processing models provided by Feigenbaum & Simon (1963) and Broadbent (1965) which contend that all information inputs require a certain amount of processing time. Very complex processes interfere with reception of the stimuli by the sensory organs and the eventual response produced—and this takes time. Carrol (1963, p. 732) in presenting his model of school learning has indicated that ". . . the degree of learning, other things being equal, is a simple function of the amount of time during which the pupil engages actively in learning." Sperling et al. (1971) in an important study found that learners extract information at approximately the same overall rate from arrays of varying complexity. These results would seem to explain why students, who received the programmed instruction and are permitted to interact with their instructional presentations for as long as they feel necessary to acquire the information being presented, achieved at a significantly higher level than do students who receive instruction externally paced.

Studies conducted by Harless et al. (1969) and Mackworth (1962) assessing the instructional effect of time on learning have generated results which indicate that the quality and quantity of information learned is a function of the rate at which the information was presented to the learners. This being the case, instruction presented in an externally paced format would impose severe restrictions on the learner's intrinsic mediational processes and subsequently interfere with information acquisition and retention. Sperling (1963, p. 30) emphasizes the importance of time in the learning process in the following manner:

> Visual processes in recall may come to be of importance only with longer exposures. Perhaps this is because following a brief stimulus exposure, most people cannot create in themselves a visual feedback loop, but they can in effect do so during a continuous stimulus exposure by looking repeatedly at certain aspects of the stimulus.

In visualized instruction where visuals are used to complement oral/print instruction, the success with which a student comprehends the information depends on how readily he can integrate the linguistic and pictorial inputs to form a common conceptual unit. Since the transmission of oral/print information is sequential and visual information is instantaneous, the student needs somewhat adequate amounts of time to integrate information presented via two sources even though they are complementary. In this respect the data provided in the cited studies provides evidence that identical types of visual illustrations are not equally effective in facilitating student achievement when used for externally paced and self-paced instruction. The method by which students receive their visualized instruction determines not only the type of visual that will be most efficient in increasing student achievement (where visuals, in fact, have been found to be beneficial in improving learning) but also determines the amount of information students can be expected to acquire from different types of visual illustrations.

SUMMARY: MAIN IDEAS

Each instructional medium has unique characteristics which should be employed to achieve specific learning objectives.

Essentially there are two basic strategies for presenting visualized materials for instructional purposes—externally paced and self-paced. In externally paced instruction the student has little or no control over the pace at which the instruction is presented. Self-paced instruction is defined as a learning situation in which each individual student controls the rate at which he proceeds through the instructional materials.

Time is an important instructional variable. Research indicates that if students are not permitted to interact with visualization for as long as is necessary for them to absorb the information contained, there are optimal levels beyond which adding additional realistic detail to visuals produces no further increases in learning and may even function to reduce learning.

The method by which students receive their visualized instruction determines not only the types of visuals that will be most efficient in increasing student achievement but also determines the amount of information students can be expected to acquire from different types of visual illustrations.

Color appears to be an important instructional variable for facilitating student achievement of specific educational objectives.

The types of visuals used in complementing instruction need to be selected with an awareness of the method to be used (externally paced or self-paced) in presenting the stimulus materials to students and with a specific idea about the type of educational objectives to be achieved by the students.

REVIEW ACTIVITIES

1. Distinguish between externally paced and self-paced instruction.
2. List several reasons why previous media research focusing on the comparative instructional effectiveness of two or more media formats have not produced conclusive results.
3. List what you consider to be the advantages and limitations associated with externally paced and self-paced instruction.
4. Discuss the general results reported in this chapter as they relate to the relative effectiveness of different methods of presenting visualized instruction.
5. Discuss how the time variable can be used to explain the results obtained in the self-paced method.
6. Discuss how the time variable can be used to explain the results obtained in the slide/audiotape and television studies.
7. Identify the types of visualization generally found to be most effective in complementing externally paced and self-paced instruction.

RECOMMENDED READINGS

Franzwa, D. 1973. Influence of meaningfulness, picture detail and presentation mode on visual retention. *AV Commun. Rev. 21:* 209-223.

Menne, J. M. & Menne, J. W. 1972. The relative efficiency of bimodal presentation as an aid to learning. *AV Commun. Rev. 20:* 170-180.

Moore, D. M. & Sasse, E. B. 1971. Effect of size and type of still projected pictures on immediate recall of content. *AV Commun. Rev. 19:* 437-450.

Wells, R. F., Van Mondfrans, A. P., Postlethwait, S. M. & Butler, D. C. 1973. Effectiveness of three visual media and two study formats in teaching concepts involving time, space and motion. *AV Commun. Rev. 21:* 233-241.

5

Studies Evaluating Externally Paced Visualized Instruction

LEARNING OBJECTIVES

Upon completion of this chapter the student will be able to:

1. *Identify and discuss the seven research questions which provided the basic experimental orientation for the slide/audiotape studies.*
2. *Summarize the results obtained from the slide/audiotape studies.*
3. *List the basic concerns which prompted the television studies.*
4. *List the major conclusions regarding the effective use of visual materials in externally paced instruction (slide/audiotape, television).*
5. *Explain why the instructional treatments complemented by the more realistic illustrations failed to improve student achievement.*
6. *List two reasons why color appears to be an important instructional variable in improving student achievement.*
7. *Explain why for some educational objectives the use of visualization to complement instruction does not facilitate increased student achievement.*

ORIENTATION

The following studies conducted by the author and his colleagues in a program of systematic evaluation are concerned primarily with externally paced visualized instruction—slide/audiotape and television. Studies cited will highlight some of the more dramatic findings in each area. The format for summarizing the studies provides: (a) a statement of the primary objective(s) for which the study was conducted; (b) the number and level of students who constituted the experimental sample; (c) the variables investigated in the study; (d) the instructional format(s) employed to present the instruction to the students, and (e) the kinds of visualized treatments involved in each study. The visual treatments coincided with the sample illustrations contained in Figure 3-4. Students in each study received the same instructional treatments and were evaluated by identical criterion measures.

A more comprehensive summary of each study is contained in an earlier text (Dwyer, 1972a) along with the complete instructional script, criterion measures, and a complete sequence of illustrations (N=37) used in the visualized treatments.

SLIDE/AUDIOTAPE STUDIES

This section describes the results obtained from studies designed to investigate the effectiveness of different types of visual illustrations, in slide format, that are used to complement oral instruction. Specifically, the studies were designed to:

1. Investigate the effectiveness of the realism continuum for visual illustrations as a reliable predictor of instructional effectiveness;
2. Determine which types of visual illustrations are most effective in promoting student achievement of different educational objectives when visuals are viewed for equal amounts of time;
3. Evaluate immediate and delayed retention resulting from the use of four different types of black and white and colored visual illustrations to complement oral instruction;
4. Determine whether identical visual illustrations are equally effective in facilitating achievement of students in different grade levels;
5. Determine whether boys and girls in the same grade level learn equally well from the same type of visual illustrations;
6. Measure the effectiveness of color as an instructional variable in facilitating student achievement of different educational objectives;
7. Investigate the validity of students' perceptions of the instructional effectiveness of different types of visual illustrations.

Some of the variables investigated in the slide/audiotape studies include: the instructional effectiveness of variations in the amount of realistic detail contained in illustrations, the effectiveness with which different types of visual illustrations facilitate student achievement of specific educational objectives, the relative effectiveness of black and white versus colored illustrations, effect of visualization on immediate and delayed retention, effect of students' sex on their ability to profit from visualized instruction, student perceptions of the instructional value of different types of visual illustrations, effect of individual difference variables on students' ability to profit from visualized instruction, etc. Throughout the entire program of evaluation the same instructional content and criterion measures were employed. In addition, the following visualized treatments were employed throughout the evaluation program (Sample illustrations are located on Figure 3-4, pp. 56-57).

Experimental Treatment Number	Type of Visualization
I	Control—oral/print presentation; *Plate 1*
II	Simple line drawing (b&w); *Plate 2*
III	Simple line drawing (color); *Plate 6*
IV	Detailed, shaded drawings (b&w); *Plate 3*
V	Detailed, shaded drawings (color); *Plate 7*
VI	Heart model photographs (b&w); *Plate 4*
VII	Heart model photographs (color); *Plate 8*
VIII	Realistic heart photographs (b&w); *Plate 5*
IX	Realistic heart photographs (color); *Plate 9*

Dwyer, F. M. (1967a) Adapting visual illustrations for effective learning. *Harvard Educational Review, 37:* **250-63.**

Objectives: 1. To determine at what point further increases in realism in the visual illustrations fail to produce significant differences in achievement of the desired types of learning.

2. To measure the relative effectiveness of three types of visual illustrations used to complement oral instruction: line drawings; detailed, shaded drawings; and realistic photographs.

3. To determine whether there is only one visual learning continuum (representing effectiveness of visual illustrations).
4. To measure immediate retention resulting from the use of visual illustrations to complement oral instruction.

Sample: 108 College Students

Variables: Variations in the amount of realistic detail contained in illustrations; different educational objectives

Treatments: I, II, IV, VIII

Results: 1. Not all types of visual illustrations are equally effective in complementing oral instruction.
2. The visual learning continuum is not an effective predictor of learning efficiency for all types of learning objectives.
3. The realistic photographic presentation was least effective in complementing the oral instruction;
4. The simple line drawing presentation was found to be the single most effective visual in complementing oral instruction.
5. For the teaching of specific types of educational objectives, oral instruction without visualization is as effective as visualized instruction.

Dwyer, F. M. (1968a) Effect of visual stimuli on varied learning objectives. *Perceptual and Motor Skills, 27:* 1067-70.

Dwyer, F. M. (1968b) An experiment in visual learning at the eleventh-grade level. *The Journal of Experimental Education, 37:* 1-5.

Dwyer, F. M. (1969a) An experiment in visual communication. *Journal of Research in Science Teaching, 6:* 67-75.

Dwyer, F. M. (1969b) The effect of stimulus variability on immediate and delayed retention. *The Journal of Experimental Education, 38:* 30-37.

Objectives: 1. To measure the relative effectiveness of eight different types of visual illustrations used to complement oral instruction.

2. To determine at what point further increases in realism in visual illustrations fail to produce significant differences in the achievement of specific educational objectives.
3. To determine whether there is only one visual learning continuum which may be utilized in facilitating the achievement of different types of educational objectives as measured at the four grade levels—ninth, tenth, eleventh, and twelfth.
4. To measure immediate and delayed retention resulting from the use of black and white and colored visual illustrations to complement oral instruction.
5. To determine whether color in visual illustrations is an important instructional variable in promoting student achievement of educational objectives as measured by the criterion tests.
6. To determine whether the realism continuum for visual illustrations proposed by the realism theories is an appropriate and reliable predictor of visual learning effectiveness when different types of visual illustrations are used to complement oral instruction presented to high school students.

Sample: 1,054 High School Students (9th, 10th, 11th, & 12th grades)

Variables: Variations in the amount of realistic detail contained in illustrations; different educational objectives; color vs. b&w treatments; different grade levels; immediate and delayed testing (two weeks later)

Treatments: I, II, III, IV, V, VI, VII, VIII, IX

Results: 1. The use of visuals to complement oral instruction is an effective way to improve student achievement of specific learning objectives; however, it must also be remembered that for some learning objectives oral instruction alone is as effective as visually complemented instruction.
2. The same types of visuals are not equally effective at different grade levels in facilitating student achievement of identical educational objectives.
3. For specific objectives and for students in certain

grade levels, color appears to be an important instructional variable for improving student
achievement.

4. In general, the differential effects attributed to the
different visualized treatments on the immediate
retention tests disappeared on the delayed retention tests.

5. The realism continuum for visual illustrations is
not a reliable predictor of learning efficiency for
high school students. The results of these studies
substantiate the hypothesis that reality may be
edited for instructional purposes.

Dwyer, F. M. (1971a) Color as an instructional variable. *Audiovisual
Communication Review, 19:* **399-416.**

Objectives: 1. To measure the relative effectiveness of four
types of visual illustrations (each in a black and
white and color version) used to complement oral
instruction at the college level.

2. To determine whether the realism continuum for
visual illustrations proposed by the realism
theories is an appropriate and reliable predictor of
visual learning effectiveness when different types
of visual illustrations are used to complement oral
instruction at the college level.

3. To determine whether there is only one visual
learning continuum which can be utilized in
facilitating the achievement of different types of
educational objectives, or whether different visuals vary in the effectiveness with which they facilitate student achievement of different educational
objectives.

4. To determine whether color in visual illustrations
is an important instructional variable in promoting
student achievement of educational objectives as
measured by the criterion tests.

Sample: 261 College Students

Variables: Variations in the amount of realistic detail in illustrations; color vs. black and white treatments; different educational objectives

Treatments: I, II, III, IV, V, VI, VII, VIII, IX

Results: In comparing the results between black and white and colored versions of the four types of visual illustrations (simple line drawings, detailed, shaded drawings, heart model photographs, and realistic photographs) on the individual criterion measures, it was found that color treatments were significantly more effective than black and white treatments in twelve comparisons, while in nine comparisons certain color treatments were found to be significantly more effective than other color treatments. The results indicate that:

1. For specific learning objectives the addition of color in certain types of visuals appears to be an important variable in improving student achievement.
2. The use of visuals (both black and white and color) to complement oral instruction does not automatically improve student achievement of all types of learning objectives.
3. Different types of colored illustrations differ in the effectiveness with which they facilitate student achievement of identical educational objectives.
4. Different types of black and white illustrations differ in the effectiveness with which they facilitate student achievement of identical educational objectives.

Dwyer, F. M. (1971b) Visual learning: an analysis by sex and grade level. *California Journal of Educational Research, 22:* **170-76.**

Objectives: 1. To determine whether boys and girls on the same grade level learn equally well from the same types of visual illustrations.
2. To determine whether identical types of illustrations are equally effective in facilitating the

immediate and delayed retention of boys and girls in the same grade level on tests designed to measure student achievement of different educational objectives.

Sample: 1,054 High School Students (9th, 10th, 11th, & 12th grades)

Variables: Sex; immediate and delayed criterion test scores; different educational objectives; grade level; variations in the amount of realistic detail contained in the different types of visuals; color vs. black and white visuals

Treatments: I, II, III, IV, V, VI, VII, VIII, IX

Results: The results indicate that, within the limits of this study—ninth through twelfth grade, boys and girls learn equally well from identical types of visual illustrations when they are used to complement oral instruction.

Dwyer, F. M. (1971c) **Student perceptions of the instructional effectiveness of black & white and colored illustrations.** *The Journal of Experimental Education, 40: 28-34.*

Objective: To determine whether or not student perceptions of the instructional value of four different types of black and white and colored illustrations were valid in terms of improving their achievement on criterion measures designed to measure specific educational objectives.

Sample: 261 College Students

Variables: Variations in the amount of realistic detail in visuals; different educational objectives; student perceptions; color vs. black and white visuals

Treatments: I, II, III, IV, V, VI, VII, VIII, IX

Results: 1. The type of visuals that students themselves perceive to be the most effective are not always the ones found to be the most effective in facilitating their achievement.

2. All types of visuals are not equally effective in improving student achievement of different learning objectives.
3. Color in visual illustrations appears to be an important instructional variable for facilitating student achievement of specific educational objectives.

Berry, L. H. (1974) An exploratory study of the relative effectiveness of realistic and non-realistic color in visual instructional materials. Doctoral dissertation, The Pennsylvania State University.

Objectives: 1. To determine the instructional effectiveness (immediate and delayed retention) of two forms of color cueing on criterion tests measuring different educational objectives.
2. To investigate the relationship between students' level of dogmatism and different types of color cueing in visualized instruction.

Sample: 224 College Students

Variables: Variations in the amount of realistic detail in illustrations; different educational objectives; immediate and delayed testing; dogmatism; realistic vs. non-realistic color in visuals

Treatments: I, IV, V, Non-Realistic Color

Results: 1. Realistic color cued materials were found to be superior in facilitating student achievement on four of the criterion measures.
2. A significant interaction was found to exist between an individual's relative level of dogmatism and his ability to learn from different types of color cued visual materials when the learning involves completion of a synthesis task.
3. Different types of color cueing devices with similar degrees of visual complexity are not equally effective in aiding learner achievement.
4. Although realistic colored visuals were instructional in facilitating immediate retention of the material, these effects disappeared after two weeks.

Dwyer, F. M. (1976a) The effect of I.Q. level on the instructional effectiveness of black and white and colored illustrations. *Audio Visual Communications Review. 24:* **49-62.**

Objectives: 1. To investigate the effect that I.Q. level has on the instructional effects of black and white and colored illustrations used to complement oral instruction.
2. To determine whether all types of visuals are equally effective in facilitating student achievement of identical educational objectives.
3. To determine whether identical visuals are equally effective in facilitating student achievement of different criterion measures.
4. To determine whether color is an important instructional variable in illustrations used to complement oral instruction.

Sample: 508 College Students

Variables: Variations in the amount of realistic detail in illustrations; different educational objectives; different I.Q. levels; color vs. black and white visuals

Treatments: I, II, III, IV, V, VI, VII, VIII, IX

Results: 1. Color is an important instructional variable for improving students achievement.
2. The instructional treatments containing the line and detailed line drawings (in color) were the treatments found to be most effective in facilitating student achievement.
3. All types of visuals are not equally effective in facilitating student achievement of different educational objectives for students in the different I.Q. levels.

BERRY, L. H. 1976. Interactive effects of color realism and learner I.Q. on visualized instruction. Paper presented at 1976 AECT National Convention, Research and Theory Division, Anaheim, California.

Objective: To determine the relative instructional effectiveness of two forms of color-cued visual instructional materials in facilitating achievement (on immediate and delayed testing) for students possessing different IQ levels.

Sample: 224 College Students

Variables: Variations in the amount of realistic detail in visuals; different educational objectives; different types of color cueing techniques; I.Q., as measured by the Otis Mental Maturity Test; immediate and delayed testing.

Treatments: I, IV, V, Non-Realistic Color

Results:
1. The use of visualization in instructional materials tends to facilitate student learning.
2. Not all types of instructional visuals are equally effective in promoting learner attainment of various educational objectives.
3. Extreme realism in instructional visuals does not appear to aid achievement of students at lower I.Q. levels.
4. Stylized or unrealistic coloring of instructional visuals serves to increase student learning only at higher I.Q. levels.
5. The realism hypothesis is generally supported as a descriptor of visualized learning by high and average I.Q. individuals when color is used as a realism dimension.
6. The realism hypothesis does not appear to be a valid predictor of performance by lower I.Q. learners when visuals are used to augment verbal instruction.
7. Neither the degree of color realism nor individual mental ability differences appear to be significant factors in facilitating the retention of material after a period of six weeks.

Dwyer, F. M. (1977c). **The effect of mental ability on student ability to profit from visualized instruction. Unpublished Research Report. University Park, Pennsylvania: The Pennsylvania State University, University Division of Instructional Services.**

Objectives: 1. To determine whether students' level of mental ability affects their achievement on criterion tests designed to measure different educational objectives.
2. To measure the effectiveness with which identical types of visualization facilitate the achievement of students possessing different mental ability levels.
3. To determine the instructional effect of color in instructional illustrations for students identified as possessing different mental ability levels.
4. To determine whether all types of visuals are equally effective in facilitating student achievement of identical educational objectives.

Sample: 268 College Students

Variables: Variations in the amount of realistic detail contained in illustrations; different educational objectives; mental ability; color vs. black and white visuals

Treatments: II, III, IV, V, VI, VII, VIII, IX

Results: 1. Not all visuals were equally effective in facilitating achievement of students identified as possessing different mental ability levels.
2. The use of specific types of visualization is an effective instructional technique for reducing student performance differences among different mental ability levels for some educational tasks.
3. Color in illustrations was found to be an important instructional variable for improving student achievement of specific educational objectives and for reducing achievement differences among students possessing different mental ability levels.
4. Students with high mental ability consistently achieved equivalent or significantly higher scores on the criterion measures than students with low and medium mental ability regardless of the type of instructional presentation they received.

TELEVISION STUDIES

Extensive research on television reviewed by Reid & MacLennan (1967) and Chu & Schramm (1967) has indicated that televised instruction is at least as effective as conventional instruction. Television, being predominately a visual medium, permits instructors to incorporate a variety of visual materials in their instructional presentations in an attempt to make learning more meaningful. Televised instruction, therefore, utilizes a vast array of different types of visual materials representing varying degrees of realistic detail: films, slides, transparencies, demonstrations, models, charts, drawings, and so forth.

The purpose of this section is to describe the results obtained from studies designed to investigate the relative effectiveness of different types of visual illustrations used to complement oral instruction presented via television. Specifically, the studies were designed to:

1. Investigate the realism continuum for visual illustrations (b&w) as a reliable predictor of instructional effectiveness;
2. Determine whether identical types of illustrations projected on different sized viewing areas (that is, approximately 1' x 1½', 3' x 5', and 4' x 6') have different effects in facilitating student achievement of different educational objectives;
3. Determine which types of visual illustrations are most effective in promoting student achievement of different educational objectives when visuals are viewed for equal amounts of time;
4. Investigate the effect that the use of motion to point out the essential learning cues in the illustrations has on student achievement of different educational objectives;
5. Measure the effect that questions, which precede visual illustrations and which are designed to focus student attention on essential learning cues in the visuals, have on student achievement of different educational objectives;
6. Determine the effectiveness of different types of cueing techniques (arrows, motion, inserted questions) in facilitating student achievement of different educational objectives.

Dwyer, F. M. (1968c) **When visuals are not the message.** *Educational Broadcasting Review, 2:* 38-43.

Dwyer, F. M. (1969c) **An analysis of the instructional effectiveness of visual illustrations presented via television.** *Journal of Psychology, 72:* 61-64.

Dwyer, F. M. (1970a) **Effect of visual stimuli in complementing televised instruction.** *California Journal of Educational Research, 21:* 43-47.

Objectives: 1. To determine whether the realism continuum for black and white illustrations is a reliable predictor of instructional effectiveness when visuals are used to complement oral instruction presented via television.
2. To determine whether the use of visual illustrations specifically designed to complement oral instruction automatically improves student achievement.
3. To measure the relative effectiveness (in facilitating student achievement on five criterion measures) of different types of visual illustrations complementing oral instruction presented via television.

Sample: 588 College Students

Variables: Variations in the amount of realistic detail in visuals; different educational objectives

Treatments: I, II, IV, VI, VIII

Results: 1. The realism continuum for visual illustrations (black & white) is not a good predictor of learning effectiveness for the types of educational objectives evaluated in the television studies.
2. The use of visualization to complement oral instruction is not an effective means of improving achievement of all types of educational objectives when college students view their respective visualized treatments for equal amounts of time.
3. The type of visual illustration found to be most effective in facilitating student achievement of a specific educational objective depends on the type of information needed by the student to achieve that objective.
4. Student achievement of specific types of learning is facilitated by the use of visualization.

Dwyer, F. M. (1969d) Motion as an instructional cue. *Audio-Visual Communications, 3:* **20-21, 41-43.**

Objectives: To determine which types of visual illustrations supplemented by motion were most effective in promoting student achievement on the five criterion measures. Motion was used in the illustrations to focus student attention on the relevant learning cues.

Sample: 139 College Students

Variables: Variations on the amount of realistic detail in visuals; different educational objectives; motion as a cueing technique

Treatments: I, II, IV, VI, VIII

Results:
1. Students who viewed the visually complemented treatments achieved significantly higher scores on the drawing, terminology, and total criterion tests than did students who received the oral presentation without visualization.
2. The use of motion as an attention gaining cue is not an effective instructional technique for improving student achievement when the instructional presentation utilizes the more realistic type of visuals and the students are limited in the amount of time they can interact with the visual information.
3. All types of visuals are not equally effective in facilitating student achievement of different educational objectives.
4. Line drawings supplemented by motion is an effective instructional technique for increasing student achievement of specific educational objectives.

Dwyer, F. M. (1970c) The effect of image size on visual learning. *The Journal of Experimental Education, 39:* **36-41.**

Objectives: To determine whether identical types of illustrations projected on different sized viewing areas (that is, approximately 1' x 1½', 3' x 5', and 4' x 6') have different effects in facilitating student achievement of different educational objectives.

Sample: 588 College Students

Variables: Variations in the amount of realistic detail in visuals; different educational objectives; different sized images

Treatments: I, II, IV, VI, VIII

Results: 1. The use of visual illustrations to complement televised instruction does not automatically improve student achievement of different types of educational objectives.
2. The type of visual illustration found to be most effective in facilitating student achievement of a specific educational objective depends on the type of information needed by the student to achieve that objective.
3. Merely increasing the size of instructional illustrations by projecting them on larger viewing areas does not improve their effectiveness, and for some educational objectives it may actually impede student achievement.

Dwyer, F. M. (1970d) Effect of questions on visual learning. *Perceptual and Motor Skills, 30:* **51-54.**

Objective: To determine which type of visual illustrations, preceded by questions, were most effective in facilitating student achievement on the five criterion measures. Questions were used to channel students' attention to the relevant visual cues in the illustrations.

Sample: 224 College Students

Variables: Variations in the amount of realistic detail in visuals; different educational objectives; questions as a cueing technique

Treatments: I, II, IV, VI, VIII

Results: 1. All types of visuals are not equally effective in facilitating student achievement of different educational objectives.
2. Line drawings supplemented by questions is an effective instructional technique for increasing student achievement on criterion measures similar

to the ones used in this study.

3. The use of questions to focus students' attention on relevant visual learning cues in the more realistic visual illustrations is not an effective instructional technique for increasing students' achievement.

Dwyer, F. M. (1977a) Effect of method in cueing televised instruction. Unpublished Research Report. University Park, Pennsylvania: The Pennsylvania State University, University Division of Instructional Services.

Objectives: To measure the relative effectiveness with which three methods of instructional cueing facilitated student achievement on the five criterion measures.

Sample: 516 College Students

Variables: Variations in the amount of realistic detail in visuals; different educational objectives; different cueing strategies; arrows, motion, and questions. In addition to cues within the instruction, students prior to receiving their respective instructional treatments, were told the specific type of learning that each criterion test was designed to measure and the type of information that they would need to obtain from the instruction in order to perform successfully on the tests.

Treatments: I, II, IV, VI, VIII

Results:
1. Different types of instructional cueing are not equally effective in facilitating student achievement of different educational objectives.
2. Different types of visualization are not equally effective in facilitating student achievement of different educational objectives.

CONCLUSIONS

A number of important conclusions emerge from the studies regarding the effective use of visual materials in externally paced instruction, i.e., slide/audiotape and televised instruction. Table 5-1 cites the studies from which the following conclusions were derived:

Table 5-1. Variables investigated in the externally paced studies.

Variable / Statement	Dwyer, 1967a	Dwyer, 1967c	Dwyer, 1968a	Dwyer, 1968b	Dwyer, 1968c	Dwyer, 1969a	Dwyer, 1969b	Dwyer, 1969c	Dwyer, 1969d	Dwyer, 1970a	Dwyer, 1970b	Dwyer, 1970c	Dwyer, 1970d	Dwyer, 1971a	Dwyer, 1971b	Dwyer, 1971c	Berry, 1974	Berry, 1976	Dwyer, 1976a	Dwyer, 1976b	Dwyer, 1977a	Dwyer, 1977c
The *realism continuum* for visual illustrations is not an effective predictor of learning efficiency for all types of educational objectives.	X	X	X	X	X	X	X	X	X	X	X	X	X	X	X	X	X	X	X	X	X	X
The use of specific types of visual illustrations to facilitate specific types of educational objectives significantly improves student achievement.	X	X	X	X	X	X	X	X	X	X	X	X	X	X	X	X	X	X	X	X	X	X
All types of visual illustrations are not equally effective in facilitating student achievement of different educational objectives.	X	X	X	X	X	X	X	X	X	X	X	X	X	X	X	X	X	X	X	X	X	
The use of visual illustrations designed specifically to complement oral instruction does not automatically improve student achievement.	X	X	X	X	X	X	X	X	X	X	X	X	X	X	X	X	X	X	X	X	X	
For specific students and for specific educational objectives the use of color in illustrations appears to be an important instructional variable for improving student achievement.			X	X	X			X	X					X	X	X						
For the teaching of specific types of educational objectives, oral instruction without visualization is as effective as visualized instruction for certain types of students.	X	X	X	X	X					X	X	X	X						X			X

In general, the differential effects attributed to the different visualized treatments on the immediate retention tests disappeared on the delayed retention test.

All types of cueing techniques are not equally effective in facilitating the effectiveness of different types of visual illustrations—some types of cueing techniques are significantly more effective than others.

Boys and girls in the same grade level learn equally well from identical types of visual illustrations.

Identical visual illustrations are not equally effective in facilitating the achievement of students possessing different levels of an individual difference variable.

The effectiveness of a particular type of visual in promoting student achievement on a specific educational objective depends, in part, on the amount of time students are permitted to interact with the visualized instruction.

For students in different grade levels, the same visuals are not equally effective in increasing achievement of identical educational objectives.

Merely increasing the size of instructional illustrations by projecting them on larger viewing areas does not automatically improve their effectiveness in facilitating student achievement.

Student perceptions of the instructional value of different types of visual illustrations are not valid assessments.

1. The realism continuum for visual illustrations applied to externally paced instruction is not an effective predictor of learning efficiency for all types of educational objectives. An increase in the amount of realistic detail contained in an illustration will not produce a corresponding increase in the amount of information a student will acquire from it.

2. The use of specific types of visual illustrations to facilitate specific types of educational objectives significantly improves student achievement of externally paced instruction.

3. All types of visuals are not equally effective in facilitating student achievement of different educational objectives when instruction is externally paced. The type of visual illustration most effective in transmitting information is dependent upon the type of information to be transmitted.

4. The use of visuals specifically designed to complement oral instruction does not automatically improve student achievement. However, for certain types of educational objectives the use of visuals designed to complement a particular instructional method and to facilitate achievement of a specific educational objective will increase student achievement of the objective.

5. For specific students and for specific educational objectives, the use of color in certain types of visuals presented via the slide/audiotape format appears to be an important instructional variable in improving student achievement. For other educational objectives, however, the added cost of color may not be justified from the instructional effectiveness standpoint.

6. For certain types of educational objectives, externally paced (oral) instruction without visualization is as effective as visualized instruction for certain types of students.

7. In general, the results obtained from the externally paced studies indicated that the differential effects attributed to the different visualized treatments on the immediate retention tests disappeared on the delayed retention tests.

8. All types of cueing techniques do not equally facilitate the instructional effectiveness of different types of visual illustrations; some types of cueing techniques are significantly more effective than others in externally paced instruction.

9. Boys and girls in the same grade level (high school) learn equally well from identical types of visual illustrations when content is presented in an externally paced format.

10. In an externally paced visualized format identical visual illus-

trations are not equally effective in facilitating the achievement of students possessing different I.Q. levels.

11. The effectiveness of a particular type of visual in facilitating student achievement of a specific educational objective depends, in part, on the amount of time students are permitted to interact with the visualized instruction.

12. For students in different grade levels who receive externally paced instruction, the same visuals are not equally effective in increasing achievement of identical educational objectives.

13. Merely increasing the size of instructional illustrations by projecting them on larger televised viewing areas does not automatically improve their effectiveness in facilitating student achievement.

14. Student perceptions of the instructional value of different types of visual illustrations are not valid assessments of their true instructional potential.

DISCUSSION

In the studies in this chapter students viewed externally paced visuals via slides and television. In these presentations all students received the same oral instruction and viewed their respective visual treatments for equal amounts of time. The results of the studies evaluating externally paced visualized instruction indicated that, in general, where the use of visuals did make a difference in improving student achievement on the criterion measures, those illustrations containing relatively small amounts of realistic detail were most effective. These findings seem to substantiate the hypothesis that reality may be edited for instructional purposes and that the realism continuum for visual illustrations is not a reliable predictor of learning efficiency—a hypothesis which has been supported in recent research and literature: Jacobson (1951), Attneave (1959), Miller et al. (1957), Broadbent (1958, 1965), Travers et al. (1964). It seems that any assumption which posits that the mere addition of stimulus units to learning situations will increase communication effectiveness is at best a very tenuous one because all stimulus cues do not seem to be equally effective in eliciting similar responses.

The available evidence from Rappaport (1957), Attneave (1954), Travers (1964, 1970) French (1954), Miller (1956), and Broadbent (1965) seems to indicate that the effectiveness of discrimination learning promoted by the addition of relevant stimuli may be limited by the information-processing capacity of the organism with learning reaching an early peak and then diminishing with the addition of relevant, but superfluous, cues. Broadbent (1958, 1965) has explained that the reduction of learning, as the cue stimulation increases, is caused by the filtering process in the central nervous system, which prevents much of the realistic stimuli from receiving active reception in the brain.

Travers and his colleagues (1964) have stated that visual information is stored in the nervous system in some form isomorphic with line drawings and that this permits the individual to more easily organize, remember, and reproduce edited information as opposed to more realistic information. Bruner et al. (1956) and Travers et al. (1964) have stated that learners do not need highly embellished stimuli in order to recognize the attributes of an object or situation. It may be that only the essentials which are initially perceived and encoded in edited form are retained over extended periods of time. Attneave's research (1954) supports this particular concept; he found that lines bordering objects provide the essence of the information to be conveyed. This would seem to indicate that those visuals closely representing line drawings would be more effective and efficient in facilitating learning than would realistic illustrations which would have to be coded initially by the central nervous system before being received.

A number of possible explanations may be proposed in an attempt to interpret the results obtained in the externally paced studies:

1. In general, in the externally paced studies the more realistic illustrations failed to facilitate student achievement. This may be attributed to the amount of realistic detail they contained, which may have had the net effect of distracting student attention from relevant and important learning cues both in the oral commentary and in the illustrations. Under these circumstances the students may be so preoccupied with the irrelevant parts of the visualized instruction that they may fail to identify, locate, and interact with crucial learning cues.
2. Students participating in the externally paced studies viewed their respective instructional treatments for equal amounts of time. If we can assume that the accuracy and the amount of information that can be perceived in a visual depend on the amount of time available for viewing, then the more realistic presentations would be at a disadvantage since the visual presentations were viewed for equal amounts of time. The process of identification and discrimination is time consuming; the more intricate the visual stimuli, the longer it takes for the

student to identify and absorb the intended information. Even though the more realistic visual illustrations contained more information than the less realistic illustrations, the students apparently did not have sufficient time to take full advantage of the information provided by the additional realistic detail. It may be that realistic illustrations containing high information content are not useful as instructional aids when students are not given adequate time to scan and interact with the information.

3. Students who perceived the more realistic illustrations as redundant and possessing an abundance of irrelevant learning cues may have considered the illustrations to be of low information value and may therefore have been reluctant to interact with them for the time necessary to absorb the information they contained.

4. Students have been exposed to oral instruction in so many learning situations that out of necessity they have developed an ability to learn from instruction without visuals. As a result, in many studies the presentation without visuals was as effective as those with visuals. The effectiveness of the oral presentation without visuals may also be explained in the following manner: when complicated content material is being presented through two channels simultaneously, the visual channel, even though it is reinforcing and illustrating the oral or print channel, may make the student block out the less familiar communication channel (the visual) and concentrate more intently on the information channel with which he is more familiar (the oral or print). Under these circumstances, visualization of content material would have little, if any, effect in improving student achievement on criterion tests measuring different educational objectives.

5. There is also the possibility that students have not been taught how to learn from the more realistic type of illustrations, their prior exposure being merely to acquaint them with reality.

6. The effectiveness with which color in the externally paced visualized presentations facilitated student achievement of different educational objectives may be explained by the fact that the realistic detail in the visuals was accentuated by color; thus, the students were better able to make the appropriate discriminations and obtain the information necessary to achieve on the criterion measures. Also, color in the visuals may have made the visuals more attractive to the students, who thus may have attended to them more vigilantly.

7. Since the differential effects attributed to the various externally paced visualized treatments on the immediate retention tests, in general, disappeared on the delayed retention tests, a number of factors should be considered to interpret this finding. It should be noted that the immediate criterion tests were completed by students immediately after interacting with the instructional unit and that the delayed criterion tests at a time 2 to 4 weeks later. No instruction occurred between the immediate and delayed testing sessions. This does not approximate the normal instructional situation in which initial learning is reinforced and extended in subsequent daily sessions. A second dimension also exists regarding the apparent ineffectiveness of visualization on tests measuring delayed retention—it may be hypothesized that certain types of visuals may produce relatively inefficient learning initially, but greater resistance to loss of retention over time. Further research involving a systematic program of delayed testing over extended periods of time is suggested as a possible strategy to investigate this hypothesis.

SUMMARY: MAIN IDEAS

The realism continuum for visual illustrations is not an effective predictor of learning efficiency for visualized instruction which is externally paced.

Specific types of visuals can be used effectively to improve student achievement of specific educational objectives. For certain types of educational objectives oral and printed instruction without visualization is as effective as visually complemented instruction.

All types of visuals are not equally effective in facilitating student achievement of different educational objectives.

For specific educational objectives, the use of color in certain types of visuals appears to be an important instructional variable in improving student achievement.

Identical visual illustrations are not equally effective in facilitating the achievement of students possessing different I.Q. levels.

Merely increasing the size of instructional illustrations by projecting them on larger viewing areas does not automatically improve their effectiveness in facilitating student achievement.

The assumption which posits that the mere addition of stimulus units to learning situations will increase communication effectiveness is at

best a very tenuous one because all cues do not seem to be equally effective in eliciting similar responses.

REVIEW ACTIVITIES

1. Discuss the implied assumptions associated with externally paced instruction.
2. Summarize the basic objectives which provided the general experimental orientation for the externally paced studies.
3. List the variables investigated in the externally paced studies (slide/audiotape and television).
4. Summarize the general findings obtained from the externally paced investigations.
5. Explain how the results obtained from the externally paced studies support or contradict the realism theories.
6. Summarize the explanations proposed to explain the results obtained in the externally paced studies.
7. Discuss how the findings obtained from the externally paced studies coincide with the findings of other researchers.

SMALL GROUP OR INDIVIDUAL OPTIONAL ACTIVITY

From the original research articles investigating the externally paced studies cited in this chapter, construct a chart illustrating the variables investigated in each study and also the type of visualization which was found to be most effective in facilitating student achievement on each criterion measure. Based on your observations of this chart state several general conclusions.

RECOMMENDED READINGS

Carpenter, C. R. 1962. Boundaries of learning theories and mediators of learning. *AV Commun. Rev. 10:* 295-306.

Conway, J. 1968. Information presentation, information processing, and the sign vehicle. *AV Commun. Rev. 16:* 403-414.

Gropper, G. L. 1966. Learning from visuals: some behavioral considerations. *AV Commun. Rev. 14:* 37-69.

Norberg, K. 1966. Visual perception theory and instructional communication. *AV Commun. Rev. 14:* 301-316.

6

Studies Evaluating Self-Paced Visualized Instruction

LEARNING OBJECTIVES

Upon completion of this chapter the student will be able to:

1. *Identify and discuss the research questions which provided the basic experimental orientation for the programmed instruction studies.*
2. *List the variables investigated in the programmed instruction studies.*
3. *Summarize the results obtained in the programmed instruction studies.*
4. *Identify and discuss the research questions which provided the basic experimental orientation for the textbook studies.*
5. *List the variables investigated in the textbook studies.*
6. *Describe in writing the main conclusions regarding the effective use of visual materials in self-paced instruction (programmed and textbook-like instruction).*
7. *List several reasons why the more realistic types of illustrations were not more effective in facilitating student achievement.*
8. *Explain the effectiveness of the oral/print presentations without visuals in both the externally paced and self-paced instructional presentations.*

ORIENTATION

Self-paced or internally paced instruction is defined as a learning situation in which each individual controls the rate at which he proceeds through the instructional materials, that is, programmed instruction, textbooks, computer-assisted instruction, workbooks, individual slide presentations, and so forth. In many instructional situations which utilize self-paced instruction it is common to employ visualization to complement the printed content material. This has the possibility of facilitating student achievement in several ways: (1) students are able to view and interact with their respective visuals for as long as they feel it is necessary to achieve a comprehensive understanding of the information being presented; (2) the visual illustrations complementing the printed instruction provide concrete referents for the content being presented; (3) the visual illustrations provide a common background of experience for students; that is, many questions resulting from ambiguous interpretations of printed statements may be answered visually, and (4) the visual illustrations have a tendency to stimulate, maintain, and focus student attention on the important aspects of the presentation.

To re-emphasize the importance associated with the method selected for presenting visualized instruction to students (externally paced vs. self-paced) the last three studies summarized in this section relate to comparative evaluations designed to investigate the relative effectiveness of different presentation formats: slide/audiotape, television and programmed instruction.

PROGRAMMED INSTRUCTION

All of the studies summarized in this chapter utilized the instructional script on the human heart. This script was linearly programmed into 37 paragraph-type frames on 8½ x 5½-inch sheets. Figure 6-1 presents sample frames from the programmed sequence. Each instructional frame contained a 2¼ x 3¼-inch illustration which presented visually the same information which was printed on the frame. The visual illustrations used in the programmed treatments were made from slides used in the previously cited externally paced studies. Information transmitted via the programmed printed channel was held constant for each presentation, and the amount of realistic detail contained within the visual illustrations was varied. To promote student interaction, each programmed booklet contained 89 fill-in questions; each frame contained from one to six questions which students were to answer mentally by reading the printed instruction and by inspecting the visual illustrations located on the same frame. Immediate feedback as to the accuracy of the mental response was provided by the appearance of the correct response(s) in the subsequent frame. The programmed booklets were identical in

Figure 6-1. Sample frames from the programmed instruction sequence complemented by simple line drawings (b&w).

LEFT VENTRICLE

HEART

AORTIC VALVE

AORTA

AORTA

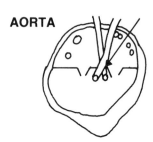

The aorta is the large artery which carries the blood from the left ventricle.

Blood is carried from the left ventricle by the artery known as the _____.

TOP

SIMULTANEOUSLY

FIRST

VALVES

CLOSE

VENTRICLE

PRESSURE

As the ventricles fill, eddies of the blood float the flaps on both the tricuspid and mitral valves out to a partially closed position.

When the ventricles begin to contract, the blood pressure within closes the flaps of both the _____ and the _____ valves.

terms of the printed content; they differed only in the type of visual used to illustrate the instructional content.

Recent research has given us some indication of the effectiveness of self-paced instruction; however, very little research has been conducted relating directly to the use of visual illustrations in improving the instructional effectiveness of this type of instruction. The primary purpose of this section is to report the results of several investigations attempting to measure the relative effectiveness of internally paced instruction complemented by various types of visual illustrations used to facilitate student achievement of specific educational objectives. Specifically, the studies were designed to:

1. Investigate the effectiveness of the realism continuum for visual illustrations as a reliable predictor of instructional effectiveness when the visualized instruction is self-paced.
2. To determine the relative effectiveness of inductive vs. deductive sequencing of visual illustrations in facilitating student achievement of different educational objectives.
3. Determine which types of visual illustrations are most effective in promoting student achievement of different educational objectives when instruction is self-paced;
4. Measure immediate retention resulting from the use of black and white and colored visual illustrations to complement self-paced instruction;
5. Measure the effectiveness of color as an instructional variable in facilitating student achievement of different educational objectives;
6. Investigate the validity of students' perceptions of the instructional effectiveness of different types of visual illustrations in facilitating their achievement on criterion measures;
7. Investigate the effect of knowledge of objectives on achievement of students receiving self-paced instruction;
8. Determine whether the amount of time students interact with their respective self-paced instructional presentations affects their achievement on criterion measures;
9. Investigate the effect of requiring students to make overt responses to questions within visually complemented self-paced instruction;
10. Investigate the effect of students' entering behavior (prior knowledge, I.Q., etc.) on their ability to profit from self-paced visualized instruction.

Dwyer, F. M. (1967b) The relative effectiveness of varied visual illustrations in complementing programmed instruction. *The Journal of Experimental Education, 36:* **34-42.**

Objectives: 1. To measure, by using five criterion tests, immediate retention resulting from the use of three types of visual illustrations used to complement programmed instruction.
2. To determine at what point in the visual learning continuum further increases of realistic detail in visual illustrations fail to produce significant differences in achievement of the desired types of learning.
3. To determine whether there is only one visual learning continuum complementing programmed instruction which may be utilized in facilitating student achievement of different types of educational objectives.

Sample: 86 College Students

Variables: Variations in the amount of realistic detail in illustrations; different educational objectives

Format: Programmed Instruction

Treatments: I, II, IV, VIII

Results: 1. Not all types of visual illustrations are equally effective in complementing programmed instruction.
2. The visual learning continuum is not an effective predictor of learning efficiency for all types of learning objectives.
3. Where visualization was found to be instrumental in improving student achievement, the realistic photographic presentation was found to be most effective.
4. For the teaching of specific types of educational objectives printed instruction without visualization is as effective as visualized instruction.

Dwyer, F. M. (1968d) The effectiveness of visual illustrations used to complement programmed instruction. *The Journal of Psychology, 70:* **157-162.**

Objectives: 1. To measure the immediate and delayed achievement (two weeks later) of students who received the varied instructional treatments.
2. To determine which types of visual illustrations complementing programmed instruction were most effective in promoting student achievement on five criterion tests.
3. To determine whether the amount of time students studied their respective treatments affected later performance.

Sample: 141 Ninth Grade Students

Variables: Variations in the amount of realistic detail in illustrations; different educational objectives; time; immediate and delayed testing

Format: Programmed and Textbook-like Booklets

Treatments: I, II, IV, VIII

Results: 1. Students who receive their instruction via programmed booklets require significantly more time to complete their instruction than do students who receive the same content material in typical textbook format.
2. Students receiving the textbook-like treatments alone achieve as well as those receiving the programmed treatments on the immediate and delayed tests.
3. When comparison was made of the effects of the programmed treatments on immediate retention, the photographic presentation was more effective than the programmed presentation without visuals in facilitating achievement on the identification and drawing tests.

Dwyer, F. M. (1969e) The effect of varying the amount of realistic detail in visual illustrations designed to complement programmed instruction. *Programmed Learning and Educational Technology,* **6:** 147-53.

Objectives: 1. To measure the relative effectiveness of eight different types of visual illustrations designed to complement programmed instruction.
2. To evaluate the realism continuum for still visuals as a reliable predictor of student learning.
3. To determine whether the amount of time that students study their respective instructional presentations affects their achievement on criterion tests.
4. To determine whether color in visual illustrations is an important variable in promoting student achievement of the five educational objectives measured in this study.

Sample: 175 College Students

Variables: Variations in the amount of realistic detail in illustrations; different educational objectives; time; color vs. black and white visuals

Format: Programmed Instruction

Treatments: I, II, III, IV, V, VI, VII, VIII, IX

Results: 1. A realism continuum of visual illustrations extending from a line drawing to the object or situation itself is not the most effective predictor of learning effectiveness for all kinds of educational objectives. Some visuals are better than others in facilitating student achievement of specific educational objectives.
2. The addition of color in specific types of visual illustrations which are to be presented to college freshmen is an important instructional variable in facilitating student achievement of specific educational objectives.
3. In general, students who receive the programmed material complemented by simple line illustrations

require longer periods of time to complete their instructional units.

Dwyer, F. M. (1969f) Student perception of the instructional value of visual illustration. *Medical and Biological Illustrations, 19:* **42-45.**

Objectives: To assess the validity of students' perceptions of the instructional effectiveness of different types of visual illustrations used to complement programmed instruction.

Sample: 88 College Students

Variables: Variations in the amount of realistic detail in illustrations; different educational objectives; visual illustration questionnaire

Format: Programmed Instruction

Treatments: I, II, IV, VIII

Results: An analysis of the data indicated that:

1. Students perceived that the programmed unit complemented with detailed, shaded drawings was the presentation which would be most effective in improving their achievement on the criterion measures;
2. The use of visual illustrations to complement the instructional units was desirable because it facilitated learning and improved understanding of the subject matter;
3. Students confirmed that the visuals they received in their instructional booklets presented visually the same information that was being presented verbally.

The data also indicated that the realistic photograph presentation was most effective in facilitating student achievement on the drawing, identification, and total criterion tests, and, therefore, students' perception that the use of visual illustrations would improve their achievement was confirmed on these three tests. However, the achievement on the terminology and comprehension tests of students who received the programmed treatment without visuals was equal to the achievement of students receiving the visually complemented treatments.

Students perceived the detailed, shaded drawings to be the visuals which would be most effective in improving their achievement. However, this perception was not found to be valid since on the three tests where visuals were found to be effective, the realistic photographs were most effective in improving achievement.

Dwyer, F. M. (1971d) Assessing students' perceptions of the instructional value of visual illustrations used to complement programmed instruction. *Programmed Learning and Educational Technology, 8:* **73-80.**

Objectives: 1. To evaluate the effectiveness of eight types of visual illustrations when students, prior to receiving their instructional units, receive specific instruction as to the type of information they are expected to obtain.
2. To evaluate the validity of student perceptions regarding the instructional value of different types of visual illustrations used to complement programmed instruction.

Sample: 259 College Students

Variables: Variations in the amount of realistic detail in visuals; different educational objectives; student perceptions; color vs. black and white visuals; specific instructions as instructional cues

Format: Programmed Instruction

Treatments: I, II, III, IV, V, VI, VII, VIII, IX

Results: 1. All types of visuals are not equally effective in facilitating student achievement of different learning objectives.
2. The use of specific instructions to focus students' attention on relevant learning cues in the more realistic illustrations is not an effective instructional technique.

3. The types of visuals that students themselves perceive as being more effective are not the ones found to be most effective in facilitating their achievement.

Dwyer, F. M. (1971e) Effect of knowledge of objectives on visualized instruction. *The Journal of Psychology, 77:* **219-21.**

Objectives: To determine which types of visual illustrations complementing programmed instruction would be most effective in promoting students' achievement on five criterion measures when students are told specifically the types of information that should be obtained from the instruction.

Sample: 259 College Students

Variables: Variations in the amount of realistic detail in illustrations; different educational objectives; time; specific instructions as instructional cues

Format: Programmed Instruction

Treatments   I, II, III, IV, V, VI, VII, VIII, IX

Results   1. An analysis of the amount of time required by students in the different treatment groups to proceed through their instructional units indicated that differences were insignificant.
2. The use of specific instructions to focus students' attention on relevant learning cues in the more realistic illustrations is not an effective instructional technique for increasing students' achievement.
3. The use of specific instructions used as cues to complement the simple line presentation (b&w) was found to be an effective technique for increasing student achievement of those educational objectives measured by the drawing and identification tests.

Dwyer, F. M. (1972b) The effect of overt responses in improving visually programmed science instruction. *Journal of Research in Science Teaching, 9:* **47-55.**

Objectives: 1. To determine which type of visual illustration used to complement programmed instruction, and followed by questions, would be most effective in facilitating student achievement on criterion measures designed to measure different educational objectives. Students were required to overtly complete a response to each question as they proceeded through their instructional booklets.

2. To measure the relative effectiveness of eight types of visual illustrations designed to focus student attention on relevant learning cues in the instruction.

3. To determine whether the amount of time students study their respective instructional presentations affects their achievement on the criterion measures.

4. To determine whether color in visual illustrations is an important instructional variable in promoting student achievement of the five objectives measured.

Sample: 266 College Students

Variables: Variations in the amount of realistic detail in illustrations; different educational objectives; time; color vs. black and white visuals

Format: Programmed Instruction

Treatments: I, II, III, IV, V, VI, VII, VIII, IX

Results: 1. All types of visuals are not equally effective in facilitating student achievement of different learning objectives.

2. The addition of color in specific types of illustrations is an important instructional variable for increasing student achievement of specific educational objectives.

3. Students who receive programmed material complemented via simple line drawings in color require significantly more time to complete their instructional units.

**Parkhurst, P. E. (1974) Assessing the effectiveness of self-paced visu-
alized instruction; a multifactor analysis on five different educational
tasks. Doctoral dissertation, The Pennsylvania State University.**

Objectives: To assess the instructional effectiveness of varying
the organizational structure of self-paced visualized
instructional units as measured by criterion tests designed to measure different educational objectives.

Sample: 332 College Students

Variables: Variations in the amount of realistic detail in illustrations; immediate and delayed testing; different
educational objectives; method of instructional
presentation; reading comprehension

Format: Programmed instruction with periodically grouped
review questions and answers; programmed instruction with periodically grouped review questions and
answers *plus* review questions and answers after
each frame; programmed instruction with periodically grouped review questions and answers *plus* review questions after each frame *plus* accessibility to
simultaneous audio presentation.

Treatments: I, II, IV, VIII

Results: 1. On both the immediate and delayed post-test
analyses of variance, significant three-way (organismic, visual realism, criterion measure) interactions were found to exist.
2. Not all methods of presenting instructional information are equally effective in facilitating student
achievement of different educational tasks.
3. The use of questions and answers as a presentation variable to focus student attention on relevant learning cues is an effective instructional

strategy for improving the achievement of students in ꞏspecific reading comprehension levels.
4. Students in the high reading comprehension level improved their performance as each method of presentation cue was added to the previous one.

Parkhurst, P. E. (1975) Students' I.Q. level and performance in self-paced instruction. Paper presented at the 1975 AECT National Convention, Dallas, Texas.

Objectives: This experiment was designed to determine whether:

1. Students' I.Q. level affects their achievement on criterion tests measuring different educational objectives.
2. Identical visuals are equally effective in facilitating the achievement of students who differ in level of intelligence.
3. Different strategies for mediating self-paced instruction are equally effective in facilitating achievement of students who differ in level of intelligence.
4. Different types of visuals are equally effective in facilitating the achievement of students who are at given levels of intelligence.

Sample: 300 College Students

Variables: Variations in the amount of realistic detail in illustrations; different educational objectives; I.Q. levels; method of instructional presentation; questions; immediate and delayed testing

Format: Four methods of presenting programmed instruction utilizing audiotape and periodic review questions

Treatments: I, II, IV, VIII

Results: 1. Not all visuals were equally effective in facilitating student achievement of different educational tasks.
2. Not all students who differed in level of I.Q. achieved at an equal level of performance on

identical criterion measures when they received identical visualized presentations.
3. Students in the high level I.Q. group consistently outperformed both the medium and low groups on all criterion measures, regardless of their instructional treatment.
4. The use of visualization to complement printed instruction seems to be an effective technique to reduce student performance differences among I.Q. levels on some educational tasks.
5. When the nature of the task and individual differences are taken into account, the realism continuum does not seem to be a valid predictor of performance. That is, an increase in visual realism is not automatically accompanied with an increase in student achievement.
6. For some levels of I.Q. and on certain kinds of educational tasks, reality in visualization may be edited with no decrement in student achievement.

Dwyer, F. M. (1975) Effect of students' entering behavior on visualized instruction. *The Journal of Experimental Education, 43:* **78-83.**

Objectives: 1. To determine whether students' level of entering behavior affects their achievement on criterion tests designed to measure different educational objectives.
2. To determine the instructional effect of color in illustrations for students identified as possessing different entering behavior levels.
3. To measure the effectiveness with which identical visuals facilitate the achievement of students possessing different levels of entering behavior.
4. To determine whether all types of visuals are equally effective in facilitating student achievement of identical educational objectives.
5. To determine whether students possessing different entering behavior require different amounts of time to complete their instructional units.

Sample: 587 College Students

Variables: Variations in the amount of realistic detail in illus-
                 trations; different educational objectives; different
                 levels of entering behavior; overt responses re-
                 quired; time

Format: Programmed Instruction

Treatments: I, II, III, IV, V, VI, VII, VIII, IX

Results: 1. Students with high entering behavior consistently
                    achieved equivalent or significantly higher scores
                    on the criterion measures than students with low
                    and medium entering behavior, regardless of the
                    type of instructional presentation they received.
                 2. For students with low and medium entering be-
                    havior the use of visualization to complement
                    programmed instruction is an effective in-
                    structional technique for reducing differences in
                    achievement on specific criterion measures.
                 3. The b&w version of the simple line drawing
                    presentation was found to be the most effective
                    presentation in reducing differences in achieve-
                    ment among students with high, medium, and low
                    entering behaviors on the drawing and terminol-
                    ogy tests. The detailed shaded drawing presenta-
                    tion (b&w) was found to be effective in reducing
                    differences among students possessing different
                    entering behavior levels on the drawing, identifi-
                    cation and comprehension tests.
                 4. Students with low and medium entering behavior
                    generally require more time to interact with the
                    more realistic instructional presentations than
                    students with high entering behavior.
                 5. Color in instructional illustrations was found to be
                    an important instructional variable for improving
                    student achievement of specific educational objec-
                    tives and for reducing achievement differences
                    among students possessing different entering be-
                    havior levels.

Dwyer, F. M. (1977b) An investigation of the instructional effect of inductive vs. deductive sequencing of varied visual illustrations. Unpublished Research Report. University Park, Pennsylvania: The Pennsylvania State University, University Division of Instructional Services.

Objectives: To determine the relative effectiveness of inductive vs. deductive sequencing of varied visual illustrations in facilitating student achievement of different educational objectives.

Sample: 210 College Level Students

Variables: Variations in the amount of realistic detail contained in illustrations; color; type of sequencing—inductively, deductively; different educational objectives

Format: Programmed Instruction

Treatments: II, II & IX, IX & II, V & II, VIII & II (combinations of different types of visualization). Each programmed booklet contained 37 illustrated frames. In the inductive format the first 18 frames contained simple line drawings (b&w) and the remaining frames contained the more realistic illustrations. In the deductive format the more realistic illustrations were positioned on the first 18 frames, the remaining frames being complemented by means of the simple line drawings (b&w).

Results:
1. Inductively and deductively sequenced visuals are not equally effective in facilitating student achievement of all types of educational objectives.
2. Where treatments consisting of combinations of visuals were found to be effective in facilitating student achievement of specific objectives, the inductive treatment (II & IX), in which students initially received the simple line drawings (b&w) and then the realistic photographs (color), was most effective. However, on the drawing and identification tests the treatment (II), which con-

tained simple line drawings (b&w) throughout, was significantly more effective in facilitating student achievement than were booklets in which two types of visuals were inductively or deductively sequenced.

TEXTBOOK-LIKE STUDIES

There is little available evidence supporting the contention that visual illustrations in textbooks currently on the market add proportionately to learning. Furthermore, there are no guidelines available to indicate where visuals should be placed in the content material, what kind of visuals should be employed, and how visualization should be organized to benefit from the use of questions, advance organizers, covert and overt responses, etc. The purpose of this section is to describe the results obtained from studies investigating the relative effectiveness of different types of visual illustrations presented in a textbook-like format.

Students participating in the textbook-like studies received instruction organized in paragraph form, and each page contained the same illustrations as those used to complement the programmed instruction studies. In the textbook studies questions were not positioned on the instructional frames to focus student attention on essential learning cues in the illustrations. However, in some studies, to investigate the instructional effectiveness of questions as advance organizers and as a means to provide the student with the opportunity to make both overt and covert responses, questions were positioned on frames which either preceded or followed the instructional frames. Specifically the studies were designed to:

1. Determine which types of visuals used to complement textbook-like materials are most effective in facilitating student achievement of different educational objectives;
2. Determine whether color in visuals used in textbook-like materials is an important instructional variable in improving student achievement;
3. Determine whether the use of questions to focus student attention on relevant learning cues is an effective instructional technique for improving student achievement of visually illustrated textbook-like content;
4. Investigate whether the amount of time students interact with their respective instructional treatments affects their achievement on the criterion measures;

5. Investigate the effect on student achievement of varying the placement of questions designed to complement visualized textbook-like material;
6. Determine whether requiring students to overtly respond to questions designed to focus their attention on essential learning cues in the illustrations is an effective technique for improving student achievement on the criterion measures;
7. Determine the effect of oral instructional cues used to complement visually illustrated textbook-like material;
8. Determine the relative effectiveness of verbal/visual feedback in facilitating student achievement of different educational objectives;
9. Investigate the instructional effects of inductive vs. deductive sequencing of varied visual illustrations.

Dwyer, F. M. (1971f) An experimental evaluation of the instructional effectiveness of black and white and color illustrations. *Didakta Medica, 3+4:* **96-101.**

Objectives:
1. To measure the relative effectiveness of eight types of visual illustrations used to complement printed instruction.
2. To determine whether all types of visual illustrations are equally effective in facilitating student achievement of different learning objectives.
3. To determine whether color in visual illustrations is an important instructional variable in improving student learning of textbook-like material.
4. To determine whether the amount of time students study their respective instructional presentations affects their achievement on criterion measures designed to measure specific educational objectives.

Sample: 262 College Students

Variables: Variations in the amount of realistic detail in illustrations; different educational objectives; color vs. black and white visuals

Format: Textbook-like Booklets

Treatments;   I, II, III, IV, V, VI, VII, VIII, IX

Results: 1. For specific objectives the addition of color in certain types of visuals appears to be an important instructional variable in improving student achievement.
2. The use of visualization to illustrate verbal instruction does not automatically improve student achievement of all types of learning objectives.
3. Different types of colored illustrations differ in the effectiveness with which they facilitate student achievement of identical educational objectives.
4. Increases in realism in a visual does not always cause a significant increase in learning. There are practical limits beyond which increased realism will not result in increased learning.
5. Analyses conducted on the amount of time students in the different treatment groups interacted with their respective instructional presentations resulted in insignificant differences.

Dwyer, F. M. (1971g) Questions as advanced organizers in visualized instruction. *The Journal of Psychology, 78:* **261-64.**

Objectives: To evaluate the effectiveness of inserted questions as advanced organizers in improving the instructional effectiveness of visualized content material.

Sample: 266 College Students

Variables: Variations in the amount of realistic detail in illustrations; different educational objectives; inserted questions; color vs. black and white visuals

Format: Textbook-like Booklets

Treatments: I, II, III, IV, V, VI, VII, VIII, IX

Results: 1. The use of questions as advance organizers in visualized instruction is not an effective instructional technique for increasing student achievement of different types of learning objectives when students are interacting with the more realistic illustrations.

2. Different types of visuals, when preceded by questions, are not equally effective in facilitating student achievement.

Dwyer, F. M. (1971h) Effect of questions on visualized instruction. *The Journal of Psychology, 78:* **181-83.**

Objectives: To measure the relative effectiveness with which different types of visuals complementing textbook-like material were able to facilitate student achievement of different educational objectives when questions, designed to focus student attention to relevant learning cues, followed each instructional page.

Sample: 272 College Students

Variables: Variations in the amount of realistic detail in illustrations; different educational objectives; inserted questions; overt responses; time; color vs. black and white visuals

Format: Textbook-like Booklets

Treatments: I, II, III, IV, V, VI, VII, VIII, IX

Results: 1. The detailed, shaded drawing presentation in color was the most efficient treatment in facilitating student achievement on the drawing test.

2. On the identification, terminology, comprehension, and total criterion tests, students receiving the presentation without visuals achieved as well as those receiving the visualized treatments.

3. There were no significant differences in the amount of time students needed to complete their respective instructional treatments.

Dwyer, F. M. (1973a) Effect of oral cues on visualized instruction. *Perceptual and Motor Skills, 37:* **843-846.**

Objectives: 1. To measure the effect that oral instructional cues have on the achievement of students receiving instruction complemented via different types of visuals.
2. To determine whether the use of questions to complement instruction in a textbook-like format facilitates student achievement.
3. To determine whether the location of questions in instruction in a textbook-like format affects student achievement.
4. To measure the relative effectiveness of different types of visuals used to complement three different instructional formats.

Sample: 799 College Students

Variables: Variations in the amount of realistic detail in illustrations; different educational objectives; oral cues; three methods of instructional presentation; color vs. black and white visuals

Format: Method 1: Textbook-like content without questions
Method 2: Textbook-like content preceded by questions
Method 3: Textbook-like content followed by questions which students were required to answer overtly.

Treatments: I, II, III, IV, V, VI, VII, VIII, IX

Results: 1. Students receiving instruction without questions achieved as well as students receiving visualized instruction complemented by questions.
2. In the two instances in which differences did occur among methods of presentation, the colored versions of the simple line presentation and the realistic photographic presentation were most effective in facilitating increased achievement.

Arnold, T. C. and Dwyer, F. M. (1973) An investigation of the relationship between stimulus explicitness and entering behavior in facilitating student achievement. *The Journal of Psychology, 84:* 129-132.

Objectives:	1. To investigate the relative effectiveness with which two types of visual illustrations facilitated students' achievement on three criterion tests measuring different educational objectives. 2. To measure the instructional effect of different types of visuals on the achievement of students differing in entering behavior.
Sample:	171 College Students
Variables:	Variations in the amount of realistic detail (stimulus explicitness) in illustrations; different educational objectives; different levels of entering behavior
Format:	Textbook-like Booklets
Treatments:	I, II, IV
Results:	1. There was a significant relationship between entering behavior and performance on criterion tests. Students identified as possessing a high entering behavior level—indicating prior knowledge of human physiology—performed more effectively than those students identified as possessing low entering behavior, regardless of the type of visual illustration they received. 2. No significant relationship was found to exist between the level of stimulus explicitness and achievement on the criterion tests. This was interpreted as meaning that visuals possessing either of the stimulus explicitness levels were equally effective in improving achievement of identical objectives for each of the entering behavior groups.

Arnold, T. C. and Dwyer, F. M. (1975a) Realism in visualized instruction. *Perceptual and Motor Skills, 40:* **369-370.**

Objectives:	To determine the relative effectiveness of two types of visuals in facilitating student achievement of different educational objectives.
Sample:	185 Tenth Grade Students

Variables:	Variations in the amount of realistic detail contained in illustrations; different educational objectives
Format:	Textbook-like Booklets
Treatments:	I, II, IV

Results:
1. Students who received the visually complemented treatments achieved significantly higher scores on the criterion tests than did students who received the presentation without visuals.
2. Some types of visuals are better than others in facilitating student achievement of specific educational objectives.

Arnold, T. C. and Dwyer, F. M. (1975b) An empirical evaluation of the use of educational objectives as guidelines for the development of instructional units. *California Journal of Educational Research, 26:* **115-119.**

Objectives:
1. To determine the feasibility of using educational objectives to provide the guidelines and establish the format of an effective instructional unit.
2. To determine the relative effect of different types of visualized treatments on achievement of educational objectives by students possessing different levels of prior knowledge (entering behavior) in the content area.

Sample:	207 College Students
Variables:	Variations in the amount of realistic detail in illustrations; different educational objectives; different levels of entering behavior
Format:	Textbook-like Booklets
Treatments:	I, II, IV

Results:
1. The use of behavioral objectives can provide viable guidelines for the development of effective instructional units.
2. Instructional units designed to facilitate student

achievement of specific educational objectives can significantly improve cognitive ability.
3. The process followed in designing the instructional unit used in this study generates a product capable of reducing differences among students possessing different levels of cognitive abilities (or entering knowledge levels).

Arnold, T. C. & Dwyer, F. M. (1976) An empirical analysis of the instructional effectiveness of stimulus explicitness in visualized instruction. *The Journal of Experimental Education, 44:* 11-16.

Objectives: 1. To explore the research potential of the Stimulus Explicitness Theory (that learning is contingent on the amount of uncertainty introduced into the learning environment by the stimuli) as a model for guiding research on visualized instruction.
2. To determine the instructional effectiveness of visual materials possessing different degrees of stimulus explicitness and also the effect on students possessing different entering behaviors.

Sample: 171 College Students

Variables: Variations in the amount of realistic detail in illustrations; different educational objectives; different levels of entering behavior

Format: Textbook-like Booklets

Treatments: II, IV

Results: 1. The mere addition of realistic detail to a visual will not automatically improve its instructional potential for facilitating student achievement of all types of educational objectives.
2. The Stimulus Explicitness Theory is not a realistic predictor of learning efficiency.
3. Students possessing high entering behaviors achieved highest on the criterion tests regardless of the type of visualization they received.

Dwyer, F. M. and Arnold T. C. (1976) The instructional effect of verbal/visual feedback in visualized instruction. *The Journal of Psychology, 94:* **39-41.**

Objectives: 1. To measure the instructional effect of verbal/visual reinforcement in facilitating student achievement of different educational objectives.

          2. To determine whether the amount of realistic detail in visualized instruction when complemented via verbal/visual reinforcement influences student achievement.

Sample: 267 College Students

Variables: Variations in the amount of realistic detail in illustrations; different educational objectives; methods of instructional reinforcement

Format: Textbook-like Booklets

Treatments: II, IV

Results: 1. Methods of presenting instructional reinforcement are not equally effective in facilitating student achievement of different educational objectives when visuals containing differing amounts of realistic detail are used to complement printed instruction.

          2. Feedback strategies may be so elaborate as to interfere with rather the facilitate student achievement.

COMPARATIVE STUDIES

This section consists of a brief synopsis of the variables, objectives, and research findings associated with the studies investigating the relative effectiveness of different methods of presenting visualized instruction to students: slide/audiotape, television, programmed instruction. Although these studies have been cited previously, the relative effectiveness of the different methods of presenting visualized instruction was not emphasized, and the variables related to the studies were not identified in their entirety.

Dwyer, F. M. (1970b) Exploratory studies in the effectiveness of visual illustrations. *Audio Visual Communication Review, 18:* **235-249.**

Objectives: To compare the instructional effects of three methods of presenting visualized instruction.

Sample: 218 College Students

Variables: Variations in the amount of realistic detail in visuals; different educational objectives; different methods of instructional presentation; time

Format: Slide/Audiotape, Television, Programmed Instruction

Treatments: I, II, IV, VIII

Results: 1. Identical visuals presented via different presentation formats are not equally effective in facilitating student achievement on the different criterion measures.
2. The amount of time that students are permitted to interact with the visualization in the instructional presentation is instrumental in determining the types of visualization which will be most effective in facilitating student achievement of the different educational objectives.
3. For certain educational objectives the use of visualization to complement oral/verbal instruction is no more effective than the instruction without visualization.

Dwyer, F. M. (1973b) The effect of method in presenting visualized instruction. *Audio Visual Communication Review, 24:* **437-451.**

Objectives: This study was designed to:

1. Measure the relative effectiveness of three methods of presenting visualized instruction (television, slides, programmed instruction) used to complement oral and verbal instruction;

2. Determine whether the same types of visuals viewed via the three presentation formats are equally effective in improving student achievement;

3. Measure the degree of effectiveness by which illustrative material presented via television, slides, and programmed instruction facilitates student achievement of different educational objectives.

Sample: 465 College Students

Variables: Variations in the amount of realistic detail in illustrations; different educational objectives; methods of instructional presentation

Format: Television, Slide/Audiotape, Programmed Instruction

Treatments: I, II, IV, VI, VIII

Results:
1. The effectiveness of specific types of visualization depends on the method used to present the material to the student.

2. Identical visualized treatments presented via the three methods are not equally effective in facilitating student achievement of the types of educational objectives measured in this study.

Dwyer, F. M. (1973c) The relative effectiveness of two methods of presenting visualized instruction. *The Journal of Psychology, 85:* 297-300.

Objectives:
1. To measure the relative effectiveness of two methods of presenting visualized instruction (slides and programmed instruction) by using criterion measures that had been designed to measure different educational objectives.

2. To determine whether color in illustrations, presented via different instructional formats, is an important instructional variable in improving student achievement on different criterion measures.

3. To determine the type of visual which is most efficient in facilitating student achievement on criterion tests measuring different educational objectives.

Sample: 520 College Students

Variables: Variations in the amount of realistic detail in illustrations; different educational objectives; different methods of instructional presentation.

Format: Slide/Audiotape and Programmed Instruction.

Treatments: I, II, III, IV, V, VI, VII, VIII, IX

Results:
1. All types of visuals are not equally effective in facilitating student achievement of different educational objectives.
2. For certain objectives the use of visualization to complement instruction does not improve student achievement.
3. The type of visualization most effective in facilitating student achievement of a specific objective is dependent on the method of instruction employed to present the information to the students.
4. The use of color in certain types of visuals which are used to facilitate student achievement of specific objectives is an important instructional variable.

DISCUSSION

A number of important conclusions emerge from both the studies focusing on the effective use of visual materials in self-paced instruction (i.e., programmed and textbook-like instruction) and the studies comparing the relative effectiveness of different methods of presenting instruction. Table 6-1 cites the studies from which these conclusions were derived.

1. The realism continuum for visual illustrations is not an effective predictor of learning efficiency for all types of educational objectives when visuals are presented via the self-paced instructional format.
2. The use of certain types of visual illustrations to complement self-paced instruction can significantly improve student achievement of specific educational objectives.
3. All types of visuals which are used to complement self-paced instruction are not equally effective in facilitating student achievement of different educational objectives. The type of

Table 6-1. Variables investigated in the self-paced studies.

Statement	Dwyer, 1977b	Dwyer & Arnold, 1976	Dwyer, 1976b	Dwyer, 1975	Parkhurst, 1976	Parkhurst, 1975	Parkhurst, 1974	Arnold & Dwyer, 1976	Arnold & Dwyer, 1975b	Arnold & Dwyer, 1975a	Arnold & Dwyer, 1973	Dwyer, 1973c	Dwyer, 1973b	Dwyer, 1973a	Dwyer, 1972b	Dwyer, 1971h	Dwyer, 1971g	Dwyer, 1971f	Dwyer, 1971e	Dwyer, 1971d	Dwyer, 1970b	Dwyer, 1969f	Dwyer, 1969e	Dwyer, 1968d	Dwyer, 1967b
The *realism continuum* for visual illustrations is not an effective predictor of learning efficiency for all types of educational objectives.	X	X	X	X	X	X	X	X	X	X	X	X	X	X	X	X	X	X	X	X	X	X	X	X	X
The use of certain types of visual illustrations to facilitate specific types of educational objectives significantly improves student achievement.	X	X	X	X	X	X	X	X	X	X	X	X	X	X	X	X	X	X	X	X	X	X	X	X	X
All types of visual illustrations are not equally effective in facilitating student achievement of different educational objectives.	X	X	X	X	X	X	X	X	X	X	X	X	X	X	X	X	X	X	X	X	X	X	X	X	X
The use of visual illustrations designed specifically to complement printed instruction does not automatically improve student achievement.	X	X	X	X	X	X	X	X	X	X	X	X	X	X	X	X	X	X	X	X	X	X	X	X	X
For specific students and for specific educational objectives the use of color in illustrations appears to be an important instructional variable for improving student achievement.			X		X							X			X	X	X		X	X		X			
For the teaching of specific types of educational objectives, printed instruction without visualization is as effective as visualized instruction for certain types of students.	X	X	X	X	X	X	X	X	X	X	X	X	X	X	X	X	X	X	X	X	X	X	X	X	X

Statement									
In general, the differential effects attributed to the different visualized treatments on the immediate retention tests disappeared on the delayed retention test.	X								
All types of cueing techniques are not equally effective in facilitating the effectiveness of different types of visual illustrations—some types of cueing techniques are significantly more effective than others.		X	X X X			X		X	X
Identical visual illustrations are not equally effective in facilitating the achievement of students possessing different levels of an individual difference variable						X		X X X X X	X
The effectiveness of a particular type of visual in promoting student achievement on a specific educational objective depends, in part, on the amount of time students are permitted to interact with the visualized instruction.					X		X		
The method by which students receive their visualized instruction determines the type of visual that will be most efficient in facilitating student achievement of specific educational objectives. Identical visual illustrations are not equally effective when used for externally paced (television, slide/audiotape) and self-paced (programmed or textbook-like format) instruction.		X		X X				X X	X
Student perceptions of the value of different types of visual illustrations are not valid assessments of their instructional effectiveness; that is, aesthetically pleasing visuals may be deceptive in their instructional value.	X	X X		X X					

visualization most effective in transmitting information is dependent upon the type of information to be transmitted.

4. The use of visuals specifically designed to complement self-paced instruction does not automatically improve student achievement of all kinds of educational objectives. Depending on the knowledge level of the students and the difficulty level of the educational objective to be achieved, some objectives can be attained from printed instruction without the use of visualization.

5. For specific students and for specific educational objectives, the use of color in specific types of visualization, presented via the self-paced presentation format, appears to be an important instructional variable in improving student achievement. For other educational objectives, however, the added cost of color may not be justified from the instructional effectiveness standpoint.

6. For certain types of educational objectives, printed instruction without visualization is as effective as visually complemented instruction. For other types of educational objectives the use of certain types of visuals designed to complement a particular instructional method and to facilitate achievement of a specific educational objective will increase student achievement of that objective.

7. In general, the differential effects in achievement attributed to the different self-paced visualized treatments disappeared on the delayed retention tests.

8. All types of cueing techniques are not equally effective in increasing the instructional effectiveness of different types of visual illustrations—some types of cueing techniques are significantly more effective than others in complementing self-paced visualized instruction.

9. The instructional effectiveness of self-paced visualized instruction depends, in part, on individual difference variables inherent within students and on variations in the amount of realistic detail within the different types of visual illustrations.

10. Where visualization is effective in facilitating student achievement of specific educational objectives, the type of visual found to be most effective is dependent on the amount of time students are permitted to interact with their respective visualization and the type of information they are required to obtain from the visualization.

11. The method by which students receive their visualized instruc-

tion determines, in part, the type of visualization that will be most efficient in facilitating student achievement of specific educational objectives. Identical visual illustrations are not equally effective when used for externally paced (television, slide/audiotape) and self-paced instruction (programmed or textbook-like formats).

12. Student perceptions of the value of different types of visual illustrations are not valid assessments of their instructional effectiveness; that is, aesthetically pleasing visuals may be deceptive in their instructional value.

The studies cited in this chapter focused on self-paced visualized instruction and on the relative effectiveness of different methods of presenting visualized instruction. In the self-paced presentations students were permitted to interact with their respective visualized presentations for as long as they felt necessary to acquire the information being presented. In the externally paced presentations students were permitted to interact with the instructional presentations for specified amounts of time. The results of these studies indicate that the realism continuum for visual illustrations is not a reliable predictor of learning efficiency when the instruction is self-paced or externally paced. These studies also emphasize the importance of the amount of time students are permitted to interact with the visualized instruction. In general, when students are given adequate time to interact with the visualized instruction, they profit maximally from the more realistic illustrations; however, this observation seems to be situational. For example, it has been found that when different types of cueing strategies are employed in self-paced visualized instruction to focus student attention on essential learning characteristics, the type of visualization that will be most effective in facilitating student achievement on a specific criterion test changes. This phenomena can be illustrated by citing the results obtained from two programmed instruction studies. In one study (Dwyer, 1967b) the visuals were cued minimally via arrows pointing to essential learning characteristics in the visualization. In a second study (Dwyer, 1971e) in addition to the arrows students were told specifically the objectives of the instruction and the types of information they would need to obtain from the instruction in order to achieve satisfactorily on the criterion measures. In the first study (Dwyer, 1967b) in which cueing was minimal, the realistic photographic presentation (b&w) was the treatment found to be most effective in facilitating student achievement on the drawing test. In situations in which cueing is minimal it may be that students are more inclined to interact conscientiously with the more realistic illustrations in absorbing the information they contain. In the second study (Dwyer, 1971e) in which students were told precisely the information that they needed to achieve on the criterion measures, the simple line drawing presentation was found to be most effective in facilitating student achievement on the drawing test. It may be that after students are aware of the specific information they need to acquire from visualization and they identify this information in the visuals, they have a tendency to cease interacting with the additional information contained in the more realistic illustrations, thereby hindering their potential learning. This is probably one reason why the more realistic illustrations are less effective than the less realistic illustrations when the visualized presentations are more than minimally cued.

In general, explanations similar in nature to those proposed in Chapter 5 for the results obtained in the externally paced studies also appear appropriate for the self-paced studies.

1. The additional stimuli contained in the more realistic type of illustrations may have interfered with the information to be transmitted, thereby reducing the effectiveness of the more realistic visuals. The initial impact of the excessive realistic detail may be sufficiently strong to detract attention from relevant and important learning cues. For example, the learner may be so preoccupied with the irrelevant parts of the visual that he may fail to identify and locate crucial learning cues.

2. Students who perceived the more realistic illustrations as redundant and possessing an abundance of irrelevant learning cues may have considered the illustrations to be of low information value and may therefore have been reluctant to interact with them for the time necessary to absorb the information they contained.

3. The effectiveness of the oral/print presentations without the visuals in both the externally and self-paced presentations may be explained in the following manner: when complicated content material, similar to that which was being measured by the comprehension test, is being presented through two channels simultaneously, the visual channel, even though it is reinforcing and illustrating the printed channel, may make the student block out the less familiar communication channel (the visual) and concentrate more intently on the information channel with which he is more familiar. Under these circumstances, visu-

alization of content material would have little, if any, effect in improving student achievement on criterion tests measuring the more complex educational objectives. Similarly, the ineffectiveness of the visualization in improving student achievement on the terminology test may be explained by the fact that students were not dependent on the visualization to acquire the kind of information measured by this type of test. Presumably, students are capable of acquiring the type of information equally well from oral or verbal instruction without visualization.

4. Students have been exposed to printed instruction in so many learning situations that out of necessity they have developed an ability to learn from instruction without visuals. As a result, in many studies the presentation without visuals was as effective as those with visuals for specific types of learning objectives. There is also the possibility that students have not been taught how to learn from the more realistic type of illustrations, their prior exposure being merely to acquaint them with reality. It is also possible that in specific instructional situations the objectives measured by the criterion tests did not require students to effectively utilize the information presented in the more realistic illustrations.

5. The effectiveness of color in visual illustrations in facilitating student achievement of different educational objectives may be explained by the fact that the realistic detail in the visuals was accentuated by color; thus, the students were better able to make the appropriate discriminations and obtain the information necessary to achieve on the different criterion measures. Color in the visuals may have made the visuals more attractive to the students, who thus may have attended to them more vigilantly.

SUMMARY: MAIN IDEAS

The realism continuum for visual illustrations presented via the self-paced instructional format is not an effective predictor of learning efficiency for all types of educational objectives.

The use of certain types of visual illustrations to complement self-paced instruction can significantly improve student achievement of specific types of educational objectives.

For certain educational objectives the addition of color in visuals used to complement self-paced instruction appears to be an important instructional variable.

The use of visuals specifically designed to complement self-paced instruction will not always improve student achievement of the content material.

The instructional effectiveness of visualization depends, in part, on the individual difference variables inherent within students and on variations in the amount of realistic detail contained within the different types of visual illustrations.

All types of cueing techniques are not equally effective in increasing the instructional effectiveness of self-paced visualized instruction.

The differential effects attributed to the self-paced visualized treatments on the immediate retention tests disappeared on the delayed retention tests.

All types of visuals used to complement self-paced instruction are not equally effective in facilitating student achievement of different educational objectives.

Identical types of visualization presented to students via different presentation formats (slide/audiotape, television, programmed instruction, etc.) are not equally effective in facilitating student achievement of identical educational objectives.

REVIEW ACTIVITIES

1. Summarize the basic objectives which provided the general experimental orientation for the self-paced studies.
2. List the alleged advantages associated with self-paced visualized instruction.
3. List the variables investigated in the self-paced studies.
4. Summarize the general findings obtained from the self-paced investigations.
5. Explain how the results obtained from the self-paced studies support or contradict the realism theories.
6. Summarize the explanations proposed to explain the results obtained in the self-paced studies.
7. Summarize the results obtained from the studies investigating the relative effectiveness of different methods of presenting visualized instruction to students.

SMALL GROUP OR INDIVIDUAL ACTIVITY

From the original research articles reporting the self-paced studies cited in this chapter, construct a chart illustrating the variables investigated in each study and also the type of visualization which was most effective in facilitating student achievement on each criterion measure. Based on your observations of this chart state several general conclusions.

RECOMMENDED READINGS

Allen, W. H. 1971. Instructional media research: past, present, future. *AV Commun. Rev. 19:* 5-18.

Carpenter, C. R. 1957. Psychological concepts and audiovisual instruction. *AV Commun. Rev. 5:* 361-369.

Strang, H. R. 1973. Pictorial and verbal media in self-instruction of procedural skills. *AV Commun. Rev., 21:* 225-232.

Travers, R. M. W. & Alvarado, V. 1970. The design of pictures for teaching children in elementary school. *AV Commun. Rev. 18:* 47-64.

7

Color as a Variable in Visualized Instruction

LEARNING OBJECTIVES

Upon completion of this chapter the student will be able to:

1. *Describe the physiological effects that color has on the human organism.*
2. *Explain how color may be a viable instructional variable in an individual's informational coding process.*
3. *Summarize the research findings relative to learner preferences for color and the use of color in instructional materials.*
4. *Cite several reasons why some research studies report that color is an important instructional variable and others report that the use of color in visualized materials is insignificant in improving student achievement.*
5. *Discuss in writing the statement that "color may be an important instructional variable in facilitating student achievement of specific educational objectives."*
6. *Explain the justification for the use of color in visual materials both as an attention gaining and an attention sustaining technique.*
7. *List three reasons why color may not be a viable instructional variable for facilitating student achievement of all types of educational objectives.*
8. *Cite six researchers whose research and writings tend to emphasize the importance of color as an instructional variable.*

ORIENTATION

Color may be considered to be a ubiquitous characteristic visible in all our daily activities. Its presence in the visualization of instruction adds a dimension unobtainable in monochromatic illustrations. Since the human organism appears to possess a limited capacity for assimilating and processing information, it would seem that the manner in which color is employed in instructional illustrations is extremely important. For example, the improper use of color can increase the complexity of the information to be transmitted beyond the information handling capacity of the student. However, the use of color judiciously and selectively employed in illustrations can be both functionally effective and aesthetically pleasing. Color not only makes illustrations attractive and emotionally appealing but it can make them instructionally more effective in facilitating student achievement of specific kinds of learning objectives. Although early research conducted on the global effectiveness of color in improving student learning provided evidence that its presence is not always necessary, subsequent research (Dwyer, 1972a) has provided substantial evidence that color is definitely a viable instructional variable for improving student achievement of specific types of learning tasks.

PHYSIOLOGICAL EFFECTS OF COLOR

Birren (1959, p. 127), investigating the measurable effects that color can have on the human organism, found that color can be used to influence the functions of the nervous system, i.e., muscular tension, cortical activation, heart rate, and respiration. Christie et al. (1972) and Symmes and Eisengart (1971) found that brain waves are affected by the complexity of visual stimuli. Fisher and Ong (1972) concluded as a result of their study that the amplitude of galvanic skin response is directly related to luminance of a visual stimulus. A further survey of the literature revealed that the perception of color has also been found to be capable of arousing definite emotional and aesthetic reactions, likes and dislikes, and pleasant and unpleasant associations (Goldstein, 1942; Kouwer, 1949; Rudisill, 1952; Collier, 1957; Smith, 1958; Gerard, 1958; Birren, 1959; Schwartz, 1960). Scanlon (1970a,b), in analyzing viewer perceptions toward television, found that students who viewed color programs included more emotional content in their written description of the programs.

COLOR CODING

Miller (1956), in summarizing several studies examining the limitations associated with the information processing capacities of the sense organs, concluded that the human organism must engage in extensive coding of incoming stimulus information. This coding is essentially a process which involves the retention of what is considered to be the most critical information and the disregarding of that stimuli considered to be redundant or irrelevant before transmission to the information processing centers occurs. Coding enables learners to organize and/or categorize stimuli into meaningful patterns which enables them to interpret and adjust to their environment.

For the learner, coding begins initially in the perceptual system where the process of information compression is initiated. Informational stimuli is subjected to compression at various stages enroute to the central nervous system. This initial coding may be considered to be a result of energy transformation since visual stimuli reaches the learner in the form of radiant energy, is converted to chemical energy in the eye, and is transmitted from the retina area to the central nervous system in a form similar to electricity. This process of transforming instructional stimuli from one form of energy to another presumably results in considerable information loss. Furthermore, since there are no direct pathways through which informational stimuli can travel through the central nervous system, additional information loss occurs as the informational impulses are transmitted along the numerous and circuitous pathways of nerve fiber. In this respect, information compression generally means that complex stimuli entering the perceptual system are simplified before being transmitted to the central nervous system. According to the verbal-loop hypothesis (Glanzer & Clark, 1963a,b, 1964), visual perceptions of an object or situation are immediately translated into a series of words, and it is these words that provide the coding structures for storage and subsequent recall. Research supporting the hypothesis that visual (print) stimuli tends to be transformed into the verbal form prior to storage has been provided by a number of researchers (Sperling, 1963; Conrad, 1964; Wickelgren, 1965a,b; Corcoran, 1967; Davies, 1969). However, Tversky's research (1969, 1973) indicates that, depending on the perceived use of the information, people can manipulate their coding strategies so that the information will be stored either verbally or pictorially.

That the process of organizing and categorizing incoming instructional stimuli is facilitated via the use of visualization can be extracted from the work conducted by Jenkins and Russell (1952),

Bousfield et al. (1957), Jenkins, Mink, and Russell (1958), and Dwyer, (1972a). The precise relationship which exists between coding and memory is not clear; however, it is rather certain that visual images are retained both in short term (Hull, 1951; Broadbent, 1958) and long term memory (Underwood, 1963, 1965). One conclusion which may be derived from the literature indicates that word associations with pictures can be instrumental in facilitating learning (Reese, 1965; Gibson, 1966; Milgram, 1967; Arnheim, 1969; Conrad, 1971; Dwyer, 1972a; Levin et al., 1976). Apparently then, one function of presenting visualization in conjunction with oral or printed stimuli is to assist the information processing machinery by providing structure whereby new information can be stored (Cofer, 1959; Deese, 1962; Cohen, 1963; Kendler, 1966).

A number of studies have been conducted which have investigated the use of color in a situation in which the color did not contribute to the message content but functioned only as a cueing or coding device for facilitating the retrieval of essential learning cues. In general, these studies found that this use of color facilitated student learning of both paired associate and concept learning tasks (Weiss & Margolius, 1954; Green & Anderson, 1956; Peterson & Peterson, 1957; Bourne & Restle, 1959; Saltz, 1963). Kanner (1968, pp. 1-2), in summarizing the results of a number of studies evaluating the effect of increasing the number of items which are color coded in serial learning (Green & Anderson, 1956; Jones, 1962; Smith, 1963; Smith & Thomas, 1964; Smith, Farquhar & Thomas, 1965), indicated that:

> A consistent finding is that as the number of color coded items increases, the value of color as a cue for selecting important information decreases. As the total number of items decreases, the value of color decreases. In other words, in a very dense visual display color coding at some minimal level helps in picking out important information, but if you increase this use of color its value as a selection cue diminishes.

The author (Dwyer, 1971a, pp. 399-400), in concluding an extensive survey of the literature relative to the use of color as a viable coding variable in visualization, indicated that:

> Although color is an important variable in the design and cost of instructional materials, the research concerning its effectiveness in increasing student learning is at best inconclusive . . . . There is very little experimental evidence as to how the addition of color to various types of visual illustrations will affect student achievement.

If instructional stimuli received by the senses must be coded before it becomes knowledge, then the process of coding becomes a very important issue to educators desiring to improve the quality of the teaching-learning process. It would seem that if information has not been adequately coded prior to being transmitted, or if the learners have not been given sufficient directions as to how to code specific types of information, or if learners have not had ample opportunity to develop the basic prerequisites to coding the incoming stimuli, learning will be, at best, less than optimum. Coding then may be considered to be a process, a set of rules, or a strategy which students need to acquire or further develop if they are to achieve maximally from visually complemented presentations. Judging from the current level of use of color in visual materials to brighten, sharpen, and to dramatize essential message characteristics, commercial and educational producers of visual materials are already convinced that color facilitates information processing by providing structures for the storage of new information and by providing categories by which familiar or already existing information can be more efficiently stored.

INFORMATION PROCESSING AND COLOR PREFERENCES

It is generally accepted that the visual material in an instructional presentation facilitates student achievement by: (a) increasing student interest and/or motivation; (b) focusing student attention on essential learning characteristics in the instruction, and (c) by providing a common background of experience so that answers from questions arising out of misinterpretations of oral/printed statements may be answered visually for the student. The individual preference syndrome regarding preferences in visualized instruction becomes apparent when one considers the use of color. Research in this area has provided evidence to support the contention that children generally prefer interacting with visualized materials which contain color (MacLean, 1930; Long, 1945; Rudisill, 1952; French, 1952; Katzman & Nyenhuis, 1972). In general, the research seems to indicate that initially children prefer simple illustrations and then develop a propensity toward the more realistic or complex illustrations. Vitz (1966) maintains individuals have preferences as to the optimum amount of complexity that should be contained in a visual; as their experience in learning from visualization increases so does the preference for the more complex types of visualization. Dember and Earl (1957) have also suggested that students have a preferred or optimal level of stimulus complexity at which they enjoy interacting with visualization and that this level of complexity is in turn based on the complexity of the subject matter, the experiential background of the learner, and the complexity of the stimulus itself. Nunnally et al. (1969) found that a relationship existed between the degree of incongruity (visual complexity) and the amount of time students will spend viewing illustrations.

Students are constantly seeking, interacting with, and processing information received from the immediate environment (Fowler, 1965; Thomas, 1965; Vitz, 1966); however, it appears that no two students learn precisely in the same manner even though they may attain the same level of achievement. Given a common stimulus field, students will perceive and react in different ways. This is so because each student enters into the formal learning situation with certain potentials for achieving and styles for learning, and the ability to process information varies from one individual to another. This fact is supported by the phenomenon that when students are presented identical instruction, some will learn quickly, others at a moderate pace, and others at a decidedly slower pace. Learners are also very individualistic in that they process that information which appears to them to be the easiest or most familiar first while disregarding that which they consider to be the most complex or least interesting. These selective processes are operative at all levels of human experience and at all stages in the communicative processes between individuals (Tyler, 1951). In this sense learning appears to be idiosyncratic in that each learner develops preferences for receiving information, e.g., oral, printed, visual, and within these preferences develops strategies for processing incoming information (Woodworth & Schlosberg, 1954; Postman & Riley, 1957; Miller et al., 1960; Ingersoll, 1970). For example, some learners prefer to receive instructional stimuli via the visual sense, others through the auditory sense. Research in this area (Otto, 1964; Bourisseau et al., 1967; Jakobson, 1967) indicates that people respond differentially to linear (words) and iconic (visual) orderings within their environment and also that they learn differentially from different methods of instruction (Tallmadge & Shearer, 1969; Doty & Doty, 1964; McKeachie, 1967). Miller et al. (1960) obtained data which indicated that the visual processing strategies follow a plan established through previous experience and conditioning. Solomon and Howes (1951) have reported evidence to support the fact that the speed of perceptual recognition is related to the frequency of prior experience with the stimuli. This finding might logically be extended to imply that if a student has established strategies for processing information presented via a specific format he might be most proficient in acquiring information presented in that manner. Consequently, it would seem apparent that the most efficient and profitable means of instruction might depend on the development and presentation of instruction which is compatible with the students' learned preferences and patterns of organizing, storing and retrieving information.

Although according to Lumsdaine (1963) the use of color in instructional materials for its attractiveness and attention-getting qualities has often been overrated, one of the primary assumptions for the use of color in media is that it increases the effectiveness of the material by making it more attractive, thereby evoking more attentive behavior on the part of the learner. This assumption that the addition of color in media can command attentive behavior has been substantiated to a degree by the Burke Marketing Research Study (1960). This study, investigating the effectiveness of color television commercials versus the same commercials viewed in black and white, found that color commercials received higher ratings and were viewed to their completion by a greater percentage of viewers. It was also found that the use of color prompted greater recall of seeing the commercial and that viewers were better able to remember specific details from the presentations (Burke Marketing Research, 1960; Kumata, 1960; Gallup & Robinson, 1965; Schaps & Guest, 1968).

Malter (1948) in summarizing the early research on color preferences indicated that children preferred color pictures to those in black and white. Rudisill (1952) in a later study concluded that children prefer: (a) the more realistically colored illustrations to uncolored illustrations; (b) realistic illustrations to abstract drawings, and (c) realistic color to unrealistic color. Additional research investigating learner preferences have found that: (a) students across a wide age range express a consistent preference for complexity and variability in visualization (Unikel & Harris, 1970; Baltes & Wender, 1971; Stevenson & Lynn, 1971), and (b) students prefer to receive color in illustrations (Dooley & Harkins, 1970; Dwyer, 1972a). The findings that students exhibit marked preferences for color is not surprising when we consider that they live in a visually colored environment. In general, reviews of color research (MacLennan & Reid, 1967; Bretz, 1970) cite corroborating evidence that students prefer color in illustrative materials.

STUDENTS' PERCEPTION OF VISUAL EFFECTIVENESS

In a study (Dwyer, 1971d) designed to evaluate the validity of student perceptions of the instructional effectiveness of eight different types of visual illustrations, eight types of black and white and colored illustrations were used to complement programmed instruction. The programmed presentation without visuals of the heart was considered the control treatment. Each student participating in this college level study received a pretest, interacted with his respective programmed instructional booklet, received four individual criterion tests, and completed a Visual Illustration Questionnaire. This questionnaire was designed to obtain student perceptions of the instructional effectiveness of varied types of visual illustrations used to complement programmed instruction. The questionnnaire consisted of seven multiple-choice questions and a sample of one of each of the various types of visuals used in the eight experimental treatment groups. Students referred to the sample visuals in answering the following questions:

1. Which type of visual illustration do you think would have best improved your achievement on the criterion tests?
2. Do you think that the visuals contained in your instructional presentation helped you to understand the content material?
3. What is your opinion of the instructional value of the visual illustrations you received in your instruction?
4. What is your reaction to the contention: the use of visual illustrations in your instructional presentation improved your learning?
5. Did the type of visual you received (color or black and white) effectively show the essential details of the subject matter? (That is, are the crucial learning cues clearly emphasized in the type of visual you received?)
6. Do you think you learned as much from the visualized presentation as you would have if the same content had been presented in the conventional manner with an instructor present?
7. How would you evaluate the adequacy of the amount of information contained in the visualization you received in the instructional presentation?

An analysis of the students' responses on the Visual Illustration Questionnaire indicated that students (Dwyer, 1971d, p. 76):

1. Perceived the detailed, shaded drawing presentation (color) and the heart model presentation (color) as containing the types of illustrations that would be most effective in improving their achievement on the criterion measures;
2. Indicated that the use of visual illustrations to complement programmed instruction was desirable because they facilitated learning and improved their understanding of the content material;
3. Indicated that they felt the black and white illustrations were ineffective and that colored illustrations would have been more effective; however, approximately half the students who received the simple line presentations

(b&w) and (colored) felt that the black and white illustrations were effective in depicting crucial learning cues;
4. Indicated that they learned more from their respective visualized presentations than they would have if the same content had been presented in the conventional manner with an instructor present;
5. Perceived that the illustrations they received in complementing their instruction contained a sufficient amount of information for them to learn . . . .

Comparisons were made between the types of visuals students indicated would be most effective in facilitating their achievement and those which were actually found to be most effective in facilitating student achievement on the individual criterion measures. The following summary is from the original study (*Ibid.*, pp. 77-80).

In comparing the effectiveness of the visualized treatments on those criterion tests where it was found that the presence of visuals did improve students' achievement, the results indicated that students who received the simple line presentation (b&w) achieved significantly higher scores on the drawing and identification tests. In comparing student perception of the instructional value of visual illustrations with the experimental data resulting from an analysis of student performance on the criterion tests, it was found that students' perceptions that the use of visual illustrations would improve their achievement was confirmed on the drawing and identification tests. However, these perceptions were not justified in regard to the terminology, comprehension, and total criterion tests, for on these tests the achievement of students who received the programmed presentations without visuals of the heart was relatively equal to the achievement of those students receiving the visually complemented treatments. Students' perceptions that colored illustrations would be more effective than black and white was not substantiated. In general, students perceived that the detailed, shaded drawings presentation (color) and the heart model presentation (color) contained the types of illustrations which would have been most effective in facilitating their achievement on the criterion measures. However, this was not found to be the case, since on the two tests where the use of visuals was found to be effective, the simple line presentation (b&w) was found to be the most effective treatment in improving achievement.

This argument is further substantiated by the fact that the students who received the simple line presentation (b&w), the presentation found to be most effective in complementing programmed instruction, indicated that they felt that the simple line presentation in color would have been more effective in improving their achievement. This result is also in agreement with previous research (MacLean, 1930; Ibison, 1952; and Rudisill, 1952) which has found that students would prefer to view colored instructional materials rather than black and white.

The inconsistencies between student perceptions and the achievement data obtained in this study are in agreement with previous findings (Elliott, 1949; Twyford, 1951; Macomber & Siegel, 1957) which suggest that student perceptions (attitudes) toward instructional media are probably not a valid indication of their instructional value since only small relationships exist between their preferred types of visualization and the level of achievement attained on the specific criterion measures. Data provided by James (1962) supports this position; he found that providing students with a preferred method of learning meaningful material makes no significant differences in the amount of learning that will occur.

INSTRUCTIONAL EFFECT OF COLOR

Color has been used as an attention gaining and an attention sustaining device in instructional situations. However, even though the use of color in the production of instructional materials is widespread, its relative effectiveness as an aid in improving student achievement still remains inconclusive and at best contradictory. The significance of the ambiguous status of color in instructional materials has been emphasized by Hoban and Van Ormer (1950), Hoban (1960), and Travers et al. (1964). Hoban (1960, p. 98), in discussing the use of color in film, has stated that generally there are no significant differences or there are contradictory results indicating that in some films color is significantly superior and in others black and white is favored.

Most of the early research relative to the use of color in instructional situations indicates that it has not been a viable instructional variable in improving student achievement. But it is important to recall that much of this early research evaluating the instructional effectiveness of color was conducted using content material which was primarily informational in nature and not designed to facilitate the achievement of specific educational objectives. The use of these kinds of materials in an empirical setting make it almost impossible to determine the instructional effects of color. For example, in several of the early experiments evaluating the relative effectiveness of color and black and white films and videotapes, entire presentations were in color. This means that both irrelevant and relevant cues were emphasized equally by the color, thus creating the situation in which the overuse of color may have contributed negatively in terms of the amount of information students were able to acquire from the instruction. The use of color in these early experiments may be considered to be merely a superfluous addition to the content material and did not in any way cue or focus student attention to relevant learning features in the instruction. A more appropriate use of color would have been to construct one version of the film in which relevant cues were colored and compare the instructional effectiveness of this version with a black and white version.

The process of simply adding color to a visual abstraction (symbol) does not intuitively seem to justify the expectation that increased learning will occur. Granted the addition of color may function as an attention gaining device and make the visual more likeable, but its presence very rarely adds substantially to increased learning (Dooley & Harkins, 1970). The results of a considerable number of empirical studies have provided evidence that no increase in learning will occur as a result of using color in instructional materials—unless color is directly related to the instructional content (MacLean, 1930; Ibison, 1952; VanderMeer, 1952, 1954; Zuckerman, 1954; May & Lumsdaine, 1958; Kanner & Rosenstein, 1960, 1961; Katzman & Nyenhuis, 1972; Reich & Meisner, 1976). Hoban (1949, pp. 4-5) summarized his impressions of the early use of color in films in the following manner:

> A photograph looks like the object photographed. It is an abstraction of visual form. Colors may make this more pleasant but do not necessarily add definition to the abstractions of form. They make the form richer and deeper and the reaction to it perhaps warmer, but there is room for doubt that the additional learning that comes to an audience viewing the saturated and perhaps distorted colors of available color film justifies the additional expense involved in the production of color films for general instruction.

> Obviously, there are situations in which colors provide the basis for a discrimination, and in such cases colors belong in a film whose object it is to teach this discrimination; but, on the whole, colors have been used indiscriminately with reference to the subject matter of the film. The purpose of the use of colors in instructional films has apparently been to increase audience attention and, perhaps, feeling tone.

Dale (1954) in discussing the use of color in visual materials has indicated that educators have precious little in terms of empirical evidence for establishing guidelines for the use of color in instructional materials. Otto and Askov (1968, p. 161), in reviewing several studies investigating the instructional effectiveness of color, have summarized their findings in the following manner: "Color has been used to carry basic information, but little has been done to make use of existing research, probably because the cue value of color in learning is still essentially unclear." Similarly, Birren (1959, p. 125), in focusing on the research related to the effects that color has on the human organism, has indicated that ". . . the literature on the subject varies from a great abundance of pure fantasy to a few and scattered research studies which might be accepted as valid."

However, there is an increasing number of studies (Table 7-1) being conducted, the results of which may be interpreted as supportive of the contention that color can be an important instructional variable in improving student achievement. Since the results from

Table 7-1. Studies supporting color as an effective instructional variable.

Van Buskirk, 1932	Jones, 1965
Long, 1945	Travers, Chan & Van Mondfrans, 1965
Weiss & Margoluis, 1954	Hake, Rodwan & Weintraub, 1966
Green & Anderson, 1956	Mackworth & Morandi, 1967
Peterson & Peterson, 1957	Rust, 1967
Anderson & Fitts, 1958	Otto & Askov, 1968
Bourne & Restle, 1959	Schaps & Guest, 1968
Exner, 1959	English, 1969
Senden, 1960	Travers, 1969
Christner & Ray, 1961	Tolliver, 1970
Saltz, 1963	Vollan, 1971
Smith, 1963	Lamberski, 1972
Underwood, 1963	Kauffman & Dwyer, 1974
Smith, Farquhar &	Berry, 1975, 1976, 1977
Thomas, 1965	Donahue, 1976

prior research investigating the instructional effectiveness of color appeared to be fragmentary and inconclusive, a number of studies conducted in a program of systematic evaluation by the author and others focused on the color variable (Dwyer, 1967c; 1968a,b; 1969a,b,c,e; 1971b,c,d,e,f,g,h, 1972b; 1973a,c; 1975; 1976b,c; Berry, 1974, 1975, 1976). These studies, although designed primarily to evaluate the effectiveness of the realism continuum in visual illustrations as a predictor of instructional effectiveness, found that in over one hundred comparisons (involving color and black and white versions of identical visual treatments) the color versions were found to be significantly more effective than the black and white versions in facilitating student achievement of specific educational objectives. These results seem to provide substantial evidence that color is, in fact, a viable instructional variable. However, this conclusion needs to be qualified. For color to have maximum effectiveness it has to be used judiciously in visuals, and the visuals themselves need to be appropriate for the type of educational objective to be achieved.

DISCUSSION

The fact that color is omnipresent is obvious. Research has established that its presence affects the human organism both physiologically and psychologically. Its importance in facilitating information processing—coding, storage, retrieval—has been confirmed. Initial research investigating the relative effectiveness of color as a significant instructional variable has questioned its usefulness. However, subsequent research, implementing acceptable experimental criteria, has provided substantial evidence which may be cited in support of the use of color in instructional materials to facilitate student achievement. Apparently what is needed is additional systematic research designed to effect a more comprehensive assessment of the instructional potential inherent in color and the ways it might optimally be employed to improve student achievement of designated educational objectives.

SUMMARY: MAIN IDEAS

Color has been used both as an attention gaining and an attention sustaining device.

Recent research investigating learner preferences have found that students across a wide age range express a consistent preference for complexity and variability in visualization.

Student perceptions of the "most desirable" types of visualization are probably not a valid indication of their instructional value since only a small relationship exists between their approval of the type of visualization from which they receive their instruction and their level of achievement of specific educational objectives.

There is an increasing amount of empirical evidence which tends to support the contention that the addition of color in visual illustrations does improve student achievement of specific educational objectives.

Research has found that people prefer to receive and interact with presentations that occur in color.

Given a common stimulus field, students will perceive and react in different ways.

REVIEW ACTIVITIES

1. State why it appears that the manner in which color is employed in instructional illustrations is extremely important.
2. Explain what is meant by the "physiological effect of color."
3. Summarize how color coding might be a useful instructional strategy for improving student learning.
4. Discuss, in writing, the relationship which exists between color and attention.
5. Summarize the relationship which exists between students' color

perceptions and their ability to learn from the preferred types of visualization.

6. State what you consider to be the general feeling toward the use of color in instructional materials.

SMALL GROUP OR INDIVIDUAL OPTIONAL ACTIVITIES

1. From the original research articles indicating color to be an important instructional variable (Table 7-1) construct a chart illustrating the specified objectives of each study, the specific variables investigated, the type of visualization employed, type of educational objectives, type of testing format, method of instructional presentation (externally paced or self-paced), level of students participating, results, and conclusions. Based on your observations of this chart construct several general conclusions.

2. From the original articles investigating color in the program of systematic evaluation (cited in this chapter), construct a chart illustrating the objectives of each study, the specific variables investigated, the type of visualization employed, type of educational objectives measured, the type of testing format used, method of instructional presentation, level of students participating, results, and conclusions. Based on your observations of this chart construct several general conclusions.

RECOMMENDED READINGS

Grover, P.L. 1974. Effect of varied stimulus complexity and duration upon immediate recall of visual material in a serial learning task. *AV Commun. Rev. 22:* 439-452.

Hockberg, J. 1962. The psychophysics of pictorial perception. *AV Commun. Rev., 10:* 22-54.

Spaulding, S. 1955. Research on pictorial illustrations. *AV Commun. Rev. 3:* 35-45.

8

Cueing as an Instructional Strategy

LEARNING OBJECTIVES

Upon completion of this chapter the student will be able to:

1. *List the physiological reactions which normally occur when an individual responds to a cue by focusing his attention.*
2. *Discuss the relationship between the results of eye movement research and the use of cues in visualized instruction.*
3. *Explain the difference between the two general types of instructional cueing.*
4. *Discuss in writing the relationship which exists among attention, visuals, and cueing in facilitating increased student achievement.*
5. *List the major variables investigated in the Instructional Film Research Program.*
6. *Discuss the instructional significance of Kendall's production principles.*
7. *List the most common cueing strategies used in education today.*
8. *Discuss in writing what research indicates about the usefulness of cueing in instructional presentations.*
9. *Cite and discuss the researchers whose research and writings have focused the attention of educators on the importance of cueing as a viable instructional variable.*
10. *List about twelve general research findings resulting from the Instructional Film Research Program which have significant implications for the design and use of visualized materials in the teaching-learning process.*

PHYSIOLOGICAL EFFECTS OF CUEING

Students, like other organisms, are in a state of constant interaction with their environment—continually performing a monitoring function by attending to and interacting with specific stimuli and ignoring others. For example, when the learner responds to a cue by focusing his attention, researchers have found that a number of physiological reactions occur; e.g., the pupil of the eye dilates, changes in galvonic skin response and heart rate occur, the auditory threshold decreases and scanning behavior is reduced (Kleitman, 1945; Kouwer; 1949; Birren, 1959; Hess, 1965; Lynn, 1966; Maltzman & Raskin, 1966; Luria & Homskaya, 1970; Meldman, 1970; Symmes & Eisengart, 1971; Fisher & Ong, 1972; Hare, 1972; Christie et al., 1972).

In the teaching-learning situation there usually exists a myriad of stimuli both relevant and irrelevant to the information to be acquired by the learner. Students when presented with visualized instruction generally spend a considerable amount of time scanning the stimuli—focusing their attention rather randomly upon specific elements; consequently, only a small portion of what is globally perceived is actually learned. Kahneman (1973) in discussing the concept of students' focusing their attention has stated:

> The allocation of attention has both instantaneous and sequential aspects. At any point in time, attention can be divided among several activities. In addition, the focus of attention changes from instant to instant, in an organized fashion. The act of looking provides a basic example of this sequential organization of selective attention. The world extends 360 degrees around us, our field of vision spans about 210 degrees, but vision is sharp only within a small foveal region of about 2 degrees, and the rate at which this narrow beam of sharp vision can be moved is limited to about 3-5/second. The question of where to direct this beam is obviously of great adaptive significance, and the mechanisms that have evolved for the control of eye position and eye movements are of exquisite precision (Kahneman, 1973, p. 50).

> Looking behavior is never random. When one's activities require the intake of visual information the movements of the eye adjust to that function. In the absense of a specific task set, the control of fixation is handled by enduring dispositions and standard routines of "spontaneous looking." These routines, many of which are probably innate, tend to select stimuli that are ecologically likely to be significant (*Ibid.*, pp. 51-52).

Since every student is a complex organism representing innumerable individual difference variables, the stimuli characteristics attended to at any given moment are governed by psychological, physiological, and personalogical characteristics along with background experiences and learning styles. The interaction of these variables influence the way the learner will react to instructional stimuli at any one moment in the learning process. In general, individual students have learned to attend to, perceive, and to react differentially to different types of stimuli. They also have learned to attach different levels of importance to different types of stimuli and to attend to certain aspects of an instructional situation.

In several studies in which students were categorized as high, medium, or low on individual difference variables (i.e., intelligence, Dwyer, 1976a; entering behavior, Dwyer, 1975; reading comprehension, Parkhurst, 1974, 1976) it was found that different types of visual stimuli facilitate the achievement of students in the different levels differentially. This finding seems to indicate that different types of visual stimuli differ in their effectiveness to attract, focus, and sustain student attention on essential learning characteristics contained in the illustrations.

EYE MOVEMENT

Eye movements are generally considered to be unconscious adjustments to the demands of attention during a visual experience. If visualization is to be used effectively to complement oral/print instruction, it is essential that information be available about how learners interact with and learn from visualized materials. A number of researchers (Llewellyn-Thomas, 1963; Mackworth & Morandi, 1967; Faw & Nunnally, 1967) have stressed the importance of individual eye movement research in the analysis of interactive behavior between the viewer and the stimulus material. This kind of data would be of critical importance to individuals charged with the responsibility to design and/or produce stimulus materials to be used for instructional purposes. Arnheim (1954) has suggested that when an individual interacts with visualized materials, neither the eye nor the mind is capable of processing all the information simultaneously. He contends that it is necessary for the learner to successively scan specific sections of the visualization absorbing critical elements as they are encountered. Enoch (1959) has provided evidence which lends support to this contention. Buswell (1935, p. 144), in commenting on the results of early eye movement studies conducted with children, has stated:

> . . . eye movements are objective symptoms of the perceptual processes of the person looking at a picture. The centers of attention from time to time during the observation of the picture can be located with objectivity and precision from the eye-movement record. While the eye-movement records give no evidence whatever

as to the quality of the mental processes going on and are considered as in no sense indicative of the type of appreciation experienced by the subject, nevertheless, they do furnish the most objective evidence available of the centers of interest within a picture.

Wolf and Knemeyer (1970) found in their investigation of eye movement that even though learners attend only to one thing at a time, they do not shift their attention equally on all areas of the visual stimuli, but focus their attention selectively on only a few regions. Within each region the eyes can shift to a new fixation point several times every second. Subsequent perceptions are based on these momentary fixations. Brandt (1953) found that the initial fixation of a viewer's eyes tended to come to rest to the left and above the center of a picture, while Niekamp's research (1971) revealed that the upper half of a visual field receives inherently more attention than does the lower half.

Hess (1965) in a series of studies provided evidence which indicated that the scanning strategies employed by individuals in interacting with differential stimuli in illustrations is sex related. For example, he found that the fixations points of men and women differ in terms of: (a) the kind of stimuli on which they will focus their attention, (b) the rank order to which they will focus their attention on identical stimuli, and (c) the amount of time they will spend interacting with the stimuli. Wolf and Knemeyer (1970) also found that differences in the attending behavior of students contributed to differences in their I.Q. levels. Caban (1971) and Coffing (1971) also obtained data which showed that individuals differ in eye movement strategies and that these strategies can be used as predictors of learning when alternative stimuli are available.

Mackworth and Bruner (1970), in investigating how adults and children search and recognize pictures, concluded that young children have inadequate eye-movement patterns when viewing and interacting with pictures. This may be one reason why young children: (a) usually experience difficulty in translating pictorial information into verbal terms (Dilley & Paivio, 1968), (b) have difficulty in making visual discriminations of spatial relations (Asso & Wyke, 1970), (c) experience problems in interpreting dimensional cues (Brown, 1969), (d) fail to recognize the distinctive features of an object in a drawing (Spitz & Boreland, 1967), (e) appear to be less capable of shutting out or ignoring extraneous stimuli presented in a visual (Maccoby & Hagen, 1965), and (f) frequently overlook or incorrectly perceive cueing devices which are used to focus attention on essential learning cues (Kennedy, 1971).

ATTENTION

For a student to learn optimally from a visualized presentation he must be able to locate, attend to, and interact with the relevant instructional stimuli while ignoring or minimizing the effect of the competing irrelevant stimuli. Although sustained attention is essential for substantial amounts of learning to occur, attention by its very nature is an elusive, fleeting, fluctuating variable. In a learning situation poor attention produces only partial learning because what is perceived may be perceived partially and/or incorrectly, thereby inhibiting the learners from comprehending accurately the information being presented.

The ability to focus one's attention on relevant cues in a learning situation is fundamental to all learning (Hewett, 1968); however, the process of obtaining and sustaining attention is not easily achieved. Dember (1960) found that student's attending responses to stimuli are characteristically of short duration. Kahneman (1973, p. 201) in reviewing the results of studies focusing on attention has summarized the main attributes of attention in the following manner:

1. Attention is limited, but the limit is variable from moment to moment. Physiological indices of arousal provide a measure that is correlated to the momentary limit.
2. The amount of attention or effort exerted at any time depends primarily on the demands of current activities. While the investment of attention increases with demands, the increase is typically insufficient to fully compensate for the effects of increased task complexity.
3. Attention is divisible. The allocation of attention is a matter of degree. At high levels of task load, however, attention becomes more nearly unitary.
4. Attention is selective, or controllable. It can be allocated to facilitate the processing of selected perceptual units or the execution of selected units of performance. The policy of allocation reflects permanent disposition and temporary intentions.

The problem of focusing student attention is further complicated by the fact that stimuli used initially to attract attention may not be the same type most efficient in sustaining it. And, unfortunately, the type of learning to be achieved in the classroom requires that sustained attention be exercised. For a visual presentation to achieve maximum instructional effectiveness efforts have to be expended to initially attract the student's attention and then to sustain the attention over extended periods of time.

CUEING VISUALIZED INSTRUCTION

Using visualization in the classroom focuses student attention, but merely using visualization in the classroom is in itself no guarantee that increased learning will occur. Some visuals which are complex in nature contain too much information, requiring that the learner constantly search for important meanings, while others contain so little information that learners quickly acquire all the available information and then become disinterested or bored. For example, simple line illustrations have the capability to generate fewer responses on the part of the student than would similar visuals containing increased amounts of realistic detail. However, arbitrarily adding superfluous detail to a visual may function to impede rather than facilitate increased learning. When a learner is interacting with complex visualization, he is being bombarded by a multiplicity of stimuli much of which may be too complicated to be comprehended instantly. In this situation the learner has a tendency to favor certain stimuli and disregard others according to his momentary preferences and needs. Osler and Myrna (1961, p. 2) have stated ". . . where alternative possibilities for categorization exist the preference, interest or experience of the student will affect his performance." Unfortunately, in many cases the stimuli that the learner selects to interact with does not enable him to acquire the intended message. The problem is not too severe if complicated (realistic) visualization is being used primarily to acquaint the learner with reality or to have him be able to identify or recognize general features (color, size, shape, etc.) of an object or situation; however, if the learner disregards many stimuli, the use of this same complicated visualization will not be very effective in facilitating student achievement of higher level learning objectives for which the student is required to exert a sustained effort in interacting with the detailed stimuli in order to perform successfully when evaluated (Dwyer, 1972a).

One of the primary reasons for the ineffectiveness of complex or highly realistic illustrations in the teaching-learning process is that when students are presented with a visualized instructional sequence, they are not conditioned to learn from it. Very rarely do learners attempt to interact totally with all stimuli to perceive and absorb all the information it contains. They interact actively with the visualization for only as long as it is necessary for them to develop an impression or a general idea of what is being presented.

Since there are limits to the amount of information (stimuli) in visualization that an individual can interact with simultaneously, one possible solution to increase the effectiveness of visualization is to limit or reduce the amount of information presented by the visual. Deleting irrelevant or superfluous information or stimuli from an illustration enables the illustration to convey its designated message quite rapidly; however, the process of reducing detail may also unintentionally eliminate detail which would have been considered as primary learning cues for some learners. Furthermore, there is a real danger in reducing information in visualization beyond a certain level. The essence of the communication may be adequately learned—but in isolation. Under these circumstances, the student may have difficulty in generalizing to realistic situations the information acquired in an edited context, and subsequently may not be able to recognize that which was learned when confronted with the same information in its natural surroundings—imbued among copious amounts of superfluous detail. In this respect Skinner (1968, p. 705) has indicated that one of the weaknesses inherent in cueing learner attention to relevant instructional characteristics ". . . is to deprive the student of the chance to learn to pay attention." He maintains that it is important for the student to be continually active in looking at and listening to the relevant stimuli.

INSTRUCTIONAL CUEING

Cueing has commonly been defined as the process of focusing learner attention on individual stimuli within the illustration to make the essential learning characteristics distinct from other stimuli. Basically, cueing strategies are utilized in visualized instruction to restrict or identify relevant stimuli, establish figure and ground relationships, screen out irrelevances, focus attention on critical learning characteristics while maintaining realistic stimulus conditions, etc. In visualized instruction cueing is essentially a technique for facilitating student search, selection, and coding of information presented visually. In any learning situation for efficient learning to occur the stimulus material for learning must be available and clearly perceivable by the learner. In this respect the instructional potential of visualization in improving student learning depends not only on the amount of information contained in the visuals but also on what specific stimuli the student identifies in the visualization as being relevant to what he is to learn. Presumably, when receiving a visualized presentation if the student could be made aware of what instructional stimuli he should interact with, he would be more inclined to perceive and interact quickly with the essential stimuli. Certainly this type of cued instruction would be more effective than instruction in which the student is given total responsibility for scanning the visual display, with the possibility that much of the ensuing interaction will occur with the irrelevant stimuli while the student is searching for the essential learning features.

Mechanic (1965) has found that learners permitted to learn incidently respond to fewer stimuli characteristics than do directed learners. Greenspoon (1955) has also obtained data which indicates that it is possible for students who are receiving reinforcing stimuli to be unaware that they are receiving it. It is apparent that students cannot efficiently respond and learn from visualized instruction if they have difficulty in identifying the crucial learning stimuli with which they are to interact. Cueing, then, is the manipulation of the stimulus environment, the purpose of which is to incite the internal motivation of the students so that they will attend to and interact with the selected stimuli and eventually acquire sufficient information to perform adequately on tests designed to measure knowledge acquisition. In this sense cueing is necessary because when essential learning stimuli are left undefined, the desired learning does not occur. When a learner is required to interact with complex stimuli and is required to guess as to what is important, occasionally he will guess incorrectly and miss the essence of the communication. Under this kind of learning condition the desired learning levels will not be attained (Cook & Spitzer, 1960). However, once the student has initially noticed what is considered to be the crucial learning features he then can make the additional cognitive responses to this stimulus prerequisite to acquiring the intended information (Wyckoff, 1959; Holland, 1957; Blair, 1958; Baker, 1960; Lindsley, 1962; Nathan & Wallace, 1965). A number of researchers in the field have emphasized the importance of cueing in the teaching-learning process (Fleming, 1970; Dwyer, 1972a; Anderson, 1972; Brown et al., 1973), and many have provided empirical data to support the use of cueing as a viable instructional technique which can improve the level of student achievement (Black, 1962; Rappaport, 1957; Travers, 1969; Dwyer, 1972a; Rosonke, 1975).

TYPES OF INSTRUCTIONAL CUEING

Over the years a wide variety of cueing strategies have been employed in an effort to improve student learning. During this time a significant number of different kinds of stimulus patterns in visualized materials have been identified as being effective in attracting and sustaining student attention for extended periods of time, i.e., change, novelty, intelligibility, familiarity, complexity, movement (Spaulding, 1955; Solley & Murphy, 1960). What seems to be apparent is that a continuous change in sensory input is important in maintaining efficient communication to receivers. For example, producers of film and commercial television have capitalized on this concept by deriving some very basic cueing techniques which have been very effective in focusing, isolating, and structuring information being transmitted. Walt Disney Productions have experienced tremendous success in the employment of many attention gaining techniques in his productions, e.g., animation, bigness, novelty, contrast, closeups, color, rapid changing of scenes, focus, isolation, multiple imagery, etc.

All these techniques plus others can be classified into two basic cueing strategies. The first consists of providing students with additional relevant stimuli to improve and make more complete their understanding of the information they are receiving. The different types of visuals of the heart used in a program of systematic evaluation (Dwyer, 1972a) can be considered to be an example of this type of cueing. In these studies the amount of realistic stimuli contained in the different types of visuals was systematically increased from the simple to the realistic, i.e., simple line drawings, detailed, shaded drawings, heart model photographs, realistic photographs of an actual heart specimen. The purpose of this type of cueing is to systematically increase the amount of stimuli contained in the visualization, the assumption being that students' subsequent achievement will increase as the amount of instructional stimuli in the visualization increases. One of the primary objectives of the program of systematic evaluation was to investigate the instructional effectiveness of this type of cueing and to identify the type of visualization (amount of realistic stimuli) needed by students to facilitate optimum achievement of specified educational objectives.

The second type of cueing does not provide additional information to the students but functions primarily to ensure that the intended instructional stimuli are emphasized in such a way so that they will be quickly perceived from among all stimuli in the student's total perceptual field. Table 8-1 identifies some of the more common cueing strategies.

Table 8-1. Common cueing strategies.

Contrast	Size	Surprise	Shading
Arrows	Animation	Oddity	Texture
Lines	Encircling	Color Cueing	Advance Organizers
Underlining	Bordering	Motion	Change
Complexity	Color Coding	Questions	Novelty
Stimulus Intensity	Dramatization	Optical Effects	Familiarity
Labeling	Ambiguity	Music	Multiple Exposure

In this type of cueing the cues are used to reduce the total number of errors students make when initially exposed to new information and to reduce the amount of time necessary to acquire the desired information.

Such cues are considered to be external stimuli whose primary function is the gaining and directing of students' attention so that they will be able to quickly identify that which is to be learned. Following is a representative list of the studies which have investigated the effectiveness of different kinds of external cueing strategies:

A. Image Size
Wagner, 1955; Woodworth & Schlosberg, 1955; Carpenter & Greenhill, 1958; Aylward, 1960; Diamond, 1962; Reede & Reede, 1963; Rosemier & Sleeman, 1965; Adams et al., 1965; Metcalf, 1967; Dwyer, 1970c; Moore & Sasse, 1971; Rosonke, 1974; Wilkinson, 1976.

B. Optical Effects
Neu, 1959; Jaspen, 1959a; Mercer, 1952; Cogswell, 1952; Sheffield, Margoluis, & Hoehn, 1961; Davis, 1965; Williams, 1965, 1968; Tiemans, 1970; Miller, 1971; Spangenberg, 1973; Salomon & Cohen, 1976.

C. Repetition
McTavish, 1949; Harby, 1952a,b; Murnin et al., 1952; Ash & Jaspen, 1953; Lumsdaine, Sulzer & Kopstein, 1961.

D. Humor/Novelty
Hoveland, Lumsdaine & Sheffield, 1949; Roshal, 1949; Nelson & Moll, 1950; Lumsdaine & Sulzer, 1951; Northrop, 1952; Cogswell, 1952; Vestal, 1952; Lathrop et al., 1953; McIntyre, 1954; Nelson & VanderMeer, 1955; Silverman, 1958; Berlyne, 1958a,b; Lumsdaine & Gladstone, 1958; Lumsdaine, Sulzer & Kopstein, 1961; Guba et al., 1964; Faw & Nunnally, 1967; Miller, 1969; Wolf, 1971; Dwyer, 1969d; Spangenberg, 1973; Kauffman & Dwyer, 1975.

E. Color
Long, 1945; VanderMeer, 1952; Bruner, Postman & Rodregues, 1951; Chan, Travers & Van Mondfrans, 1965; Dwyer, 1967c; 1968a,b; 1969a,b,c,e; 1971a,b,c,d,e,f,g,h; 1972b; 1973a,c; 1975; 1976a; 1977b,c; Black, 1966; Chen, 1971; Birren, 1963; Isaacs, 1969; Link, 1961, Scanlon, 1970a,b; Tolliver, 1970; Pearce, 1970; Chan et al., 1970; Katzman & Nyenhuis, 1972; Lamberski, 1972; Snowberg, 1973; Berry, 1974, 1975, 1976, 1977; Kauffman & Dwyer, 1975.

F. Music
Hoveland, Lumsdaine & Sheffield, 1949; Lumsdaine & Gladstone, 1958; Freeman & Neidt, 1959.

G. Questions
Kurtz, Walter & Brenner, 1950; Allen, 1952; Michael & Maccoby, 1953; Kantor, 1960; Vuke, 1962; Anderson, 1967, 1970; Rothkopf & Bisbicos, 1967; Frase, 1967, 1968a,b; Rothkopf, 1965, 1971; Dwyer, 1970d, 1971g,h, 1972a; Boker, 1974; Parkhurst, 1974, 1975; Shavelson et al., 1974; Koran & Koran, 1975; Dwyer & Arnold, 1976.

H. Visual Embellishments/Complexity
Zuckerman, 1949; Jaspen, 1950a,b; Neu, 1951; Mercer, 1952; Cogswell, 1953; VanderMeer, 1950a, 1953; McIntyre & McCoy, 1954; Greenhill & Kepler, 1955; Greenhill, 1955b; Carpenter & Greenhill, 1958; Hoban, 1965; Yarbus, 1967; Overling & Travers, 1967; Wohlwill, 1968; Brown & Gregory, 1968; Baker, 1970; Devor & Stern, 1971; Attneave, 1971; Gorman, 1973; Dunathan & TenBrink, 1974.

I. Arrows
Jaspen, 1950a; Lumsdaine & Sulzer, 1951; VanderMeer & Thorne, 1964; Dwyer, 1972a; Rosonke, 1974.

J. Advance Organizers/Feedback
Wittich & Folkes, 1946; Jaspen, 1950b, Kurtz et al., 1950; Allison & Ash, 1951; VanderMeer, 1951; Northrop, 1952; Harby, 1952b; Lathrop et al., 1953; Michael & Maccoby, 1953; Gibson, 1954; McNiven, 1955; Christensen & Stordahl, 1955; Cook & Spitzer, 1960; Stevenson & Siegel, 1960; Ausubel & Fitzgerald, 1962; King & Russell, 1966; Milgram, 1967; Anderson & Faust, 1967; Johnson, 1968; Dalis, 1970; Anderson, Kulhavy & Andre, 1971; Dwyer, 1971d,e,g; Schuyler & Long, 1973; Kaplan & Rothkopf, 1974; Barnes & Clawson, 1975; Dwyer & Arnold, 1976; Ksobiech, 1976.

K. Dramatization/Incongruity
McIntyre, 1954; Carpenter, 1954; Fletcher, 1955, Berlyne, 1957, 1958; Day, 1965, 1966.

L. Meaningfulness
Van Mondfrans, 1964; Fleming & Sheikhian, 1972; Dwyer, 1972a; Franzwa, 1973.

M. Method of Presentation
Beach, 1960; Van Mondfrans & Travers, 1965; Tallmadge & Shearer, 1969, 1971; Schlater, 1970; Gorman, 1973; Wells et al., 1973; Franzwa, 1973; Fradkin, 1974; Brown et al., 1975; Koran et al., 1976.

N. Captions/Summaries

Hall, 1950; Christensen & Stordahl, 1955; Freed, 1963; Hershberger, 1964; Chan & Travers, 1966.

THE INSTRUCTIONAL FILM RESEARCH PROGRAM

In 1947 under the directorship of C. R. Carpenter the Instructional Film Research Program was initiated at The Pennsylvania State College, now The Pennsylvania State University, University Park, Pennsylvania. This endeavor was among the first attempts to systematically investigate film characteristics and their differential effects on learning. Figure 8-1 presents the general parameters which provided the orientation under which research was conducted in the program.

In addition, the Instructionaf Film Research Program may be considered to be the first systematic program of investigation which focused on evaluating the instructional effectiveness of different kinds of cueing strategies. Smith and Van Ormer (1949, pp. 8-9), in providing the specific structure which served as the orientation for the investigators in the program who did research in the area of film characteristics, stated:

> Films have certain attributes not readily related to one or two learning principles, but instead related to a considerable number of them. The effects of some of these film variables on learning from instructional films are perhaps best investigated by means of hypotheses relating to the film characteristics themselves. The purpose of such investigations would be to determine the relative effectiveness of these film variables under various conditions of learning. Representative film characteristics which lend themselves to evaluation are:
>
> A. *Color:* in portraying natural characteristics, stressing certain parts or features, enhancing esthetic appeal, etc.
> B. *Music*
> C. *Emphasizers to direct attention:* novelty, size, contrast, isolation, rhythm, rhyme, etc.
> D. *Voice Characteristics*
> E. *Multiple sensory presentation:* i.e., presenting material through both picture and sound track.
> F. *Esthetic tone or artistic qualities*
> G. *Emotional tone*
> H. *Dramatic vs. factual presentation*
> I. *Humor*
> J. *Personalized commentator:* well-known person, commentator off stage, commentator shown in picture, lip-synchronous dialogue.
> K. *Units clearly marked off:* with use of pauses, fadeouts, titles, statements by commentator, etc.
> L. *Pacing and rate of development*

Figure 8-1. Areas of research in the Instructional Film Research Program (Carpenter, 1949, p. 53).

I. Learning Principles

A. MOTIVATIONS AND INCENTIVES
   1. Effectiveness of goals
   2. Knowledge of progress
   3. Praise and reproof
   4. Suggestion
   5. Realism and practicability
   6. Anticipation of early use
   7. Examination set
   8. Challenge
B. SELF ACTIVITY
   1. Mental practice
      a. Verbalizing task
      b. Visualizing task
      c. "Feeling" task
   2. Raising and answering questions
   3. Learner protagonist
C. SEEING-ORGANIZING
   RELATIONSHIPS
   1. Meaningfulness
      a. Meaningfulness (generally)
         (1) Use of simple words
         (2) Relating past to present
         (3) Preliminary overview
         (4) Learner position
         (5) Emphasis on details
         (6) Reasons "why?"
         (7) How it works
         (8) Reviews and summaries
      b. Meaningfulness (in case of
         concepts)
         (1) Varied experiences
         (2) Simplified symbols
         (3) Personalization
         (4) Contrasts and similarities
   2. Patterning
      a. Functional
      b. Spatial
      c. Temporal
      d. Logical
   3. Identifiability
D. PRINCIPLE OF EFFECT
   1. Checking or "ok" by learner
   2. Demonstration of wrong method
E. PRACTICE AND REPEATED
   PRESENTATION
   1. Exercise under favorable
      conditions
   2. Overlearning
   3. Realistic practice
   4. Part-whole practice
   5. Spaced practice
   6. Minimum delay of practice
   7. Reviews

F. GENERALIZATION
   1. Generalization set
   2. Recognized similarity
G. CHARACTERISTICS OF LEARNER
   1. General mental ability
   2. Educational level
   3. Knowledge or skill
   4. Special aptitudes
   5. Learning through eye or ear
   6. Attitudes and interests
   7. Experience with teaching
      techniques

II. Film Characteristics

A. COLOR
B. MUSIC
C. EMPHASIZERS
D. VOICE CHARACTERISTICS
E. MULTIPLE SENSORY PRESENTATION
F. ESTHETIC QUALITIES
G. EMOTIONAL TONE
H. DRAMATIC VS. FACTUAL
I. HUMOR
J. PERSONALIZED COMMENTATOR
K. UNITS CLEARLY MARKED OFF
L. PACING AND RATE OF
    DEVELOPMENT
M. VERBALIZATION CHARACTERISTICS
N. TIME RELATION: SOUND AND
    PICTURE
O. FACT FREQUENCY AND FILM LENGTH
P. ANIMATION
Q. MODIFIED MOTION
R. CAMERA VIEWPOINT AND
    PERSPECTIVE

III. Development of New Research
        Equipment and Procedures

IV. Utilization of Films in
        Instruction

V. Reviews of Pertinent
       Literature

M. *Verbalization characteristics:* relative amount and kind of verbal commentary, level of difficulty, personal reference, use of nomenclature, etc.
N. *Time relations of sound track and picture*
O. *Fact frequency and film length*
P. *Animation:* e.g. use of animation sequences to achieve simplification, or to show things which cannot be actually photographed.
Q. *Modified motion:* slow motion, speed-up motion.
R. *Camera viewpoint and perspective:* 0° vs 180°; use of wide angle, long focus lenses for special perspective effects.

Following is a partial list of authors and the titles of the research which they conducted in the Instructional Film Research Program. The studies listed attempted to answer specific questions relating to the use of cueing in the teaching-learning process.

Lathrop & Norford, 1949	*Contributions of film introductions and film summaries to learning from instructional films.*
McTavish, 1949	*Effect of repetitive film showings on learning.*
Roshal, 1949	*Effects of learner representation in film-mediated perceptual-motor learning.*
Vincent, Ash & Greenhill, 1949	*Relationship of length and fact frequency to effectiveness of instructional motion pictures.*
Zuckerman, 1949	*Commentary variations: level of verbalization, personal reference, and phase relations in instructional films on perceptual-motor tasks.*
Hoban & Van Ormer, 1950	*Instructional film research 1918-1950.*
Jaspen, 1950a	*Effects on training of experimental film variables, Study I: verbalization, rate of development, nomenclature, errors, "how-it-works," repetition.*
Jaspen, 1950b	*Effects on training of experimental film variables, Study II: verbaliza-*

tion, "how-it-works," nomenclature, audience participation, and succinct treatment.

Kurtz, Walter, & Brenner, 1950 — *The effects of inserted questions and statements on film learning.*

Nelson, & Moll, 1950 — *Comparison of the audio and video elements of instructional films.*

Neu, 1950 — *The effect of attention gaining devices on film mediated learning.*

Allison & Ash, 1951 — *Relationship of anxiety to learning from films.*

Ash & Carlton, 1951 — *The value of note-taking during film instruction.*

Twyford, 1951 — *Film profiles.*

VanderMeer, 1951 — *Effects of film-viewing practice on learning from instructional films.*

Carpenter, 1952 — *Logistics of sound motion pictures for military training.*

Cogswell, 1952 — *Effects of a stereoscopic sound motion picture on the learning of a perceptual-motor task.*

Harby, 1952a — *Evaluation of a procedure for using daylight projection of film loops in teaching skills.*

Harby, 1952b — *Comparison of mental practice and physical practice in the learning of physical skills.*

Hirsch, 1952 — *The effects of knowledge of test results on learning of meaningful material.*

Mercer, 1952 — *The relationship of optical effects and film literacy to learning from instructional films.*

Murnin, Hayes & Harby, 1952   *Daylight projection of film loops as the teaching medium in perceptual-motor skill training.*

Northrop, 1952   *Effects on learning of the prominence of organizational outlines in instructional films.*

VanderMeer, 1952   *Relative effectiveness of color and black and white in instructional films.*

Ash & Jaspen, 1953   *The effects and interactions of rate of development, repetition, participation and room illumination on learning from a rear-projected film.*

Stover & Tear, 1953   *Evaluation of two kinescopes.*

VanderMeer, 1953   *Training film evaluation: comparison between two films on personal hygiene: TF8-155 and TF8-1665.*

Carpenter, 1954   *Evaluation of the film: military police support in emergencies (riot control) TF19-1701.*

McIntyre, 1954   *Training film evaluation: FB254–cold weather uniforms: an evaluation of special effects and appeals.*

McIntyre & McCoy, 1954   *The application of sound motion pictures for recording billet analysis information.*

Fletcher, 1955   *Profile analysis and its effect on learning when used to shorten recorded film commentaries.*

Greenhill, 1955a.   *The recording of audience reactions by infra-red photography.*

Greenhill, 1955b   *The evaluation of instructional films by a trained panel using a film analysis form.*

Greenhill & Kepler, 1955 — *A study of the feasibility of local productions of minimum cost sound motion pictures.*

Hurst, 1955 — *Relative effectiveness of verbal introductions to kinescope recordings and training films.*

Kale & Grosslight, 1955 — *Exploratory study in the use of pictures and sound for teaching foreign language vocabulary.*

Lefkowith, 1955c — *The validity of pictorial tests and their interaction with audio-visual teaching methods.*

McCoy, 1955 — *An application of research findings to training film production.*

McNiven, 1955 — *The effects on learning of the perceived usefulness of the material to be learned.*

Nelson & VanderMeer, 1955 — *The relative effectiveness of differing commentaries in animated film on elementary meterology.*

Rimland, 1955 — *Effectiveness of several methods of repetition of films.*

Vris, 1955 — *A comparison of principles training and specific training using several types of training devices.*

As a result of these studies a number of relevant findings have been derived. Although the studies focused primarily on variables in film, the implications for the design and use of visualized materials in the teaching-learning process are significant. Following is a synopsis of these findings (Carpenter & Greenhill, 1956, pp. 3-5).

1. *Camera Angle.* Show a performance on the screen the way the learner would see it if he were doing the job himself (Roshal, 1949; McCoy, 1955).
2. *Rate of Development.* The rate of development of a film should be slow enough to permit the learners to grasp the material as it is shown (Jaspen, 1950a; Ash & Jaspen, 1953).

3. *Succinct Treatment.* Presenting only the bare essentials or rapid coverage of subject matter may be very ineffective (Jaspen, 1950b).

4. *Show Errors.* Learning performance skills from films will be increased if you show common errors and how to avoid them (Jaspen, 1950a; Harby, 1952a).

4. *Repetition.* Organize a film so that important sequences or concepts are repeated (Jaspen, 1951a; Ash & Jaspen, 1955; Rimland, 1955). Repetition of films, or parts within a film, is one of the most effective means for increasing learning to a required level (McTavish, 1949).

6. *Organizational Outline.* Films which treat discrete factual material appear to be improved by the use of an organizational outline in titles and commentary (Northrop, 1952).

7. *Introductions.* Present relevant information in the introduction and tell the viewer what he is expected to learn from the film (Lathrop & Norford, 1949).

8. *Summary.* Summarize the important points in the film in a clear concise manner. Summaries probably do not significantly improve learning unless they are complete enough to serve as a repetition and review (Lathrop & Norford, 1949; Kurtz, Walter & Brenner, 1950).

9. *Visual Potentialities.* Take advantage of the ability of the motion picture medium to show motion, to speed up and slow down motion, to telescope and otherwise control timing of events and processes, to bridge space, and to organize events and actions (Hoban & Van Ormer, 1950; Carpenter, 1952). The visuals and commentary in a film should reinforce each other (Nelson & Moll, 1950).

10. *Picture-Commentary Relationship.* The commentary of a typical informational film appears to teach more than only the pictures of that same film when learning is measured by verbal tests (Nelson & Moll, 1950). This does not necessarily mean that the commentary has greater inherent effectiveness than pictures; it may mean that producers are currently relying more heavily on commentary than on pictures or on the optimum integration of the two. With films designed to teach performance skills, where learning is measured by nonverbal tests, the pictures appear to carry the main teaching burden (Zuckerman, 1949).

11. *Concentration of Ideas.* Ideas or concepts should be presented at a rate appropriate to the ability of the audience to comprehend them (Vincent, Ash & Greenhill, 1949).

12. *Commentary.* The number of words (per minute of film) in the commentary has a definite effect on learning. Care should be taken not to "pack" the sound track (Zuckerman, 1949; Jaspen, 1950a,b). Application of readability formulas to improve a commentary may not do so (Nelson & VanderMeer, 1955).

13. *Use of Personal Pronouns.* Use direct forms of address (imperative or second person) in film commentaries. Avoid the passive voice (Zuckerman, 1949).

14. *Nomenclature.* Introduction of a new names or technical terms in a film imposes an additional teaching burden on learners, and may impede the learning of a performance skill (Jaspen, 1950a,b).

15. *Special Effects.* Special effects used as attention getting devices have no positive influence on learning (Neu, 1950).

16. *Optical Effects.* A film in which such optical effects as fades, wipes, and dissolves have been replaced by straight cuts teaches just as effectively as a film which uses these effects (Mercer, 1952).

17. *Stereoscopic Films.* In the one experiment conducted, the addition of stereoscopic vision did not increase learning of a motor skill performance (Cogswell,

1952). For teaching a complex motor skill a three-dimensional model may be better than a two-dimensional model which may be better than a two-dimensional aid (Vris, 1955).

18. *Color.* Experimentation has not yet demonstrated any general over-all increased learning as a result of using color in instructional films (VanderMeer, 1952).

19. *Music.* Preliminary experimentation suggests that music does not add to the instructional effectiveness of an informational film (Hoban and Van Ormer, 1950).

20. *Pre-testing.* Scripts, workprints, demonstrations and final prints can be evaluated quickly using the learning profile method of film evaluation which requires a group of trainees to estimate their own learning (Twyford, 1951; Stover & Tear, 1953; Fletcher, 1955). A film analysis form should be used for pre-production evaluation of films (Greenhill, 1955b). Audience reactions to films can be economically obtained using infra-red photography (Greenhill, 1955a).

21. *Film Loops.* Short film loops, which can be repeated continuously as many times as desired, appear to be a good way of teaching difficult skills (Harby, 1952a,b; Murnin, Hayes & Harby, 1952).

22. *Participation.* Learning will increase if the viewer practices a skill while it is presented on the screen, provided the film develops slowly enough, or provided periods of time are allowed which permits the learner to practice without missing new material shown on the screen (Jaspen, 1950a; Ash & Jaspen, 1953; Rimland, 1955).

23. *Dramatic Sequences.* Incorporation of dramatic sequences such as comedy, singing commercials, or realistic settings in films to teach factual information will not improve the film (VanderMeer, 1953; McIntyre, 1954; Fletcher, 1955).

24. *Filmographs.* Filmographs which incorporate still shots rather than motion may be equally effective and be less expensive (McIntyre, 1954; Kale & Grosslight, 1955).

25. *Visual Recordings.* Films may be produced to make a visual recording of a task that may be difficult to describe with words alone (McIntrye & McCoy, 1954).

26. *Inexpensive Films.* Because color, optical effects and dramatic effects have little to do with increasing learning from films it is possible to eliminate them. Films prepared in this manner can be made inexpensively and can be produced quickly (McIntyre & McCoy, 1954; Greenhill & Kepler, 1955; Greenhill, 1955a).

PRODUCTION PRINCIPLES

Kendall (1952) has summarized and assessed the results of technical and progress reports generated by the Instructional Film Research Program in light of their possible significance for other types of media production as well as for instructional films. Following is a brief discussion of the nine principles which have been derived (*Ibid.*, pp. 437-441).*

*Quoted by permission from the May 1952 *Journal of the SMPTE.* © 1952 by the Society of Motion Picture and Television Engineers, Inc.

First Principle—Films possess their greatest influence when their content has been designed to reinforce and extend the previous knowledge, attitudes or motivations of the viewer.

Discussion. A film will not substantially influence the behavior of a person unless that person can respond to the film in terms of what he already knows— or what he can do—or how he feels—or what he wants. The film can be designed to help change his attitudes and opinions, his knowledge and his skills, provided that it extends or reinforces those elements which he already possesses.

The effects of any motion picture depend on the reinforcing of the viewer's experiences which preceded, follow or are coincident with the actual film showing. Tests have shown that the influence of any one film is limited while the influence of several films is cumulative in the dynamics of learning.

A second principle is that the behavior-influencing impact of film is usually specific and not general.

Discussion. The principle that films have a specific effect holds for all informational objectives. The cumulative effect of related films shown over a period of time and/or reinforced by other means of instruction may be general. Even here, however, this general influence is limited to the area of the instructional content of the films.

The third principle is that required film influence increases directly as the content of the film matches the specific audience response required by the sponsors.

Discussion. The subject of the film and the way that subject matter is treated is instrumental always and only to a specific end product of audience response. This means that the behavior pattern that the film is intended to produce must be directly related to the content and treatment of the film.

The fourth principle is that variations in the prejudices or predispositions of the audience influence the reactions to a specific motion picture.

Discussion. Some elements of these variations depend upon audience literacy, abstract intelligence, formal education, age, sex, or previous experience in the subject. Differences in heredity and social experience mean equivalent differences in reaction to the film, and these differences seem to increase with maturity.

It has been found that intelligence and formal education are directly related. Viewers of above-average intelligence and education learn more from films than those with average or below-average education.

Below-average education viewers learn very much better from films than from verbal instruction.

The retention of film content has been found to decline with age after a certain point.

Sex differences in response occur when the values or occupations shown in the film are sex-typed.

A film has bias but the bias of the audience also counts. The recollection tendency of the viewer depends on his acceptance, rejection or indifference to the bias of the film.

Tests show that the more an audience knows about a given subject the more it will learn from a film on that subject.

An interesting point which the research has brought to light concerns the influence of many films on the same viewer. The first principle showed that a series of related film experiences all operating in the same direction is cumulative. However, the fourth principle exemplifies the fact that the more films of any type which are seen the more the viewer tends to learn from any single film. People learn to learn from films.

The fifth principle is in two parts:
1. Both audio and visual elements of films are effective channels of communication. Neither channel is consistently better than the other. Each channel is uniquely capable of conveying certain types of information and the two should be properly integrated.
2. The overall influence of the motion picture is thought to be primarily in the picture and secondarily in the accompanying language. It is relatively unaffected by the slickness of productions.

Discussion. The measurements indicated that the presentation of a film as a whole or the presentation of either the audio or the visual channel alone resulted in significant learning.

Both channels together were consistently better than either one alone. This "both" factor has been identified. It is established that some items are learned jointly from the audio and visual elements working together. Evidence also exists to show that items are often taught via both audio and visual channels in an overlapping sense, in which case the cumulative value of the "both" factor is reduced.

Color film has not been demonstrated as generally superior in information and instruction to black-and-white film.

Attention-gaining devices, either visual or auditory, have not been found to add significantly to learning in an otherwise correctly made informational film.

Optical effects and other film tricks have not been found to contribute significantly to learning from informational films.

Too much or too little talking in words per minute of film has been found to detract from the teaching effectiveness of a film. The optimum word rate is about 100 words for each minute of film.

The sixth principle is that the recollection of a film depends on the viewer's feeling that the action is significant and is in a familiar background.

Discussion. Not everything shown or said in a motion picture is seen or heard by the viewer. His response to film is selective not photographic. Scenes and sequences are best recalled when the pictorial background is familiar to the viewer and when the action has specific meaning to him. What counts is not the action but the importance of the action, not the close-up but the significance of the objects in the close-up, not the manner of performing the task but the meaning of the task to the viewer.

The seventh principle is that an intense, efficient and predictable response occurs when the picture content has a personal relationship to the viewer.

Discussion. It has been found that the influence of the film on the attitude and factual learning of the viewer is related to the prestige attached by the viewer to the role of the principal character.

The position of the viewer, or zero camera angle, should be used instead of the 180° angle which is so frequently used in informational films. It has been found that the subjective approach is important to long-term recollection.

Showing the errors likely to be made when carrying out the task improves the instructional value of a training film.

Direct instructions or direct address to the viewer should be used. The third-person, passive voice has been found to retard learning.

The eighth principle is that the rate of development of a film's message must be slow rather than fast.

Discussion. Where recollection, learning or information rather than entertainment is involved, a slow rather than a rapid rate of development is important. Rapid development of the presentation of a film subject reduces the amount of learning very materially.

The ninth principle is that instructional techniques built into the film or applied by an instructor substantially increase learning.

Discussion. The research conclusively shows that the following techniques add to the effectiveness of instructional films:

1. An orienting introduction and a relevant summary of the content of the film are of significant value.
2. An opening announcement of a check-up or quiz on the learning from the film measurably improves the recollection value.
3. Repeated film showings and/or repetition within the film showings and/or repetition within the film itself, materially improve its recollection value.
4. Audience participation or practice during or following the film showing "locks in" the teaching.
5. Presenting the viewer with a knowledge of the results of his learning is of great significance.

DISCUSSION

Research on instructional cueing has established that visualization varying in stimulus intensity (amount of realistic detail) varies in its capacity for attracting and sustaining learner attention (Vitz, 1966) and in improving student achievement (Dwyer, 1972a). Fitts et al. (1956) has provided corroborating evidence that stimulus redundancy does not always improve discrimination and that the type of redundancy employed in an illustration may alter considerably the ease with which visual forms are identified, the implication being that student attention is either affected by or is a function of the complexity of the stimulus material. Therefore, it is not merely sufficient to use a specific type of visual in a presentation and expect that its presence will ensure intense, sustained, and appropriate interaction between learner and instructional stimuli so that optimum amounts of learning will be realized. The possibility is very real that there are competitive interactions occurring between the amount of complexity contained in the visualization and the type of cueing techniques employed to focus student attention. These interactions may function to impede rather than to facilitate student learning. Even though students appear to be attracted to rich stimulus sources, especially if the stimulus materials are varied, novel, and contain substantial amounts of information (Hershenson et al., 1965; Fowler, 1965), the evidence indicates (Vitz, 1966) that the addition of realistic detail beyond a certain point in instructional visualization has little effect in sustaining student attention and in improving student achievement (Dwyer, 1972a).

In addition to increasing the number or the quality of cues within a visual, a wide variety of cueing strategies have evolved which contribute no additional information to the visual but have been found to be very effective in capturing the momentary attention of students. Unfortunately, many kinds of learning require sustained attention. It is possible that sustained attention can be achieved, however, by sequencing different cueing techniques in various combinations and by alternating visuals containing different amounts of realistic stimuli. It may be that with cues focusing student attention and change employed in the learning situation by alternating different kinds of cues and visualization containing various amounts of realistic stimuli, student attention can be secured and maintained, and increased learning will be realized. These techniques may highlight the characteristics to be learned and reduce the possibility of boredom on the part of the student.

Again, however, it would seem illogical to presume that all types of cueing techniques would be equally effective in gaining and sustaining student attention so as to improve all kinds of learning circumstances. Also it would seem that there must be optimal levels beyond which adding additional cueing techniques to a visualized presentation produces no further increases in learning. It may be that different kinds of cueing techniques are more or less effective for different stages of the learning process and for different kinds of educational objectives. Considerable research needs to be conducted on the attention gaining and attention sustaining strengths of different cueing techniques and also how different types of cues might be sequenced to achieve maximum student attention (and learning) over extended periods of time. Maximum learning from a visualized presentation may depend on the judicious juxtaposition of several different kinds of cueing techniques rather than upon the simple nature of the stimuli contained within the visualization itself.

SUMMARY: MAIN IDEAS

Students are in a state of constant interaction with their environment continually performing a sort of monitoring function by attending to and interacting with specific stimuli and ignoring others.

Individual students have learned to attend, perceive, and react in certain ways, e.g., to react differentially to different types of stimuli.

Student eye movements are important instructional variables in their interaction with visualized instruction.

The ability to focus ones attention on relevant cues in a learning situation is fundamental to all learning.

For a visualized presentation to achieve maximum instructional effectiveness, efforts have to be expended to initially attract the student's attention and then to sustain the attention over extended periods of time.

Cueing is defined as the process of focusing student attention on individual stimuli within a visual illustration to make them distinct from other stimuli.

Research on instructional cueing has established that visualization varying in a stimulus intensity vary in their capacity for attracting and sustaining learner attention and in improving student achievement.

Maximum learning from a visualized presentation may depend on the judicious juxtaposition of several different kinds of cueing techniques rather than on the simple nature of the visual stimuli contained within the visualization itself.

The research conducted in the Instructional Film Research Program has provided a number of important instructional strategies which should be incorporated in the design and use of visual materials.

REVIEW ACTIVITIES

1. List several physiological characteristics of students which, in part, determine how they will react to instructional stimuli in the learning process.
2. Summarize what the research says regarding eye movements as it relates to student interaction with visual stimuli.
3. State how attention is related to learning in visualized instruction.
4. Explain the rationale for using visuals in the cueing process.

5. Describe the two different types of cueing; give examples.
6, Summarize the kinds of cueing strategies investigated in the Instructional Film Research Program.
7. State several generalizations which have resulted from the research findings related to the instructional effectiveness of cueing.

OPTIONAL SMALL GROUP OR INDIVIDUAL ACTIVITY

Utilizing the list of studies which investigated the effectiveness of different kinds of external cueing strategies, construct a chart for each of the cueing strategies investigated, illustrating the objectives of each study, the types of students involved, specific types of cueing strategies employed, method of instructional presentation, type of objectives to be achieved, type of testing involved, results, and conclusions. Based on your observations of this chart summarize your findings.

RECOMMENDED READINGS

Allen, W. H. 1967. Media stimulus and types of learning. *Audiovisual Instruction. 12:* 27-31.

Perrin, D. G. 1969. A theory of multiple-image communication. *AV Commun. Rev. 17:* 368-382.

Severin, W. 1967. Another look at cue summation. *AV Commun. Rev. 15:* 233-245.

9

Cueing in the Program of Systematic Evaluation

LEARNING OBJECTIVES

Upon completion of this chapter the student will be able to:

1. *Identify and discuss the main reasons why the method of cueing visualized instruction may be considered an important instructional variable.*
2. *Explain in writing why for some types of educational objectives cueing does not appear to be a viable instructional technique for improving student achievement.*
3. *Identify the types of cueing strategies found to be most effective in facilitating student achievement of specific educational objectives in externally paced and self-paced instruction.*
4. *Discuss the relative effectiveness of different types of cueing strategies used to complement self-paced instruction.*
5. *Identify the types of cueing strategies which do not appear to be effective in facilitating student achievement of specific educational objectives in self-paced and externally paced instruction.*
6. *Explain the statement, "Learning does not appear to conform to a linear relationship which is dependent on the number or complexity of the cues employed."*

ORIENTATION

The primary justification for using cues in visualized instruction is that student learning will be most efficient if their attention can be focused quickly and precisely on the crucial learning cues in the visualization from which they are expected to learn. Research evidence in the previous chapter substantiates the use of cues as viable instructional variables which, if judiciously employed, will function to improve student achievement. However, this is not meant to imply that merely using cues in a visualized presentation will automatically improve student learning. Cueing is but one variable to be considered in the learning process and if the criticisms leveled at previous media research (Chapter 3) are not controlled adequately, the instructional effect of cueing on student performance may not be possible to detect.

Just as it is not reasonable to expect that all kinds of visualization will be equally effective in improving student achievement of different educational objectives, there is no reason to expect that all kinds of cueing strategies will be equally effective in facilitating student achievement of different educational objectives. One of the objectives of the systematic program of evaluation pursued by the author and his colleagues was the investigation of the relative effectiveness with which different types of cueing techniques, presented in externally paced and self-paced instructional formats, facilitated student achievement of different types of educational objectives. For example, studies employing the externally paced format investigated cueing strategies such as image size, motion, arrows, and advance organizers.

The following sections summarize some of the findings relative to the instructional effectiveness of different kinds of cueing strategies.

IMAGE SIZE

Previous research relative to the effectiveness of image size in televised instruction (Carpenter & Greenhill, 1958; Aylward, 1960; Greenhill, Rich, & Carpenter, 1962; Reede & Reede, 1963) provided results which indicated that no significant differences in achievement occur when students receive their instruction on regular television monitors as opposed to viewing identical instruction on a very large screen.

In an attempt to explore the instructional effects of image size as a cueing variable, three individual studies involving television were conducted by the author (Dwyer, 1968c; 1969c; 1970a). For each study the oral presentation without visuals was considered to be the control treatment, and the four black and white visualized treatments of the heart were considered to be the experimental treatments, i.e., the simple line presentation, the detailed, shaded draw-

Figure 9-1. Size relationships of the viewing areas for the television studies.

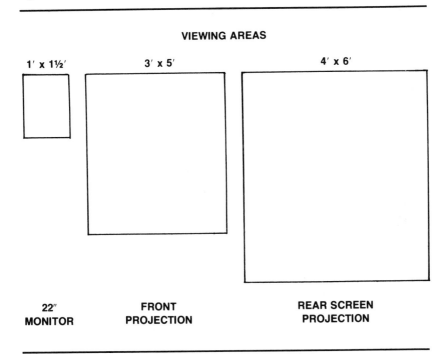

ing presentation, the heart model presentation, and the realistic photographic presentation. College students participated in these studies. Students in each of the three studies received the same instructional treatments; however, the method by which students received their respective instructional presentation differed for each study (Figure 9-1). In the first study (Dwyer, 1968c) students viewed their instruction in conventional television classrooms via 22-inch monitors. In the second study (Dwyer, 1969c) students received their instruction by means of a Telebeam Model A-912 television projector, which provided a 3-foot by 5-foot front projector image. Students in the third study (Dwyer, 1970a) also received instruction by the Telebeam projector which was arranged to project a 4-foot by 6-foot rear screen image.

In each of the three studies the same pattern of results occurred (Table 9-1): the oral presentation without visuals of the heart was found to be as effective as the visually complemented treatments on four of the five criterion tests. The exception was the drawing test, for which in all three studies the simple line presentation was signifi-

Table 9-1. Presentations most effective in facilitating achievement on each criterion measure for the television studies.

Criterion Measures	Instructional Treatments
Terminology Test	Oral Presentation
Identification Test	Oral Presentation
Drawing Test	Simple Line Drawing
Comprehension Test	Oral Presentation
Total Criterion Test	Oral Presentation

cantly more effective than the oral presentation in facilitating student achievement.

A number of possible explanations may be proposed to explain the results obtained in these studies.

1. If we can assume that the accuracy of perception and the amount of information that can be perceived in a visual illustration depends on the amount of time available for viewing, then the detailed, shaded drawing and photographic presentations would be at a disadvantage. Even though the more realistic visual illustrations contained more information than the line drawings, the fact that students viewed their respective televised presentations for equal amounts of time may have prevented them from having sufficient time to study, comprehend, and profit from the additional information contained in the more realistic types of visuals (Dwyer, 1969c, p. 63; 1970a, p. 47).
2. Since college students are generally selected from the upper two-thirds of the population in terms of verbal and conceptual ability, it may be that they are in a highly favorable position in terms of being able to learn from oral instruction. If this assumption is accurate, then the use of visual illustrations *structured as they were* in the cited studies are not necessary to complement oral instruction designed to promote achievement of learning objectives similar to those measured by the identification, terminology, comprehension, and total criterion tests (Dwyer, 1968c, pp. 40-41).
3. The realistic detail contained within the visual illustrations used to complement the oral instruction may have had the net effect of distracting the attention of the students from the essential learning cues, thereby interfering with rather than facilitating student achievement (*Ibid.*, p. 41).

IMAGE SIZE: COMPARATIVE EFFECTIVENESS

To investigate the effectiveness of identical visualized treatments presented in different image sizes a more comprehensive study (Dwyer, 1970c) was designed involving 588 college level students. The same instructional treatments employed in the previous studies were used in this evaluation, and instruction was presented using the same modes as in the previous studies: Mode 1—22-inch Monitor,

Mode 2—Front Projection, Mode 3—Rear Projection. An analysis of the data obtained in this study replicated exactly the findings of the three individual studies cited previously. (Refer to Table 9-1.) In an attempt to assess the effect of image size on student achievement, analyses were conducted across the three modes of presentation. Comparisons were conducted among students receiving identical instructional treatments via the three different modes of presentation. Table 9-2 illustrates where significant differences in achievement occurred among students receiving identical instruction via the different instructional modes. The results indicate that where mode of presentation made a difference in achievement, students receiving instruction by Mode 1, the 22-inch monitors, achieved significantly higher scores on the drawing and identification tests than did students receiving the same instruction on the larger viewing areas— Mode 2 and Mode 3. The blank areas in Table 9-2 indicate that significant differences in achievement did not occur among students viewing visualized presentations of different sizes.

Table 9-2. Analysis of the effectiveness of visual presentations of different sizes (Dwyer, 1970c, p. 38).

| | *Instructional Treatments* | | | | |
| | *Oral* | *Simple* | *Detailed* | *Heart* | *Realistic* |
Criterion Measures	*Presentation*	*Line*	*Shaded*	*Model*	*Photograph*
Terminology Test					
Identification Test	1 > 3	1 > 2	1 > 3	1 > 2	
Drawing Test	1 > 3	1 > 3			
Comprehension Test					
Total Criterion Test					

Mode 1: 22″ Monitor (1′ x 1½′)
Mode 2: Front Projection (3′ x 5′)
Mode 3: Rear Screen Projection (4′ x 6′)

Table 9-2 illustrates the fact that merely increasing the size of instructional illustrations by projecting them on larger viewing areas does not automatically improve their effectiveness. In fact, for certain educational objectives, the use of the larger images inhibited student achievement.

The success of the instruction presented via Mode 1 (22-inch monitors) may be explained by the fact that the increased size of the visual images projected by Modes 2 and 3 produced larger viewing areas which in turn required the students to spend more time searching the images for the relevant information being discussed orally. Since all the televised presentations were externally paced and of the same time duration, students viewing the larger images apparently spent more time searching and/or scanning the visuals in order to locate the essential learning cues, leaving proportionally less time to study and interact with these same cues once they were located. Apparently, the ability to be able to perceive clearly and quickly the relevant instructional characteristics is a prerequisite when students are interacting with their respective instructional presentations for equal amounts of time.

EFFECT OF MOTION

In this study (Dwyer, 1969d) television was employed to investigate the instructional effectiveness of arrows plus motion in visual illustrations used to focus student attention on the relevant learning cues. The five instructional treatments employed in this study were the same as were used in the previously cited study. The audiotaped oral instruction was identical for all treatments; it contained audio signals which cued the changing of slides so that the appropriate visuals appeared simultaneously with the oral instruction they were designed to complement. While the treatments were being videotaped, the investigator physically pointed out on each illustration the relevant instructional cues as they were being described orally. The treatment groups received their respective videotaped treatments in conventional classrooms via 22-inch television monitors. Table 9-3 presents the results obtained in this investigation.

Table 9-3. Presentations most effective in facilitating achievement on each criterion measure.

Criterion Measures	Instructional Treatments
Terminology Test	Simple Line Drawing
Identification Test	Oral Presentation
Drawing Test	Simple Line Drawing
Comprehension Test	Oral Presentation
Total Criterion Test	Simple Line Drawing

The following summary of the results is from the original publication of the research study (*Ibid.*, p. 42).

The results indicate that students who viewed the visually complemented treatments achieved significantly higher scores on the terminology, drawing, and total criterion tests than did students who received the oral presentation without visuals of the heart (See Table 9-3). In terms of economy and instructional effectiveness, the line presentation was found to be the most effective treatment in facilitating the achievement of objectives measured by these three criterion measures. The success of the line drawings complemented by motion may be attributed to the fact that students viewed their respective instructional presentations for equal amounts of time. The line drawings presented succinctly the relevant information, and the use of motion focused the students' attention on the important aspects of the instruction.

If we can assume that the accuracy and the amount of information that can be perceived in a visual depends on the amount of time available for viewing, then the realistic drawings and photographs would be a disadvantage. Apparently, the use of motion as an attention gaining cue is not an effective instructional technique for improving student achievement when the instructional presentation utilizes the more realistic visuals and the students are limited in the amount of time they can interact with the visual information.

EFFECT OF QUESTIONS

Television was also used with college students to determine the effectiveness of different types of visuals in facilitating student achievement of different educational objectives when questions preceded each visual illustration (Dwyer, 1970d). In this study students viewed a printed question designed to focus their attention on the crucial learning characteristic of the visualization prior to receiving the visually complemented oral instruction. The same five instructional treatments with black and white visuals used in the previously cited studies were used in this study, and students viewed their respective instructional presentations on 22-inch monitors for equal amounts of time. Table 9-4 summarizes the results obtained in this study.

Two important generalizations emerge from the results obtained in this study which have relevance for the use of questions as a means

Table 9-4. Presentations most effective in facilitating achievement on each criterion measure.

Criterion Measures	Instructional Treatments
Terminology Test	Simple Line Drawing
Identification Test	Simple Line Drawing
Drawing Test	Simple Line Drawing
Comprehension Test	Simple Line Drawing
Total Criterion Test	Simple Line Drawing

of complementing visualized instruction presented via television: (1) the use of questions to focus students' attention on relevant visual learning cues in the more realistic visual displays is not an effective instructional technique for increasing students' achievement; and (2) the use of questions to complement simple line illustrations is an effective instructional technique for increasing student achievement on criterion measures similar to the ones used in this study.

CUEING TELEVISED INSTRUCTION

Another study (Dwyer, 1977a) was designed to investigate the relative effectiveness of three methods of cueing televised instruction. In addition to cues within the visualization (arrows), students, prior to receiving their respective televised treatments, were told the specific type of learning that each criterion test was designed to measure and the type information that they would need to obtain from the instruction in order to perform successfully on the tests. The same five instructional treatments previously cited were used in this study. Students received their respective instructional presentation via 22-inch monitors and viewed their respective treatments for equal amounts of time.

The purpose of this study was to evaluate the effectiveness of different methods of cueing televised instruction.

Method 1: Students received their respective instructional presentations in a conventional manner. The visualized presentations contained arrows focusing student attention to the relevant learning cues.

Method 2: Students received instructional presentations identical to those received by students in Method 1. In addition, they viewed motion in their respective visualized presentations; that is, the investigator physically pointed out in each illustration the relevant instructional cues as they were being described via the oral commentary.

Method 3: Students received the same instructional presentation as in Method 1; however, prior to each visual they viewed a question designed to direct their attention to relevant learning cues in the visual illustrations of the heart.

Specifically, this study was designed to measure the relative effectiveness on different criterion measures of three methods of cueing televised instruction: visuals complemented by arrows, visuals complemented by arrows and motion, visuals complemented by arrows and questions.

The data obtained from the three methods of cueing televised instruction were analyzed across methods, comparing the achievement on each criterion measure of the students receiving their televised instruction via the conventional format complemented with arrows (Method 1) with the achievement of those students receiving identical instruction complemented with arrows plus motion (Method 2) and the achievement of students receiving arrows plus inserted questions to complement their visualized instruction (Method 3). Table 9-5 summarizes the results.

Table 9-5. Method of presentation most effective in facilitating achievement on each criterion measure.

Instructional Treatments	Criterion Measures				
	Terminology Test	Identification Test	Drawing Test	Comprehension Test	Total Criterion Test
Oral Presentation					
Simple Line Drawing					
Detailed, Shaded Drawing					
Heart Model					
Realistic Photographs	2 > 1			2 > 1	2 > 1

Method 1: Conventional Television
Method 2: Television and Motion
Method 3: Television and Inserted Questions

In interpreting the results obtained from this study it is necessary to remember that this study differs from the previous study in that the students prior to receiving their differentially cued instruction were told specifically the type of information they needed to obtain from the instruction in order to perform successfully on the criterion measures. Table 9-5 shows where significant differences in achievement occurred among students receiving the different methods of presentation. The blank areas indicate where significant differences in achievement did not occur among the three cueing methods. When differences did occur, students receiving the televised presentation containing motion (Method 2) achieved significantly higher scores on specific criterion measures than did students receiving the conventional instruction complemented via arrows (Method 1). The results of this evaluation indicated that when realistic illustrations are used to complement televised oral instruction, motion that is used to point out essential learning cues to students becomes an effective instructional technique for improving student achievement. Apparently, motion in the visualized presentation enabled students to identify the important instructional cues in a minimum amount of time and enabled them to make those discriminations necessary to obtain the information that would permit them to achieve successfully on the criterion tests. Once the relevant instructional cues were located, the most realistic treatment (the realistic photograph presentation) was found to be most effective in facilitating student achievement—probably because (a) these illustrations possessed more inherent information which could be transmitted to the students who were interacting with them; (b) student attention was effectively focused on the relevant learning characteristics by the oral instructions, and (c) the use of motion acted as a reinforcing agent, again emphasizing the crucial content characteristics to be learned.

PROGRAMMED INSTRUCTION: QUESTIONS AS CUES

Self-paced instruction is defined as a learning situation in which each individual controls the rate at which he proceeds through instructional materials; for example, programmed instruction booklets, textbooks, computer-assisted instruction, individual slide presentations, etc. Students receiving instruction in this format are permitted to interact with their respective instructional materials for as long as they feel necessary to comprehend the content being presented.

The visual illustrations (prints) used in the self-paced studies were made from the slides produced for the previously cited externally paced studies. Students in the self-paced studies received exactly the same content material as did the students receiving the externally paced instruction; however, to further cue student attention to essential learning characteristics in the visuals, each programmed booklet contained 89 fill-in questions. Each frame in the programmed booklet contained from one to six questions which students were to answer mentally by reading the printed presentation and by inspecting the visual illustration located on the same frame. Immediate feedback as to the accuracy of the mental response was provided in the form of the correct response on the subsequent frame.

The initial study involving programmed instruction (Dwyer 1967b) was conducted to determine the effect of the 89 fill-in questions requiring covert responses on students' ability to profit from visualized instruction. This study was conducted with college level students and involved a control group, which received no visualization, and three black and white visualized treatments: simple line drawings, detailed shaded drawings, and realistic photographs. The data obtained from this study (Table 9-6) indicates that the realistic photograph presentation was the most effective treatment in facilitating student achievement on the identification, drawing and total criterion tests. The programmed instructional presentation without visuals of the heart was found to be as effective as the visually complemented treatments in facilitating student achievement on the terminology and comprehension tests.

Table 9-6. Presentations most effective in facilitating achievement on each criterion measure.

Criterion Measures	*Instructional Treatments*
Terminology Test	Program Without Visuals
Identification Test	Realistic Photographs
Drawing Test	Realistic Photographs
Comprehension Test	Program Without Visuals
Total Criterion Test	Realistic Photographs

The results of this study can be explained by the fact that since students progressed through the instructional booklets at their own rate, they could interact with the instructional materials for as long as they felt necessary to acquire the information. Since the realistic photographs contained more inherent information, students interacting with this presentation were able to achieve significantly more than did students who received the less realistic illustrations. The illustrations used in the simple line and detailed, shaded drawing presentations possessed less realistic detail and were, therefore, limited as to the amount of information they were able to transmit to the students, regardless of how long they were permitted to view and study their respective illustrations.

In another study (Dwyer, 1969e) the number of visualized programmed treatments was expanded to include an additional black and white treatment (the heart model presentation) and four colored treatments. The same procedure and evaluation strategy was employed. Table 9-7 presents the instructional treatments found to be

Table 9-7. Presentations most effective in facilitating achievement on each criterion measure.

Criterion Measures	Instructional Treatments
Terminology Test	Program without Visuals
Identification Test	Heart Model (color)
Drawing Test	Simple Line Drawing (b&w)
Comprehension Test	Program without Visuals
Total Criterion Test	Heart Model (color)

most effective in facilitating student achievement on the different criterion measures.

OVERT RESPONSES

The purpose of this study (Dwyer, 1972b) was to determine whether requiring students to make overt responses to cues improved their achievement on the different criterion measures. Each instructional frame in each of the programmed treatments was followed by question frame, which contained a question designed to cue the student's attention to information he should have obtained from the preceding illustrated frame. Students were required to overtly complete a response to each question as they proceeded through their instructional booklets. Students were permitted to look back at the preceding illustrated frame to make certain that their responses to the questions were correct. Students were allowed to interact with their instructional booklets for as long as they felt necessary; however, they were asked to indicate on the cover of the booklet the time they started and completed the instructional unit. Table 9-8 presents the treatments found to be most effective in facilitating achievement on each criterion test in this study. The following quotation provides a summary of the results obtained in this study (*Ibid.*, p. 51):

> The data collected in this study appear to support the contention that an increase in the amount of realistic detail in visual illustrations will not arbitrarily improve student achievement. The results regarding the effectiveness of the simple line drawings (color) are in agreement with research literature (Attneave, 1954, 1959; Travers, 1964) which suggest that visuals similar in nature to those viewed by students receiving the simple line presentation would be most effective in facilitating student achievement. . . . Since the color in the simple line drawings provided no additional information, it seems plausible that the effectiveness of the colored treatment may be attributed to the fact that color increased student interest and motivation in interacting with the content material. Acknowledging the method of presentation in this study, it appears that the use of color in the simple line draw-

ing presentation may be considered an important instructional variable for promoting increased student achievement of learning objectives similar in nature to the ones measured by the drawing and total criterion tests. The success of the simple line drawings may also be attributed to the fact that students could readily identify the relevant instructional cues in the visuals and learn from them.

Table 9-8. Presentations most effective in facilitating achievement on each criterion measure.

Criterion Measures	Instructional Treatments
Terminology Test	Program Without Visuals
Identification Test	Program Without Visuals
Drawing Test	Simple Line Drawing (color)
Comprehension Test	Program Without Visuals
Total Criterion Test	Simple Line Drawing (color)

Relative to the amount of time used by students for the instructional presentations, the results indicate (Dwyer, 1972b, pp. 51, 54):

... that students who received the programmed instruction presentation complemented by simple line drawings in color required significantly more time to complete their instruction than did students who received the programmed presentation without visuals and the programmed treatments complemented by the more realistic type of illustrations. This data might be interpreted as an indication that students do not know how to learn from detailed drawings and photographs; consequently, they do not spend much time interacting with or studying them.

The failure of the visually complemented treatments to facilitate student achievement on the terminology, identification and comprehension tests may be explained in several ways (*Ibid.*, p. 51):

1. Since student attention was focused on the relevant learning cues by the questions, it may be that once students located the answer to the specific question they ceased to interact with the additional information in the more realistic illustrations.
2. The type of learning measured by these criterion tests does not require students to utilize effectively the information presented in the more realistic illustrations.
3. It may have been that the additional detail in the more realistic illustrations distracted the students from identifying the essential learning cues and thereby hindered their efficient acquisition and retention of the intended information.

In additional studies Parkhurst (1974, 1975, 1976), utilizing the programmed materials on the human heart, explored the use of questions as cue variables on three levels (Parkhurst, 1974, pp. 3-4):

Level one subjects received five questions of a fill-in-the-blank nature after approximately every 10-12 frames. Worksheets were provided on which the students made their responses. Answers were found in the upper left corner of the following frame. Questions covered only that material in the preceding 10-12 frames; no attempt was made to question subjects on material covered in a previous review.

Level two subjects received the identical format as level one; however, there were additional fill-in questions immediately following each frame's instructional content. The number of fill-in blanks ranged from two to four depending on the amount of information presented. Answers were found in the upper left corner of the following frame.

Level three subjects received identical format as level two plus simultaneous presentation of the instructional content via audiotape. All three groups were internally (self) paced and there was no time limit for interacting with the instructional material.

The data generated from Parkhurst's studies indicate that students given the opportunity to interact at their own rate with differentially cued materials will achieve differentially on criterion measures designed to measure different educational objectives. The studies provide evidence that all methods of cueing visualized instruction are not equally effective for facilitating student achievement of identical learning tasks.

ORAL INSTRUCTIONS

The process of telling students, prior to their receiving an instructional unit, about the specific types of information they are expected to obtain from the instruction is becoming a common instructional technique. A study (Dwyer, 1971e) utilizing the programmed instruction format and the black and white and color treatments previously cited used this technique; the study was designed to investigate what effect telling students specifically the types of information they should obtain would have on facilitating their achievement on different criterion measures. Students were permitted to proceed through their respective treatments at their own rates; however, they were asked to record on the programmed booklet the amount of time it took them to complete their instruction.

An analysis of the amount of time required by students in the different treatment groups to proceed through their instructional units indicated that differences were insignificant. Table 9-9 presents the instructional treatments found to be most effective in facilitating student achievement on the different criterion measures.

The data provided by this study indicates that when visualization was effective in facilitating student achievement, the simple line drawing presentation (b&w) was the most effective treatment. The failure of the visually complemented treatments to facilitate

Table 9-9. Presentations most effective in facilitating achievement on each criterion measure.

Criterion Measures	Instructional Treatments
Terminology Test	Program Without Visuals
Identification Test	Simple Line Drawing (b&w)
Drawing Test	Simple Line Drawing (b&w)
Comprehension Test	Program Without Visuals
Total Criterion Test	Program Without Visuals

achievement on the terminology, comprehension, and total criterion tests may indicate that when students are told precisely the type of information they need to obtain in order to achieve successfully on criterion tests they are capable of interacting purposefully with the printed instruction and thereby acquire the intended information.

TEXTBOOK INSTRUCTION: QUESTIONS AS ADVANCE ORGANIZERS

Students participating in the textbook-like studies received the same heart content as did students participating in the programmed instruction studies; however, unlike the programmed treatments, the textbook treatments did not contain the 89 questions used in the programmed treatments to focus student attention on essential learning cues in the illustrations.

In the initial study (Dwyer, 1971g) nine textbook-like treatments were employed to evaluate the effectiveness of inserted questions as advance organizers in improving the instructional effectiveness of the visualized content. In this study each illustrated page in the instructional booklet was preceded by a question frame to which the students were to respond covertly. Questions in this study were used as orienting stimuli designed to focus attention on relevant cues in the illustrations. The specific purpose of this study was to determine which types of visual illustrations preceded by questions were most effective in promoting student achievement on the five criterion measures when students were permitted to interact with their respective instructional booklet for as long as they felt necessary to comprehend the information being presented.

The results of this study indicated that significant differences did not exist in the amount of time students studied their respective instructional units. The analysis also indicated that the simple line drawing presentation (b&w) was the presentation most efficient in facilitating student achievement of the type measured by the drawing test. The textbook format without visuals of the heart was found to be as effective as the visualized treatments in facilitating achievement on the terminology, identification, comprehension and total criterion tests. Table 9-10 illustrates the results obtained in this study.

Table 9-10. Presentations most effective in facilitating achievement on each criterion measure.

Criterion Measures	Instructional Treatments
Terminology Test	Instruction Without Visuals
Identification Test	Instruction Without Visuals
Drawing Test	Simple Line Drawing (b&w)
Comprehension Test	Instruction Without Visuals
Total Criterion Test	Instruction Without Visuals

In summarizing the data obtained in this study, it may be concluded that questions can be effective in focusing student attention on essential learning characteristics in the printed instruction. Questions may also function as a deterent in visualized instruction since once the students acquire sufficient information to answer the questions they achieve a sense of closure and feel no further need to interact with the additional information contained in the different types of visuals.

In a second study (Dwyer, 1971h) the same textbook-like instructional units used in the previous study were employed, and questions designed to focus student attention to relevant learning cues followed each instruction page. Students were asked to record on their instructional booklets the amount of time they required to complete working through their respective instructional treatments. Total time included the time they needed to study the content material and complete a written response on the question page following the instructional page. In this study students were permitted to look back in the booklets to make certain the answer they wrote in response to the question was correct.

An analysis of the data obtained in this study (*Ibid.*, p. 182) indicated that:

1. . . . the detailed, shaded drawing presentation in color was the most efficient treatment in facilitating student achievement on the drawing test . . . .
2. On ther terminology, identification, comprehension, and total criterion tests, students receiving the presentation without visuals achieved as well as did those receiving the visualized treatments.
3. There were no significant differences in the amount of time students needed to complete their instruction.

Explanations similar to those advanced for the previous study may be proposed for this study (*Ibid.*, p. 182).

These results may be attributed to the fact that questions effectively reinforced relevant learning cues. However, it may be that when students answered the specific questions, they ceased to interact with the visualization for additional information and, as a result, the visuals lacked effectiveness. The effectiveness of the detailed, shaded drawing presentation (color) may be explained in the following manner: the type of learning measured by the drawing test required visualization and the color in this visual depicted vividly the information needed by the students to achieve on the criterion measure.

The results indicate that when questions follow textual material and focus student attention on relevant learning follow textual material and focus student attention on relevant learning cues, visualization of the content material is not a necessary instructional technique for facilitating student achievement of all types of learning objectives.

EFFECT OF CUE FORMAT

This study (Dwyer, 1973a) involved college students and was designed to investigate the effectiveness of using questions to complement visualized content material organized in regular textbook-like format. The difference between this study and the two preceding studies is that in this study, prior to receiving their instructional treatments, students were told specifically what types of criterion tests they were to receive as well as the kind of information they would need to obtain from the instruction in order to perform successfully on the tests. Two methods using questions were compared with one method containing no questions:

Method 1. Illustrated booklets received by students contained no questions.

Method 2. Illustrated booklets received by the students contained a question frame, preceding each content frame, which was designed to focus attention on the relevant learning cues in the visual.

Method 3. Illustrated booklets received by students contained the same questions received by students in Method 2; however, in Method 3 the questions followed the instructional frame. Students in Method 3 were asked to write a complete answer to each question and were permitted to refer to the booklet to make certain their answers were correct.

Table 9-11 illustrates where significant differences in achievement occurred among students receiving the different methods of presentation (*Ibid.*, p. 845). The blank areas indicate that significant differences did not occur among students receiving the different methods of presentation. As the table shows, students receiving in-

Table 9-11. Method of presentation most effective in facilitating achievement on each criterion measure.

		Instructional Treatments							
		Simple Line Drawing		Detailed Drawing		Heart Model		Realistic Photograph	
Criterion Measures	*Verbal*	*b&w*	*color*	*b&w*	*color*	*b&w*	*color*	*b&w*	*color*
Terminology									1 > 3
Identification		1 > 3							
Drawing									
Comprehension									
Total Criterion									

Method 1: Textbook-like content material without questions.
Method 2: Textbook-like content material preceded by questions.
Method 3: Questions followed textbook-like material; students were required to overtly complete the questions.

struction without questions achieved as well as or significantly better than did students receiving the visualized instruction complemented by questions. It is interesting to note that in the two instances where differences did occur among methods of presentation, it was the colored versions of the simple line presentation and the realistic photographic presentation that were most effective in facilitating increased student achievement.

The failure of any one method of presentation to consistently be more effective than another may be because all students were informed as to what the criterion tests would be like and the type of information they would need in order to achieve successfully. This information may have enabled students receiving instruction via the three methods to focus more accurately on the printed information; consequently, they were less dependent on the questions to guide their attention to the relevant cues.

VISUAL REINFORCEMENT

Skinner's research (1958) dealing with programmed instruction has demonstrated the usefulness of providing students with printed reinforcement attesting to the correctness of incorrectness of their responses; however, very little research has been focused on the comparative effectiveness of printed vs. visual reinforcement used to complement visualized programmed instruction and its subsequent effect on student achievement of different educational objectives.

Therefore, a study conducted by Dwyer and Arnold (1976) was designed to measure the instructional effect that different reinforcement cueing strategies (printed/visual) had on improving student achievement of different objectives and to determine whether the amount of realistic detail in the visualization influences the amount of student achievement when complemented via printed/visual reinforcement.

Two types of visuals were used in this study—simple line drawings and detailed line drawings (b&w). Three methods of instructional presentation were employed, each method containing only one type of visual:

Method 1.   Textbook-like content material with simple line drawings and no questions.

Method 2.   Programmed instruction material complemented via line drawings, questions, overt responses, and printed reinforcement.

Method 3.   Programmed instruction complemented via the detailed, shaded line drawings, questions, overt responses, and visual reinforcement.

Instructional presentations presented via Methods 1 and 2 each contained thirty-seven illustrations. Students receiving Method 1 interacted with the textbook-like printed content and the accompanying illustration located on each frame. Students receiving Method 2 interacted with visually complemented programmed units. Each programmed frame contained from one to six fill-in questions (N=89) to which students were to respond on a separate piece of paper. Immediate feedback as to the accuracy of their responses to each question was provided by the appearance of the correct response printed in the upper left hand corner of the subsequent frame.

Students receiving instruction via Method 3 received the same instructional script as Method 2; however, Method 3 employed 53 illustrations. Every frame, other than the first frame which contained only one illustration, contained two illustrations. The questions asked on each frame were different in nature and substance from those received by students in Method 2. Each frame contained the following question and directions:

Does the picture of the heart in the upper right corner correctly illustrate the printed material you just read on this page?

   a. yes
   b. no

*Look at the picture on the upper left corner of the next page to
see if you answered correctly.*

Students interacted with the printed instruction on each frame and
recorded their response to the question (either yes or no) on an accompanying answer sheet prior to checking the accuracy of their response. Students received immediate feedback as to the accuracy of
their response by the appearance of a visual in the upper left corner
of the subsequent frame. These reinforcement visuals were accompanied either by the words *picture correct* or *corrected picture*. Regardless of how the student responded he received the correct visualization as reinforcement; that is, correct visualization reinforced
the correct response, or the correct visualization clarified visually
the student's initial incorrect response.

Table 9-12 presents the results obtained in the study and shows
where significant differences in achievement occurred among students receiving the different reinforcement (cueing) techniques.
Blank areas in the table indicate that significant differences did not
occur among the treatment groups.

Table 9-12. Feedback technique most effective in facilitating achievement on
each criterion measure (Dwyer & Arnold, 1976, p. 41).

	Instructional Treatments		
Criterion Measures	*Text line drawings*	*P.I. line drawings*	*P.I. detailed line drawings*
Terminology	2 > 3	2 > 3	3 > 1, 2 > 1
Identification	—	—	—
Drawing	2 > 1	2 > 3	2 > 3, 1 > 3
Comprehension	2 > 1, 2 > 3	2 > 3	2 > 1, 2 > 3
Total criterion	—	—	—

Note: Numbers in table represent presentation methods as follows:
Method 1. Textbook-like content material with simple line drawings and no questions.
Method 2. Programmed instruction material complemented via line drawings, questions,
overt responses, and printed reinforcement.
Method 3. Programmed instruction complemented via the detailed, shaded line drawings,
questions, overt responses, and visual reinforcement.

Results from this study may be generalized to indicate that all
reinforcement (cueing) techniques are not equally effective in
facilitating student achievement of identical educational objectives,
and that specific cueing techniques are more effective than others

for specific educational objectives when visuals containing different amounts of realistic detail are used to complement the instruction. Essentially, the results indicate that learning does not conform to a linear relationship which is dependent upon the number or complexity of the cues employed in a teaching-learning situation. The relationship appears to be curvilinear in that it appears that an increase in cues beyond a certain point has a tendency to inhibit rather than to facilitate student achievement. This observation can be illustrated by the fact that: (a) Method 2, the illustrated programmed format with printed reinforcement, was found to be consistently more effective than the more elaborate programmed version providing visual reinforcement, and (b) even though one programmed format was found to be more effective in facilitating student achievement than the other on several criterion measures, neither was found to be significantly more effective than the more simplified textbook-like format.

DISCUSSION

Chapter nine presented a sampling of the types of cueing strategies investigated in the program of systematic evaluation. In general, the results obtained from these studies indicate that all cueing techniques are not equivalent in their potentiality for increasing student achievement of all types of educational objectives—some types of cueing being more or less effective for specific types of educational objectives. The results also indicate that students learn best when they are involved in looking and/or listening for specific information in an instructional situation rather than merely looking and listening. This condition is evidenced by the fact that when students are properly cued as to the type if information they are expected to learn, they can acquire this information quite readily from oral or printed instruction without the use of accompanying visualization.

In the studies reported it was also noted that when the number of cues included on each frame is increased, and these same types of cues are continued on each frame throughout the instructional unit, increased learning does not conform to a linear relationship which is dependent upon the number or complexity of the cues employed in the teaching-learning environment. However, it is possible that the use of a variety of different types of cueing strategies systematically and intermittently intergrated into visualized instruction might function to create a linear relationship between specific kinds of cue combinations and subsequent student achievement of specific types of educational objectives. At present the research opportunities related to the design and implementation of effective cueing strategies is unlimited. Only through sustained research in the future will the true potentials of cueing be realized and eventually be incorporated into the design and use of visualized materials.

SUMMARY: MAIN IDEAS

All kinds of cueing strategies are not equally effective in facilitating student achievement of different educational objectives when the content to be learned is presented via different instructional formats.

The accuracy of perception and the amount of information that can be perceived and absorbed from visualized instruction depends on the amount of time available for viewing.

Excessive realism in visuals used to complement oral instruction may distract student attention from essential learning cues, thereby interfering with rather than facilitating student achievement.

Merely increasing the size of instructional illustrations by projecting them on larger viewing areas does not automatically improve their instructional effectiveness.

All methods of cueing visualized instruction are not equally effective for facilitating student achievement of identical learning tasks.

Learning does not conform to a linear relationship which is dependent upon the number or complexity of the cues employed in a teaching-learning situation. The relationship appears to be curvilinear in that it appears that the increasing of cues beyond a certain point has a tendency to inhibit rather than to facilitate student achievement.

REVIEW ACTIVITIES

1. List the types of cues investigated in the program of systematic investigation.
2. Construct a chart of the types of instructional presentations (externally paced studies) found to be most effective in facilitating student achievement of the different educational objectives, and relate the chart to the following cueing strategies: image size, motion, questions, and method of presentation.
3. Construct a chart of the types of instructional presentations (self-paced studies) found to be most effective in facilitating student achievement of the different educational objectives, and relate the chart to the following cueing strategies: questions, overt

responses, oral instructions, advanced organizers, and visual reinforcement.
4. Identify the similarities and differences relative to cueing obtained
   in the research on externally paced and self-paced instruction.
5. List the explanations cited as to why cued visualization was able
   to facilitate student achievement for specific educational objectives.
6. Summarize the explanations concerning the ineffectiveness of
   cueing strategies in facilitating student achievement of specific
   educational objectives.
7. Discuss the relative advantages and disadvantages of cueing visualized instruction.

RECOMMENDED READINGS

Gropper, G. L. 1963. Why is a picture worth a thousand words? *AV Commun. Rev. 11:* 75-95.

Conway, J. K. 1967. Multiple-sensory modality communication and the problem of sign types. *AV Commun. Rev. 15:* 371-383.

Hartman, F. R. 1961. Single and multiple channel communication: a review of research and proposed model. *AV Commun. Rev. 9:* 235-262.

10

Aptitude-by-Treatment Interaction

LEARNING OBJECTIVES

Upon completion of this chapter the student will be able to:

1. *Define what is meant by aptitude-by-treatment interaction.*
2. *List and discuss the different types of interaction.*
3. *Construct graphs depicting the different types of interaction.*
4. *State the major objectives of aptitude-by-treatment interaction research.*
5. *Cite three reasons why aptitude-by-treatment interaction research has not been very fruitful.*
6. *List several instructional variables which have been found to interact disordinally.*
7. *Explain what the implications would be for instructional product development if aptitude-by-treatment reasearch achieved its major objectives in the future.*
8. *List the basic issues associated with aptitude-by-treatment interaction research which need to be resolved prior to the development of instruction adaptable to individual differences.*

ORIENTATION

It is a well known biological concept that individuals differ along a multitude of dimensions and that each student represents a totality of individuality with respect to both cognitive and non-cognitive variables. Human learning is considered to be an active and unitary process which involves the total organism—e.g., aspirations, motives, attitudes, emotions, needs, etc.—all interacting with sensory impressions and intellectual abilities jointly to determine what and how much information will be acquired from an instructional presentation. DuBois (1962, p.66) in discussing the importance of individual differences has indicated that such variations need to be considered by those concerned with human learning, and when they are ignored ". . . investigations of learning are limited to the study of a relatively narrow range of topics, chiefly the effect of variations of internal drives and of external stimuli, including rewards and reinforcement, on changes in behavior."

There is at the present time an increasing awareness on the part of educators of the importance of individual differences and their relationship to instructional practice; that is, the learning process and subsequent acquisition of information by students is significantly affected by individual difference variables. For example, the effects of individual differences can be clearly illustrated in a typical classroom in which one can observe the rate difference at which students within a "homogeneously-grouped" class proceed through a given set of instructional materials. An analysis of their performance on a criterion measure would also substantiate the fact that students exposed to identical instruction achieve at different levels. Practical exposure to classroom situations provides evidence that students differ in their ability and capacity to learn, the implication being that individual differences in aptitude must be considered by educators in designing instructional presentations. Allen (1975, p. 165), in discussing the research as it relates to individuals of low and high mental ability, has indicated that:

> There seems to be a consistency of findings that points logically to one kind of media design approach for one class of learners and to another kind for the opposite class, with a substantial area of overlap shared by both.

APTITUDE DEFINED

Aptitudes, or individual difference variables, are a complex set of personal characteristics which result from a combination of natural ability and environmental experiences upon which it is suspected that individuals will differ in terms of their learning potential. The potential number of aptitudes which may be related to learning is overwhelming since there are many categories (preferences, intellectual abilities, personality traits, interests, attitudes, etc.) from which discrete constructs may be derived (Allport & Odbert, 1936; Cattell, 1963, 1971; Guilford, 1967; Vernon, 1969).

Aptitude can be defined as the ability to learn quickly and easily and is directly related to what an individual learns, how he learns it (learning style), how much he learns, and how rapidly he acquires content information from a specific instructional presentation. Of the many different types of aptitude a person's intelligence or general aptitude affects almost everything he does. General aptitude is commonly considered to consist of three special aptitudes, i.e., spatial aptitude—the ability to manipulate shapes, sizes and distances in the absence of verbal and numerical symbols; numerical aptitudes—the ability to think with numerical symbols such as those used in algebra, chemistry, and statistics, and verbal aptitude—the ability to think with words.

General aptitude functions selectively; for example, a person possessing high general aptitude may acquire a significant amount of content material from a specific instructional treatment while a person possessing a low general aptitude may experience extreme difficulty in acquiring the same information from the same instructional presentation. As an individual difference variable, aptitude can facilitate learning in some students and interfere with learning in others. In essence, the higher the general aptitude of an individual the more likely he will be successful in a specific instructional presentation or in a specific problem solving situation. Consequently, an individual's level of general aptitude is a significant factor which may influence the quality of interaction he will have with an instructional presentation.

APTITUDE-BY-TREATMENT INTERACTION

It is generally agreed that since human behavior is so complex and the teaching process so subtle, to deal with them successfully necessitates the utilization of complicated techniques. Researchers by means of an experimental technique known as aptitude-by-treatment interaction are attempting to identify the interrelationships among variables which tend to make the learning process so complex; e.g., what specific kinds of learning tend to be facilitated or inhibited by specific individual difference variables when students receive their respective instructional presentations by means of different instructional formats. One contention of ATI researchers is that individual difference variables are the primary source of variation in the evaluation of innovative and traditional methods of instruction; whenever instruction is presented to groups of students, individual differences are bound to affect the outcomes. Essentially, one of the primary purposes of ATI research is to facilitate the identification, organization, and management of instructional variables in facilitating optimal student achievement of different educational objectives.

This concern with different types of instructional strategies (i.e., television, programmed instruction, computer assisted instruction, large lecture format, etc.), individual difference variables associated with efficient learning, and the different types of educational objectives to be achieved appears to be of primary importance since logically it seems that different kinds of instructional strategies will be more or less effective in facilitating student achievement of different kinds of educational objectives. Gagné (1967, p. 30) has stated, "Learning is an individual act, a set of events which take place entirely within the learner. In fact, it is a highly idiosyncratic event, and depends very much on the nature of the learner, particularly on his own learning."

Gagné (1970a,b) and others (Bloom et al., 1956; Mager, 1962; Krathwohl, 1964; Dwyer, 1972a) have very convincingly identified various learning conditions which must be established relative to optimum achievement of different learning objectives. The concept of different learning conditions providing an optimum learning environment for different educational objectives has within it the basic assumption that specific instructional strategies need to be identified which will provide the "best fit" in terms of providing those conditions prerequisite for maximum acquisition of specific types of information. Stanley (1960) and Tiemens (1970) have cautioned educators against only considering interactions which exist between organismic variables inherent within individual students and instructional variables inherent in different presentation strategies. Acknowledging that individuals differ in a multitude of ways, the implication is that different instructional strategies are most efficient when they can be matched to patterns of individual difference characteristics which have been identified as being influential in facilitating student achievement. Rhetts (1974, p. 339) has stated that:

> A basic assumption underlying the aptitude-treatment-interaction concept is that individuals are indeed meaningfully different and that with sufficient conceptual and methodological tools these differences can be significantly utilized in the design of instruction. The aptitude-treatment-interaction believer rejects the notion that there is one best instructional procedure for teaching all individuals.

OBJECTIVES OF APTITUDE-BY-TREATMENT INTERACTION RESEARCH

Educators have long been pursuing the discovery of the one best way to teach. However, the current belief is that different students will profit differentially from identical presentations and there is no single best instructional process or format which will produce optimal learning for all students (Cronbach, 1967; Gagné, 1967; Jensen, 1968; Dwyer, 1972a). The rationale for aptitude-by-treatment interaction research is the contention that students learn from instructional presentations to the extent that their aptitudes enable them to interact with the materials. This being the case, it should be possible to develop a number of alternate instructional units each focusing on facilitating student achievement of identical educational objectives. A student then would be assigned to those treatments identified as being most beneficial for his particular configuration of aptitudes.

The ATI movement suggests that it will be possible to identify which individual difference variables interact with specific types of instructional presentations as joint determiners of academic achievement so that it eventually will be possible to match students to alternate specifically designed instructional formats which will ensure maximum levels of achievement. Heidt (1977, p. 13) in using the terminology trait-treatment interaction synonymously with aptitude-by-treatment interaction has characterized the typical trait-treatment interaction study in the following way.

> First, a personality trait is chosen (e.g., visualization ability) and by appropriate testing one tries to ascertain to what degree the experimental groups have this ability. Then for each subject matter or task at least two instructional treatments are chosen which have to differ with regard to one variable (e.g., verbal vs. graphic presentation). The instructional results are represented for each treatment by means of regression analysis. To prove a trait-treatment interaction it is necessary to detect a disordinal interaction, that means, that the regression lines of the different treatments must cross within the personality domain investigated.

Essentially, the ATI thrust as it relates to mediated (visualized) instruction is focused on identifying individual difference variables which interact with: (a) different types of instructional presentation formats (e.g., self paced—programmed instruction, externally paced—film, lecture, TV), (b) different types of educational objectives (terminology, concepts, rule learning, problem solving, etc.), (c) different amounts of realistic detail contained in visualization used to illustrate instructional content (e.g., line drawings, detailed line drawings, realistic photographs), (d) different media production variables (e.g., camera angle, color vs. black and white, realism vs. animation, etc.) and (e) different techniques of organizing and managing the media (e.g., the use of repetition, structure of the message, advance organizers, rate of presentation, types of cueing techniques, etc.).

Once data is obtained it will be possible to identify the kinds of stimulus situations most appropriate for promoting the achievement of students possessing specific aptitude configurations. It may also then be possible to identify the kinds of stimulus inputs which would have to be integrated into a stimulus situation to ensure that students not possessing the prescribed aptitude configuration would also have ample opportunity to achieve maximally.

TYPES OF INTERACTIONS

Fundamental to the development of the ATI philosophy is the necessity to produce evidence of significant statistical interactions among individual difference variables which are related to increased student achievement. Proponents of this philosophy generally agree that aptitude data is not very useful in adapting instruction to individual differences unless aptitude and instructional treatments interact (Lubin, 1961; Kropp et al., 1967; Bracht & Glass, 1968; Bracht, 1969, 1970; Salomon, 1972a,b; Tobias, 1976; Cronbach & Snow, 1969, 1977). Figures 10-1, 10-2, and 10-3 referred to in the following paragraphs illustrate possible relationships between an individual learner variable (e.g., level of background knowledge) and achievement level (e.g., score on criterion test) when identical instruction is presented by means of two different instructional formats—television and programmed instruction.

Figure 10-1 serves to illustrate no interaction between treatment type (programmed instruction or television) and level of students' background knowledge in the content area (high or low). Given two hypothetical groups of students, one group having been identified as low (A) in background knowledge in a specific content area and the other group (B) identified as high in background knowledge, assume that the low background knowledge group (A) is randomly split in half and that one half receives the televised instruction while the other half receives the programmed instruction. Their mean scores are plotted as A_1 and A_2. The high background knowledge group of students (B) is also randomly split in half with one half receiving the televised instruction and the other receiving the programmed instruction. Their mean scores are plotted as B_1 and B_2 respectively. As is apparent from this hypothetical graph, students who receive the televised instruction perform better regardless of their level of background knowledge. In addition, the differences in performance between the television and programmed instruction groups at each background knowledge level are approximately the same; that is, the television groups (A_1, B_1) are superior to the programmed instruction groups (A_2, B_2) at both ability levels. Note that the lines are parallel in this example of no interaction between type of in-

Figure 10-1. No interaction.

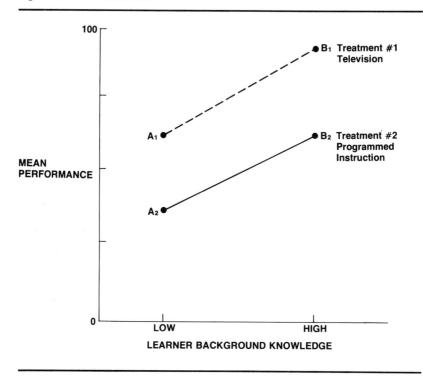

structional treatment and level of background knowledge.

Figure 10-2 and 10-3 illustrate cases in which interactions are present. Interactions are evidenced by the fact that the lines in each graph are not parallel. In Figure 10-2, the television treatment is still better overall; that is both low and high background knowledge students do better receiving the television treatment. However, the difference between the television and the programmed treatments is smaller for low background knowledge students and greater for high background knowledge students. In this situation, there is a different difference at each end of the two ability levels. Such a pattern is called an ordinal interaction because one method (television) is still superior at both knowledge levels.

Figure 10-3 represents the case in which average student performance is about the same for both treatments, i.e., if you calculated the means using points A_2 and B_1 (the television treatment) compared to points A_1 and B_2 (the programmed treatment). However, such a simple description of the results clearly misses the obvious

Figure 10-2. Interaction significant (nonsymmetric-ordinal).

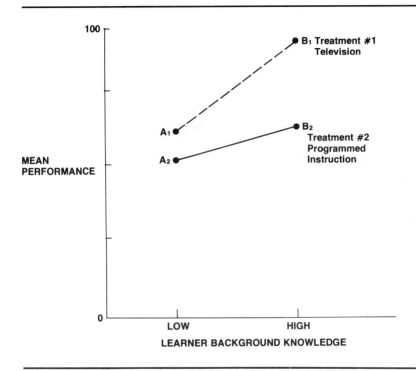

point that for low background knowledge students the programmed instruction treatment produced significant positive results (point A_1) whereas high background knowledge students performed better receiving the television treatment (point B_1). This type of pattern is called a disordinal interaction because the order of superiority of the instructional treatments depends on the level of the students' background knowledge—the programmed instruction treatment being best and the television treatment poorest for low background knowledge students. However, for the high background knowledge the reverse order is found to exist—the television treatment being best and the programmed instruction poorest. By assigning students possessing low levels of background knowledge in the subject area to the programmed instruction treatment in which they can proceed at their own rate and interact with the content material for as long as they feel necessary to acquire competency, and by allowing students possessing high background knowledge to receive the televised format, maximum learning is achieved for the majority of students.

Figure 10-3. Interaction significant (symmetrical-disordinal).

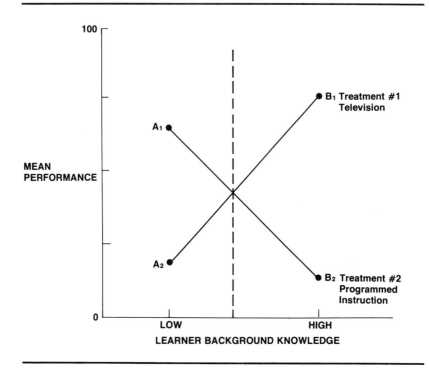

REPRESENTATIVE APTITUDE-BY-TREATMENT INTERACTION STUDIES

Clark (1975, pp. 199-202), in surveying the research literature on interactions between media attributes and individual differences (Table 10-1), found very few studies testing such interactions. In general, he found:

> First, the studies were primarily atheoretical and the results are thus difficult to explain. Second, before 1970 treatments involving gross media attributes—such as pictures vs. text vs. verbal presentations—were overwhelmingly popular. Since 1970, however, both individual difference measures and media attributes have been specified more exactly. Finally, a majority of these studies used gross trait measures such as age or grade level and/or general abilities, even when very specific mental skills and operations were required from subjects.

To date there have been a number of ATI studies conducted but generally the results have not been impressive. An extensive synthesis of this problem has been reported by Cronbach (1967) and Cron-

Table 10-1. Selected studies hypothesizing media attribute-trait/aptitude interactions. (Clark, 1975, pp. 200-201).

Authors	*Media Attribute*	*Trait(s) & Aptitude(s)*	*Dependent Measures*
	Audio vs. Visual vs. Reading		
Allen (1970)	Motion visuals vs. verbal	General mental ability tests	Identification
Allen, Filep, & Cooney (1967)	Motion picture/verbal modes vs. concrete/abstract content	General mental ability tests	Learning definitions
Bourisseau, Davis, & Yamamoto (1967)	Pictorial vs. verbal	Racial group	Number of sensory responses
Carterette & Jones (1967)	Auditory vs. visual	Grade level	Word recognition
Cooper & Gaeth (1967)	Reading/listening	Grade level	Paired-associate learning
Dilley & Paivio (1968)	Pictures vs. words	Age/grade level	Recognition
Gagné & Gropper (1965)	Motion picture vs. verbal instruction	Verbal ability/pre-achievement level	Learning
James (1962)	Reading vs. listening	Channel preference	Learning
Jenkins, Stack, & Deno (1969)	Picture vs. word	Age	Recognition
Koran, Snow, & McDonald (1971)	Video vs. written modeling	Film memory/general fluid ability	Acquisition of teaching skills
Marantz & Dowaliby (1973)	Filmed vs. lecture presentation of verbal material	Hidden figures	Recall
Snow, Tiffin, & Seibert (1965)	Filmed vs. live instruction	14 individual difference measures of ability, prior knowledge, and attitude	Immediate and delayed recall
Thalberg (1964)	Reading/listening vs. difficulty level	General mental ability tests	Learning
	Motion Variables		
Feldman (1971)	Simulations of map reading skills	Subcultural group membership	Map reading
Guba et al. (1964)	Moving vs. static visual presentation	IQ	Eye fixation
Salomon (1972)	"Zooming in on objects" "laying out objects in space" (motion vs. static presentation)	Verbal ability cue attendance & embedded figures information search	Memory for cues "laying out objects" hypothesis generation

Authors	*Media Attribute*	*Trait(s) & Aptitude(s)*	*Dependent Measures*
Salomon (1973)	Visual modeling: 1. visually changing points of view 2. relating components to wholes visually 3. novel vs. redundant formats etc.	Social class, field dependency, picture arrangement, age	Learning

Table 10-1. (Continued)

Color vs. Black/White			
Farley & Grant (1973) (post hoc discussion)	Black/white vs color pictures	Arousal potential/ stimulation seeking	Arousal/delayed effects
Kanner & Rosenstein (1960)	Color vs. black/white TV	General mental ability tests	Learning
Travers (1967) (review)	Variations in color	Age	Preference

Pictorial Design Variables			
Dwyer (1970b)	Various pictorial attributes (e.g. drawing detail, color-black/white, modes vs. photographs)	Grade level	Learning
Elkind, Koegler, & Go (1964)	Differing size of objects in pictures	Age	Object
Samuels (1970) (literature review)	Various types of pictorial representation	Reading ability	Reading performance

Figural vs. Symbolic vs. Verbal Materials			
Frederick, Blount, & Johnson (1968)	Figural vs. symbolic vs. verbal notation	General ability	Learning
Peterson & Hancock (1974)	Figural, symbolic or verbal modes	Pretests figural, verbal and symbolic aptitudes	Immediate and delayed retention

Novelty & Complexity			
Clark (1970)	Variations in stimulus complexity	Locus of control & dogmatism	Information seeking
Salomon & Sieber (1970)	Randomly spliced vs. "ordered" motion pictures	Cue attendance and hyphothesis generation abilities	Number of cues and hyphotheses elicited

Organizers & Prompts			
Ausubel & Fitzgerald (1962)	Advanced organizers	Verbal ability	Retention
Grippin (1973)	Strong vs. weak prompt techniques	Field dependence impulsivity	Learning

bach and Snow (1969, 1977). Following is a list of some of the research studies in which identification was made of instructional variables which interacted:

Researchers   *Interaction*
Snow, Tiffin, Seibert (1965)   Attitude toward instructional films, ascendency, responsibility, numerical aptitude, verbal aptitude, past experience with entertainment films, and past use of instructional films in-

	teracted significantly with instructional treatments (film vs. line presentation conditions).
Getzel & Jackson (1962)	Academic ability interacted with creativity.
Krumboltz & Yabroff (1965)	Levels of ability (high and low on the Miller Analogies Test) interacted with two alternate instructional formats (inductive/deductive).
Lubin (1965)	Autonomy and instructional reinforcement schedules.
Knight & Sassenrath (1966)	Test anxiety and pretest ability.
Cooper & Gaeth (1967)	Audiovisual materials, grade level, and content meaningfulness.
Buckland (1967)	I.Q. and instructional formats employing different response modes (reading, thinking, and writing).
Ripple, Millman & Glock (1969)	Student characteristics (anxiety, compulsivity, exhibitionism, convergent-minus-divergent thinking style) and instructional mode (programmed vs. conventionally structured learning tasks.)

Cronbach & Snow (1969, p. 193) provided an extensive review of ATI studies and concluded:

> Progress toward the goal of identifying and understanding ATI has been slight . . . . There are no solidly established ATI relations even on a laboratory scale, and no real sign of any hypothesis for application and development.

Bracht (1969) in reviewing the literature identified 90 studies designed to detect aptitude-by-treatment interactions, and of these only five were found to reveal disordinal interactions. Bracht (1970, p. 636) reported the following results obtained from the five studies in which disordinal interactions were found to occur:

> 1. In the experiment by Atkinson and Reitman (1956), Ss low on affiliation motive performed better with the achievement orientation treatment ($p<.10$), and Ss high on affiliation motive performed better with the multi-incentive treatment ($p<.05$).

2. Hovland, Lumsdaine and Sheffield (1949) found that presenting one side of an issue was more effective for changing the opinion of the men who initially favored the opinion of the program (p<.05), but presenting both sides of an issue was more effective for changing the opinion of the men who initially opposed the opinion of the program.

3. In the experiment by Marshall (1969), Ss from poor educational environments performed better on the high-interest task (p<.05) and Ss from good educational environments performed better on the low-interest task (p<.05).

4. Thompson and Hunnicutt (1944) reported that introverts obtained higher cancellation scores when they received praise (p<.05) and extroverts obtained higher cancellation scores when they received blame (p<.01).

5. Van De Riet (1964) found that underachievers performed better when they received reproof (p<.01) and normal achievers performed better when they received praise or were asked unrelated questions (p<.01).

One of the problems inherent in attempting to distill useful information from studies which have generated disordinal interactions, similar to the studies cited above, is caused by the types of individual difference variables which interact, e.g., need of affiliation, a pretest of opinion, educational aspects of the social environment, introversion-extroversion, etc. Most educators would experience difficulty in utilizing this information to improve the effectiveness of the teaching-learning process. The generalizability and usefulness of ATI research results is further complicated by the fact that a considerable amount of research dealing with individual differences has focused on criterion tasks not similar to those expected to be achieved by students in a typical instructional situation, e.g., paired-associate learning, auditory-visual digit span tasks, manual key depressing tasks, visual discriminations, matching paradigms, etc.

DILEMMA OF APTITUDE-BY-TREATMENT INTERACTION RESEARCH

Salomon (1972b, p. 327) in discussing one of the primary problems related to ATI has stated:

> Researchers in the field of instruction are becoming more amenable to the idea of aptitude-treatment interactions (ATI) as opposed to the search for the one "best" method or instructional treatment. In fact, the number of studies in which ATI's are deliberately sought is increasing rapidly. Yet, ATI research still seems to work on the basis of trial and error. . . . no conceptual tools have been developed with which specific ATI's can be either theoretically interpreted or deduced from a rationale.

Recently, Allen (1975, p. 139) in summarizing the work of Bracht

(1970) and Cronbach & Snow (1977) relating to aptitude-treatment interaction has stated:

> . . . there is little definitive evidence from the aptitude-treatment interaction research that point conclusively to the employment of practices that might guide the selection of the more general instructional strategies, much less lead to the design of specific instructional media. The research results are so fragmentary and diverse that generalizations from these alone are virtually impossible.

Similiarly, Heidt (1977, p. 13) in summarizing the reviews of Cronbach and Snow, 1969; Bracht, 1970; Berliner and Cahen, 1973; and Hunt, 1975, concludes:

> Only very few significant interactions have been experimentally proved to date. Results are not only contradictory, but even positive studies, i.e., those that detect a ATI effect, are so inconsistent that they cannot be summarized in any general way. Nearly all researchers and reviewers attribute the absence of conclusive evidence for ATI effects primarily to haphazardness in the selection and combination of treatment and personality variables.

For the ATI movement to succeed, disordinal interactions among variables have to be identified. However, at this point research has not been able to identify which specific variables interact consistently to facilitate maximum student achievement in a mediated learning environment (Jelden, 1971). One explanation might be that for many of the tasks which students are to perform they are not given enough time for the interaction to reveal itself—individual difference variables are just not given sufficient time to operate.

In addition, a further problem has been identified. Lindquist (1953, p. 124) has indicated that a significant interaction between two or more treatments in an experiment may only be partially explained by the differences in the instructional effectiveness of the two treatments. He contends that there are three possible causes of treatment-by-level interaction. The first is the situation in which true interaction exists between two variables and they effect a third variable; second, a significant interaction can occur by chance; and third, a significant interaction can occur as the result of some uncontrollable variable influencing one level of an experimental treatment and not the other. In discussing the implications of significant interactions Lindquist (*Ibid.,* p. 124) has commented that:

> . . . significance, however, does not enable us to say whether the interaction is intrinsic or extrinsic, or a mixture of both. In nearly all experiments of this type, a significant interaction is a mixture of intrinsic and extrinsic interaction, but there is no way of determing from the experiment alone what proportion is intrinsic and what extrinsic.

Anderson et al. (1975, p. 445-449), in commenting on the apparent limitations of ATI (Trait-Treatment-Interaction as used by Anderson et al. is synonomous with ATI) have stated:

> While a great deal of attention has been paid to the notion of TTI, relatively few investigators have designed their studies or analyzed their data with the identification of possible interactions in mind. The few who have investigated the phenomenon have only occasionally found significant interactions, and some of these have not held up in replication. There are probably several overlapping reasons for this state of affairs. First, the conceptualization, design, and conduct of TTI research is complex, requiring attention to multiple input, context, program, and outcome variables and use of *Multivariate Analyses*. Second, TTI is probably a relatively subtle effect. The measures and descriptors of both students and programs that are used in much evaluative research may be too gross to reveal it. Finally, of course, no matter how appealing the notion of trait-treatment interaction is, it simply may not exist in many practical situations or with most students (e.g., most students may be flexible enough to benefit from either treatment, or treatments may be so eclectic that they include "something for everyone"). Certainly further empirical investigation and theoretical analyses of the concept are needed at this stage. However, the lesson for evaluation is clear: they should at least look for differential effects of a program on subgroups of students. A program may appear to have no effect if the evaluator simply looks at average gains, whereas a closer inspection of the data might reveal that the program has significant benefits for learners.

Gulliksen (1961, p. 99) in commenting on two unpublished studies conducted by Stake (1958) and Allison (1960) which were designed ". . . to determine how many different learning abilities there are, and to see how these learning abilities are related to the abilities measured by aptitude and achievement tests" concluded:

> First we can say that, as a result of these two studies, the learning area is definitely a complex area that cannot be represented in terms of one learning ability. There are many different kinds of learning ability—how many we will not know until a good many more studies have been made. Second, it is clear that some of the abilities required for the learning tasks are not represented in any of the intelligence measures. The nature and the importance of these abilities that have been missed by the one-shot aptitude and achievement measure constitutes a very important problem for further investigation.

DISCUSSION

A number of basic issues associated with ATI have yet to be resolved if we are to effectively pursue the concept of developing instruction adaptable to individual differences in aptitude and learning style.

1. Is it economically feasible to produce different instructional treatments to accomodate differences in aptitude levels, or do

we integrate into a single presentation those conditions which will be appropriate for a majority of the students?

2. What learner characteristics are most closely related to the learning process; what characteristics are germane only to specific instructional situations, methods of instruction, etc.?

3. What specific student aptitudes are positively related to achievement of different types of educational objectives?

4. Once a specific aptitude has been identified as being influential in facilitating achievement, how should students be grouped to ensure that they will respond approximately the same way to identical instructional presentations?

5. What specific aptitudes interact optimally with different independent variables (instructional and methodological)?

6. Do identical aptitudes interact differentially with different types of instructional presentations? For example, do students identified as being at similar aptitude levels achieve equally well from different instructional formats, e.g., externally-paced television versus a self-paced programmed unit?

7. Are there specific combinations of aptitudes which maximize achievement of some learners while inhibiting the achievement of others?

Rhetts (1974, p. 339), while acknowledging that the pressing question related to ATI research is to identify and verify patterns of characteristics which are both (a) consistently ascribable to or manifested by an individual and (b) related to performance difference on some task(s), contends that the most potentially informative research should be focused on the following questions:

1. For a given task, what identifiable and replicable patterns of characteristics among individuals are associated with significantly different levels of performance on the task?

2. Are such patterns of individual-difference characteristics involved in aptitude interactions across a variety of tasks or are they task specific?

3. Are performance differences eradicable (partially or completely) by changing or modifying the task environment?

SUMMARY: MAIN IDEAS

Each student represents a totality of individuality on a number of cognitive and non-cognitive variables.

There is an increasing awareness on the part of educators of the importance of individual differences and their relationship to instructional practice.

As an individual difference variable, aptitude can facilitate learning in some students and interfere with learning in others.

One purpose of ATI research is to facilitate the identification, organization, and management of instructional variables that will interact maximally with individual learner variables in facilitating optimal student achievement of different educational objectives.

To date the results of research on aptitude-by-treatment interaction has not been impressive.

Fundamental to the development of the ATI philosophy is the necessity to produce evidence of significant statistical interactions (disordinal) among individual difference variables which are related to increased student achievement.

The investigation of the more complex forms of learning eventually leads to the search for variables which are farther and farther removed from the classroom situation and which tend to exist as previously acquired individual difference capabilities of the students.

REVIEW ACTIVITIES

1. Define aptitudes; list several examples.
2. Explain what is meant by aptitude-by-treatment interaction.
3. List the objectives associated with aptitude-by-treatment interaction research.
4. Describe the different types of interactions; construct graphs illustrating each type.
5. List the possible instructional implications of aptitude-by-treatment interaction research.
6. Summarize the results of the aptitude-by-treatment interaction studies cited in this chapter.
7. Explain the dilemma of aptitude-by-treatment interaction research.
8. Discuss the basic issues associated with aptitude-by-treatment interaction which have to be resolved if the concept of developing instruction adaptable to individual differences in aptitude and learning style are to be realized.

RECOMMENDED READINGS

Clark, R. E. 1975. Constructing a taxonomy of media attributes for research purposes. *AV Commun. Rev. 23:* 197-215.

Koran, M. L. 1972. Varying instructional methods to fit trainee characteristics. *AV Commun. Rev. 20:* 135-146.

Shapiro, K. R. 1975. An overview of problems encountered in aptitude treatment interaction (ATI) research for instruction. *AV Commun. Rev. 23:* 227-241.

Snow, R. E. & Salomon, G. 1968. Aptitudes and instructional media. *AV Commun. Rev. 16:* 341-357.

11

Individual Differences and Visualized Instruction

LEARNING OBJECTIVES

Upon completion of this chapter the student will be able to:

1. *Discuss in writing why no single instructional technique will provide optimum learning conditions for all students.*
2. *Identify the types of visualization most effective in reducing differences among students identified as possessing high, medium, and low levels of individual difference characteristics (reading comprehension, intelligence, and entering behavior—level of prior knowledge in the content area).*
3. *Explain the statement that "visuals containing different amounts of realistic detail that are functionally indistinguishable (in terms of increased student achievement) are functionally identical."*
4. *Explain why students' sophistication level in a content area in an important instructional variable in their ability to profit from visualized instruction.*
5. *State several reasons why it will not be necessary for educators to develop unique instructional modules to coincide with each student's individual variabilities.*
6. *Explain why the realism continuum for visual illustrations is not a reliable predictor of learning efficiency for students possessing different levels of individual difference characteristics.*
7. *Explain how high, medium, and low individual difference variables possessed by students affect their capacity to profit from visualized instruction.*

ORIENTATION

Given the variety of different types of instructional variables present in the typical learning situation (differences in students, educational objectives to be achieved, methods of presentation, types of visualization available to illustrate content, etc.), it is plausible that some students will achieve greater success from one method of instructional presentation while others will be more successful when receiving instruction from a totally different mode of presentation. In considering the instructional implications of visualized instruction, it may be that students possessing different levels of specific individual difference variables will profit differentially from instruction complemented by visuals containing different amounts of realistic detail.

When in a learning situation, each student responds to instructional stimuli according to his own background. Previous experience, I.Q., and age have been found to be among the major individual difference variables which influence both the quantity and quality of information students acquire from visualized instruction (Dwyer, 1972a). Differences in individuals is the primary reason why a specific learning situation has multiple outcomes (Tyler, 1951) and why different students possessing different levels of a individual difference variable profit differentially from different types of visuals used to complement identical content material. For example, what a learner already knows in a given content area (prior experience) determines not only what will be learned, how it will be learned, and how rapidly the content will be learned, but prior knowledge also is the determining factor in the amount of realistic detail which should be contained in the visualization so that optimum student learning will occur. The mature or sophisticated learner in any specific content area possesses a large vocabulary and is capable of conceptualizing and integrating new content, etc. The mature learner is different from the novice in that while the novice is interacting with primary cues in a visualized presentation, the mature learner has already assimilated the primary information and has proceeded to interact with the secondary cues in acquiring a more complete and comprehensive understanding of the information being presented. It is for this reason that learners being introduced to relatively new content profit from simple or basic illustrations while the more advanced learners are able to learn more comprehensively from the more realistic illustrations.

Collins (1970) in studying the effect of age on achievement indicated that young children are readily distracted from the essential learning cues in a program of instruction by responding more actively to peripheral details. As a child gets older he becomes more capable of attending selectively to those features in an instructional presentation that have the greatest potential for enhancing his learning of desired information (Feldman, 1961; Wohlwill, 1962; Neisser, 1964; Maccoby & Hagen, 1965; Miller et al., 1960; Gibson & Yonas, 1966; Siegel & Stevenson, 1966; Gibson, 1969; Hale & Morgan, 1973; Hale & Taweel, 1974).

Research by Klausmeier & Check (1962) found that when learning tasks are adjusted in difficulty to the learner's achievement level, differences attributed to I.Q. level are diminished. Inherent in this conclusion is the logical extenion—that the learning potential of an individual at any particular moment depends not solely on individual difference variables but also on the type of learning he is expected to achieve. Allen, Cooney, and Weintraub (1968), Parkhurst (1974), and Dwyer (1972a) found that when instruction is not specifically designed to coincide with specific individual differences (i.e., mental ability, entering behavior, reading comprehension), significant differences in the amount of information acquired by the students will result and the amount of learning achieved diminishes as the difficulty of the learning objectives increases.

Acknowledging that individual differences may make a difference, it follows then that a greater proportion of students would achieve a specified criterion level if the method by which they received their respective instructional presentation was adapted to compensate for individual difference variables and for the different types of educational objectives to be achieved by students (Dwyer, 1972a). However, this should not be interpreted as a suggestion that unique teaching conditions have to be established for each individual student. Since there are enough similarities among students at any given educational level, a given visualized presentation may be effective over a wide band of individual difference variables and probably for more than one type of educational objective.

INDIVIDUAL DIFFERENCE VARIABLES

Acknowledging the ATI philosophy—that no single instructional technique will facilitate optimal learning for all students—it was hypothesized further that (a) no one type of visualization would be equally effective in facilitating the achievement of students possessing different quantities (levels) of the same individual difference variables, and (b) different types of visualization—possessing varying amounts of realistic detail—would not be equally effective in facilitating student performance on criterion tests measuring achievement of different types of educational objectives. To explore these hypotheses a number of studies have been conducted by the author and his colleagues in a program of systematic evaluation which relate directly to the issue of whether students possessing different levels of an individual difference characteristic profit differentially from different types of visuals (Arnold & Dwyer, 1973, 1975, 1976; Kauffman & Dwyer, 1975; Parkhurst, 1974, 1975, 1976; Berry, 1976; Dwyer, 1975, 1976). In these studies a number of different individual difference variables have been investigated: student entering behavior (prior knowledge in the content area), intelligence, and reading comprehension. Levels of individual difference variables—high, medium, and low—have been defined by establishing cut-off points one-half standard deviation on each side of the group mean achieved on the test used to measure individual difference variables. The following sections contain a synopsis of a number of the cited studies.

READING COMPREHENSION

Parkhurst (1976), in his study of the effect of reading comprehension level on student achievement, investigated the effectiveness with which three types of black and white illustrations (simple line drawings, detailed, line drawings, and photographs of a three dimensional model) facilitated achievement on the different criterion tests. Figure 11-1 illustrates graphically how students possessing different levels of reading comprehension achieved on the five different criterion tests when they received their respective programmed instructional presentation complemented by visualization possessing different amounts of realistic detail.

Based on an analysis of the data Parkhurst (1976, pp. 9-11) concluded:

1. Not all visuals were equally effective in facilitating student achievement on different educational tasks.
2. Not all students who differed in level of reading comprehension achieved at an equal level of performance on identical criterion measures when different visuals were available.
3. On most of the educational tasks, the simple or less realistic visuals reduced the overall significant differences in achievement between the high, medium, and low level reading comprehension groups.
4. The high level reading comprehension group achieved their lowest performance on all educational tasks when they received line drawings.
5. The high level reading comprehension group's achievement improved as the degree of realism in visuals increased from line drawing to detailed shaded drawing to realistic model.

Figure 11-1. Plots of the treatment means for different reading comprehension levels on each criterion measure (Parkhurst, 1976, pp 9-10).

In Figure 11-1, the letters H, M, and L represent the levels of reading comprehension (high, medium, low) possessed by the students, and the points 1.0, 2.0, 3.0, and 4.0 represent the programmed treatments employed in the study (no visualization, line drawings, detailed, shaded drawings, and realistic model respectively.

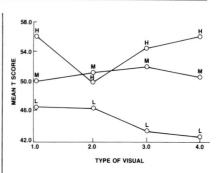

Plate 1.
Terminology Test.

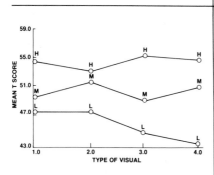

Plate 2.
Identification Test.

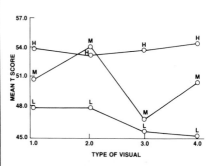

Plate 3.
Drawing Test.

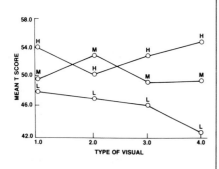

Plate 4.
Comprehension Test.

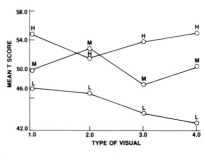

Plate 5.
Total Criterion.

6. The low level reading comprehension group's achievement decreased as the degree of realism in visuals increased from no visuals to the realistic model.
7. The pattern of student achievement for the medium level reading comprehension group was inconsistent and irregular on each of the educational tasks as the amount of visual realism increased from no visuals to realistic model.

INTELLIGENCE

Dwyer (1976a) investigated the instructional effect that different levels of intelligence have on student performance when eight types of visual illustrations were used to complement oral instruction. In this study, instruction was presented by means of synchronized audiotape slide presentation (externally paced format). Figure 11-2 illustrates how students possessing different levels of intelligence per-

Figure 11-2. Plots of the treatment means for the different I.Q. levels on each criterion measure.

In Figure 11-2, the symbols △—△ , ■—■, and ○—○ represent levels of I.Q. (high, medium, low) possessed by the students, and the numbers 1, 2, 3, etc. correspond to the following visualized instructional treatments:

1. Line drawings (b&w)
2. Line drawings (color)
3. Detailed line drawings (b&w)
4. Detailed line drawings (color)
5. Heart model (b&w)
6. Heart model (color)
7. Realistic photograph (b&w)
8. Realistic photograph (color)

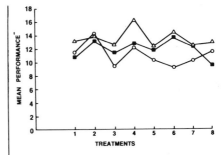

Plate 1.
Plot of the Treatment Means on the
Terminology Test

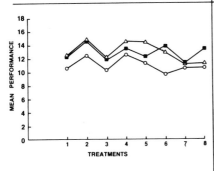

Plate 2.
Plot of the Treatment Means on the
Identification Test

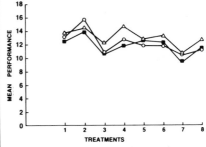

Plate 3.
Plot of the Treatment Means on the
Drawing Test

Figure 11-2. (Continued)

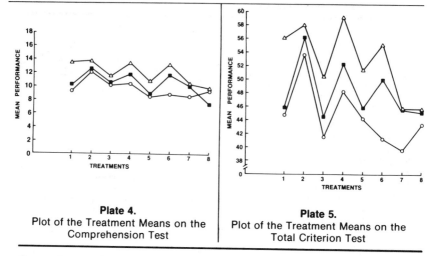

Plate 4.
Plot of the Treatment Means on the
Comprehension Test

Plate 5.
Plot of the Treatment Means on the
Total Criterion Test

formed on criterion tests when they received their respective instructional presentations complemented by different types of visualization.

A number of summary statements can be made concerning the results obtained in this study (Dwyer, 1976a, pp. 59-60):

1. Not all visuals were equally effective in facilitating student achievement on the different criterion tasks. It is interesting to note that in general the colored version of the line drawing, detailed line drawing, and heart model presentation were consistently most effective in facilitating student achievement across all criterion measures.
2. Students in the high I.Q. level consistently achieved equivalent or significantly higher scores on the criterion measures than students in the medium and low I.Q. levels regardless of the type of instructional presentations they received. Apparently, identical visual illustrations are not equally effective in facilitating the achievement of students possessing different intelligence levels.
3. In terms of instructional effectiveness, economy, and simplicity of production, the simple line drawing presentation (color) was found to be the treatment most effective in facilitating student achievement on the five criterion measures.

ENTERING BEHAVIOR

In another study (Dwyer, 1975) an attempt was made to assess the instructional effect of different levels of entering behavior (prior knowledge in the content area) on student performance. The same instructional treatments as the previous study were used; however, in this study the instruction was presented to students via programmed booklets—a self-paced instructional format. Figure 11-3 illustrates how students in the high, medium, and low levels of entering behavior performed on the different criterion measures as a result of receiving the differentially complemented visualized treatments.

224

Figure 11-3. Plots of the treatment means for the different entering behavior levels on each criterion measure.

In Figure 11-3, the symbols △—△, ■—■, and ○—○ represent levels of entering behavior (high, medium, low) possessed by the students, and the numbers 1, 2, 3, etc. correspond to the following instructional treatments:

1. Line drawings (b&w)
2. Line drawings (color)
3. Detailed line drawings (b&w)
4. Detailed line drawings (color)
5. Heart Model (b&w)
6. Heart model (color)
7. Realistic photograph (b&w)
8. Realistic photograph (color)

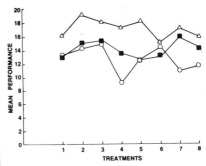

Plate 1.
Plot of the Treatment Means on the Terminology Test.

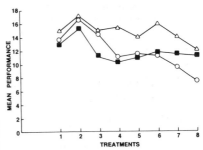

Plate 3.
Plot of the Treatment Means on the Drawing Test.

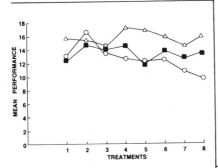

Plate 2.
Plot of the Treatment Means on the Identification Test.

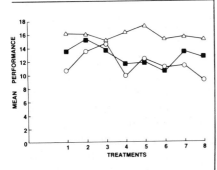

Plate 4.
Plot of the Treatment Means on the Comprehension Test.

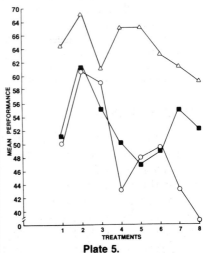

Plate 5.
Plot of the Treatment Means on the Total Criterion Test.

A number of summary statements can be made concerning the results obtained in this study (Dwyer, 1975, pp. 82-83):

1. Students with low and medium entering behavior generally require more time to interact with the more realistic instructional presentations than students with high entering behavior.
2. Students with high entering behavior consistently achieved equivalent or significantly higher scores on the criterion measures than students with low and medium entering behavior regardless of the type of instructional presentation they received. Apparently, identical visual illustrations are not equally effective in facilitating the achievement of students possessing different levels of entering behavior.
3. The use of visualization to complement programmed instruction is an effective instructional technique for reducing differences in achievement between students with low (level 3) and medium (level 2) entering behavior on the five criterion measures. The detailed, shaded drawing presentation (b&w), the heart model presentations (b&w and color), and the detailed, shaded drawing presentation (color) were effective in reducing differences in achievement on four of the five criterion measures. The realistic photographic presentations (b&w and color) were the two presentations found to be least effective in reducing differences in achievement between students with low and medium entering behavior.
4. The b&w version of the simple line and detailed, shaded drawing presentations were found to be most effective in reducing differences in achievement among students with high, medium and low entering behavior—i.e., differences in achievement were reduced on the drawing and terminology tests for students receiving the simple line presentation (b&w) and on the drawing, identification, and comprehension tests for students receiving the detailed, shaded drawing presentation (b&w).

CONCLUSIONS

A number of summary statements can be derived from the data obtained from these studies relating to the relationship which exists among visuals containing varying degrees of realistic detail, individual difference variables and different types of educational objectives:

1. Students differ in their ability to learn from different types of visual illustrations. Students identified as possessing high levels of an individual difference variable (intelligence, reading comprehension, entering behavior) consistently achieve equivalent or significantly higher scores on the criterion measures than do students identified as possessing medium and low levels of the individual difference variable regardless of the type of visualized instructional presentations they receive.
2. In terms of improving student achievement by means of visualized instruction a variation in the amount of realism contained in the visual has to make a difference (in terms of increased student achievement) to be considered different. Visuals containing varying amounts of realistic detail that are functionally

indistinguishable (neither is significantly more effective than the other in improving student achievement of a specific educational task) are functionally identical.

3. There are specific types of visuals which can be designed and used to complement both self-paced and externally paced instruction which will significantly improve student achievement of specific educational objectives and will be optimally effective in reducing achievement differences among students in the high, medium, and low individual difference variable levels.

4. In general, the simple line drawings (b&w and color) and the detailed, shaded drawings (b&w and color) were found to be consistently effective in reducing differences in achievement among students in the high, medium and low categories of individual difference variables.

5. In terms of economy and simplicity of production, the simple line drawing presentation (b&w and color) was found to be the single most effective type of visual for facilitating student achievement and for reducing differences in achievement on all criterion measures among students in the high, medium, and low individual difference levels.

6. In general, students identified as possessing different levels of an individual difference variable (e.g., intelligence, reading comprehension, and entering behavior) achieve differentially from different types of visualization.

DISCUSSION

Individual difference characteristics in learners appear to be crucial variables which influence the quality and quantity of learning that will occur in a particular instructional situation. Even though the results of the cited studies found that students possessing different levels of an individual difference variable profit differentially on specific educational objectives from identical types of visualization, the data also supported the contention that for other objectives specific types of visualization seem to be suitable across a wide range of individual difference levels—high, medium and low.

Bruner (1957) has indicated that the differential perception and encoding strategies employed by the learner influence the learner's coding and information processing capabilities. If information being presented to students is known, familiar, or somewhat related to what they already know, visualization of the content material offers no advantage. When the content being presented is new, and the student is required to develop new structures or associations to facilitate coding and storage, his information processing capacity is somewhat slower but possibly may be improved via the use of simple illustrations. This might be considered as one reason why the presentations complemented by means of simple line illustrations in the cited studies were so successful in facilitating student achievement—the students possessed very little background knowledge in the content area and were able to profit maximally from the line drawings. When the density of information contained in the visualization was high (photographs of the heart model and realistic photographs), the abundance of realistic stimuli in the visual distracted from rather than focused student attention on essential learning cues.

In situations in which students do possess the basic building blocks of a content area, e.g., facts, definitions, concepts, etc., and the new information being presented is complicated requiring that the student manipulate and integrate information extensively, visualization is beneficial in improving achievement. However, in attempting to facilitate this more complex type of learning with the use of visualization, it is necessary that the student be given adequate amounts of time to interact with the visualization and to participate in this type of information processing. In this context Feigenbaum and Simon (1963) present the idea that all inputs of stimuli impinging upon the perceptual system require a certain amount of processing time. Since it is often contended that information processing occurs within a single channel, the information processing capacity of the learner is limited, necessitating the need for additional time for the learner to alternate effectively between channels to acquire a maximum amount of information. Homer (1946) and Dwyer (1972a) have indicated that the amount of time and effort required by students to achieve different types of educational objectives, ranging from the simple to the complex, varies directly with the complexity of the stimuli presented and with the present knowledge level of the students. Under these circumstances content complexity would be considered a function of the degree of familiarity which the learner has with the content being presented.

SUMMARY: MAIN IDEAS

Individual differences among students appear to be crucial variables which influence whether or not a student will learn in a particular instructional situation.

Students differ in their ability to learn from different types of visual illustrations.

As a child gets older, he becomes more capable of attending selectively to those features in an instructional presentation that have the greatest potential for enhancing his learning of desired information.

The simple line drawings (b&w and color) and the detailed, shaded drawing presentations (b&w and color) were the presentations found to be most consistently effective in reducing differences among students in the high, medium, and low categories of different individual difference variables.

There are sufficient commonalities among students so that instruction complemented by a specific type of visualization may be used effectively for students representing a rather wide band of a specific individual difference variable.

Visual illustrations containing different amounts of realistic detail can transmit the same amount of information without providing the same amount of visual stimulation.

The learning potential of an individual at any particular moment depends not only on individual difference variables but also on the type of learning the student is expected to achieve.

REVIEW ACTIVITIES

1. Describe the relationship which exists between individual differences and visualized instruction.
2. List the individual difference variables investigated by the author and his colleagues in the program of systematic evaluation.
3. Explain the meaning of the statement, "Visuals containing different amounts of realistic detail that are indistinguishable in terms of facilitating student achievement are functionally identical."
4. Develop several generalizations from your observation and study of Figures 11-1, 11-2, 11-3 as they relate to the selection and use of visualized instruction for students identified as possessing different levels of an individual difference variable.
5. Identify the two types of visualization (Figures 11-1, 11-2, 11-3) which appear to be least consistent in facilitating student achievement on the criterion measures.
6. From information contained in Figure 11-1, construct a chart identifying the visuals most and least effective in facilitating student achievement on each criterion measure for each reading comprehension level. Also, identify the types of visuals which are approximately equal in facilitating student achievement for two or

more levels of reading comprehension on each criterion measure.

7. From information contained in Figure 11-2, construct a chart identifying the visuals most and least effective in facilitating student achievement for each I.Q. level on each criterion measure. Also, identify the types which are approximately equal in facilitating student achievement for two or more levels of I.Q. on each criterion measure.

8. From information contained in Figure 11-3, construct a chart identifying the visuals most and least effective in facilitating student achievement on each criterion measure for each entering behavior level. Also, identify the types of visuals which are approximately equal in facilitating student achievement for two or more levels of entering behavior on each criterion measure.

RECOMMENDED READINGS

Allen, W. H. 1975. Intellectual abilities and instructional media design. *AV Commun. Rev. 23:* 139-170.

Haskell, R. W. 1971. Effect of certain individual learner personality differences on instructional methods. *AV Commun. Rev. 19:* 287-297.

Hsia, H. J. 1969. Intelligence in auditory, visual and audiovisual processing. *AV Commun. Rev. 17:* 272-282.

Randhawa, B. S. 1971. Intellectual development and the ability to process visual and verbal information. *AV Commun. Rev. 19:* 298-312.

12

Visual Testing

LEARNING OBJECTIVES

Upon completion of this chapter the student will be able to:

1. *List four reasons why educators are currently focusing considerable attention on visual testing.*
2. *Explain why visual testing is not currently being implemented extensively.*
3. *Summarize the theoretical justification for visual testing.*
4. *Discuss the statement "visual testing has to be related to specific types of educational objectives."*
5. *Summarize the research findings relative to visual testing.*
6. *List the types of variables associated with visual testing that have been investigated.*
7. *List several advantages that pictorial tests have over verbal tests, equipment tests, and printed pictorial tests.*

ORIENTATION

Many of the world's cultures are becoming more sensitive to and capable of learning from visual stimuli, and visual media for instructional purposes has become an instructional strategy employed worldwide within the teaching-learning process. However, one of the major criticisms of this phenomena is that most evaluation strategies currently in use to evaluate mediated instruction are of the pencil and paper type and are highly verbal, rather than visual, in nature. Apparently, there is an urgent need for systematic examination of the relationship which exists among different types of visual teaching-testing formats and the level of student achievement of different types of educational objectives.

ADVANTAGES OF VISUAL TESTING

Proponents of the visual testing movement question the validity and reliability of verbal printed tests used to measure the instructional effects of visualization employed in the teaching-learning process. Their contention is that the contribution of visualization to student learning can most appropriately be measured visually. Gross (1969, p. 35) arguing in favor of visual testing of visualized instruction has stated:

> The verbal testing of visually presented material is often frustrating to the student and is not a true measure of what he actually knows. In a way, this verbal testing in the presence of visual presentation stimuli is akin to the older IQ tests which are not a measure of general intelligence but largely a measure of white middle-class vocabulary standards.

Similarily, Gibson (1947) has indicated that there are several functions which are particularly amenable to motion picture (visual) testing:

1. Discrimination of visual motion and locomotion;
2. Perception of space and distance;
3. Maintaining orientation during locomotion;
4. Ability to learn a procedure;
5. Ability to react to a changing situation;
6. Ability to perform under emotional stress.

Lefkowith (1955a, p. 15-21), in summarizing literature and research related to pictorial testing, has derived theoretical advantages in three general areas: (a) pictorial test over verbal test, (b) pictorial tests over equipment tests, and (c) projected tests over printed pictorial tests. Following is a summary of his conclusions:

A.   PICTORIAL TESTS OVER VERBAL TESTS
   1. Pictorial tests are more accurate and more easily understood.
   2. Pictorial tests can be used to ask good questions about some things which cannot be described or set-up adequately by words alone.
   3. Pictorial tests reduce the emphasis on reading which often tends to prevent the measurement of non-verbal abilities.
   4. Pictorial tests often provide a more interesting and motivating situation.

B.   PICTORIAL TESTS OVER EQUIPMENT TESTS
   1. Pictorial tests take less time to administer.
   2. Pictorial tests can be used with any size group.
   3. Pictorial tests make administration of the test less cumbersome.
   4. Pictorial tests are less expensive since equipment need not be set up repeatedly for each group.

5. Pictorial tests can be administered anywhere as opposed to an equipment test for which equipment or subjects must be transported.

C.   PROJECTED PICTORIAL TESTS OVER PRINTED PICTORIAL TESTS
1. Projected pictorial tests are cheaper than printed pictorial tests.
2. Projected pictorial tests can be used with groups of any size.
3. Projected pictorial tests are more durable.
4. Projected pictorial tests will not be marked up with "give away" symbols.
5. Projected pictorial tests have better security or secrecy potential.
6. Projected pictorial tests can more easily control the order of the questions.
7. Projected pictorial tests can more easily control the amount of time spent on each question.
8. Projected pictorial tests can be more easily stored.
9. Projected pictorial tests are usually easier to transport.
10. Additional advantages accrue when the projected pictorial tests become more complex since color, motion, sound, and even a third dimension can be added extending the scope of the testing potential.

A THEORETICAL FOUNDATION FOR VISUAL TESTING

One of the perennial problems associated with the teaching-learning process is the determination of how learners acquire, store and recall information. As a result, a number of information acquisition strategies have been proposed which attempt to explain how learners acquire and retrieve information. For example, Tversky (1969, 1973) has found that verbal and visual information are encoded differently depending on the learner's perceived use of the information. Glanzer and Clark (1963b) have advanced the notion of a single information processing system (verbal-loop hypothesis) which contends that visual information is translated into and stored in verbal/symbolic form. When this information is to be retrieved, it is retranslated from the verbal symbolic form back to the original visualization. A number of specific research studies have been conducted which can be interpreted to be supportive of this orientation (Glanzer & Clark, 1963a,b, 1964; Lantz & Stefflre, 1964; Smith & Larson, 1970).

Paivio, Rogers and Smythe (1968) have suggested the possible existence of dual encoding and retrieval systems each functioning as a separate entity with the capability of working in unison with each other. Basically, this orientation (Paivio et al., 1968; Paivio, 1971) proposes a model involving two independent memory systems: one having the capability of processing verbal symbols, the other having the capability of processing visual information. Although the dual encoding and retrieval systems are perceived as functioning as separate entities, they also possess the capability of functioning in unison with each other. Depending on the nature (form) of the information to be retrieved, action with the specific memory system would be initiated. Similarly, a number of research studies have been conducted which may be interpreted as being supportive of the dual encoding and retrieval systems (Bahrick & Boucher, 1968; Paivio & Csapo, 1969; Bahrick & Bahrick, 1971; Cermak, 1971; Ternes & Yuille, 1972; Levie & Levie, 1975).

Keele (1973, p. 17) in commenting on the literature relating to the area of information acquisition states:

> The evidence reviewed indicates that once information is perceived a great deal of flexibility exists for the form of recoding. Verbal materials are often coded in an articulatory form, even when presentation is visual. Spatial material may· be visually coded, even when presentation is auditory. Although the new code may be a different mode than the presentation mode, evidence is accumulating that a transformation in mode is not necessary.

The justification for using visual testing in situations where visualization is used to complement oral/print instruction appears to have its generic roots in the sign similarity hypothesis and the cue summation principle of learning. The sign similarity hypothesis (Carpenter, 1953, p. 41) contends that, ". . . films, signals, signs, and symbols [which] have high degree of similarity (iconicity) to the objects and situations which they represent will be more effective for most instructional purposes than those films whose signals, signs, and symbols have low degrees of iconicity." In general, the essence of the cue summation principle of learning is that (Severin, 1967b, p. 237): ". . . learning is increased as the number of available cues or stimuli is increased." The strategy of attempting to use visualization both in the presentation and evaluation phases of instruction is an attempt to implement the stimulus generalization phenomena which contends that the amount of information that will be acquired by students increases as the testing situation becomes more similar to the situation in which the students received their instruction (Hartman, 1961a; Severin, 1967a).

VISUAL TESTING RESEARCH

Over the years a considerable amount of research has been conducted in an attempt to determine whether, in fact, there is a difference in achievement scores between students who receive visualized instruction and are evaluated verbally and those who are evaluated visually (Thurstone, 1941; Thalen, 1945; Brown, 1947, 1949; Ebel, 1951; Lefkowith, 1955a; Dwyer, 1972a). Researchers investigating the visual testing phenomenon have explored a number of different dimensions. Studies conducted on the reliability, validity (Carpenter et al., 1954; Lefkowith, 1955b; Torrence, 1976), and administration (Pessinger, 1969; Hill, 1976) of visual tests have established that visual tests are indeed reliable, valid, and capable of being administered with a reasonable amount of success.

Strategies involving a number of different formats have been employed in investigating the parameters of visual testing: film (Carpenter et al., 1954), realistic photographs and line drawings (Lefkowith, 1955a; Dwyer, 1972a), television (Hopkins, Lefever & Hopkins, 1967; Stallings, 1972), slides (Lumsdaine & Gladstone, 1958; Stoker et al., 1968; Tanner & Dwyer, 1977). Most of the findings from these studies indicate that no significant differences occur in student performance as a result of their being evaluated visually rather than in the conventional verbal format. These general findings along with the time and expense involved in constructing visual tests have succeeded in preventing, if only temporarily, the impact that visual testing may eventually make on educational evaluation as we know it today.

PROGRAM OF SYSTEMATIC EVALUATION

Just as it has been found that there is no one best type of instructional procedure, type of visual, method of content organization, etc. which will produce optimum student achievement of all types of educational objectives, it may also be true that no one type of testing format will be equally effective in accurately assessing student achievement of all types of educational objectives. It may be that some students are so capable that they can achieve all types of educational objectives equally well. There is also the possibility that some students will achieve optimally on some educational objectives when tested visually. In general, most of the previous research conducted on the relative effectiveness of the verbal-print vs. visual testing phenomenon merely required learners to recognize or recall visual content. Very little effort has been expended in attempting to relate the advantages of visual testing to specific types of educational objectives. It may be that the use of visual testing procedures would be a more valid assessment technique for assessing student performance levels of specific types of educational tasks, e.g., visual reasoning, manipulation, problem solving, etc.

For example, consider the results obtained in three studies (Dwyer, 1970b; 1971e; 1971f) conducted in his program of systematic evaluation (Table 12-1). The conclusions presented in Plate 1 illus-

Table 12-1. Presentations most effective in facilitating student achievement on each criterion measure.

Criterion Measures	Instructional Treatments
Terminology Test	Oral Presentation
Identification Test	Oral Presentation
Drawing Test	Simple Line Drawing
Comprehension Test	Oral Presentation
Total Criterion Test	Oral Presentation

Plate 1. (Dwyer, 1970b, p. 244).

Criterion Measures	Instructional Treatments
Terminology Test	Program Without Visuals
Identification Test	Simple Line Drawing (b&w)
Drawing Test	Simple Line Drawing (b&w)
Comprehension Test	Program Without Visuals
Total Criterion Test	Program Without Visuals

Plate 2. (Dwyer, 1971e, pp. 220-221).

Criterion Measures	Instructional Treatments
Terminology Test	Presentation Without Visuals
Identification Test	Detailed, Shaded Drawing (color)
Drawing Test	Simple Line Drawing (color)
Comprehension Test	Presentation Without Visuals
Total Criterion Test	Presentation Without Visuals

Plate 3. (Dwyer, 1971f, p. 99).

trate that visualization was effective in facilitating student achievement on the drawing test. Plates 2 and 3 reveal that visualization was effective in facilitating student achievement on both the drawing and identification tests. However, in each of the three studies cited, the presentation without any type of visualization was found to be as effective as the visualized presentations on the total criterion test. When the sub-scores achieved on the different criterion tests are pooled together to provide a total criterion test score, the variances among the different test scores are cancelled out yielding insignificant differences on the total criterion tests. This observation may be offered as a partial explanation as to why so many studies investigating the effectiveness of visually mediated instruction yield insignificant results. Many of these studies employed a global test which yielded one test score even though the test was measuring student achievement of different kinds of educational objectives. If in the three studies cited only the total criterion test was administered to students as a measure of academic attainment, subsequent analyses would indicate that the presentations without visualization were as effective as the visualized presentations in facilitating student achievement. Clearly this is not the case since visualization was found to be effective in facilitating student achievement on the drawing test in one study and on the drawing and identification tests in the two other studies.

The drawing test and the identification tests may be considered to be forms of visual testing since the drawing test required students to draw a representative diagram of the heart and position the various parts in their respective positions, and the identification test required students to recognize parts of the heart from a detailed line drawing. When students were evaluated by these visual tests, their achievement was found to be significantly greater. These findings indicate that student achievement of specific types of educational objectives can be facilitated by the use of visualization and that this learning can most appropriately be assessed through some form of visual testing.

Other studies conducted in the program of systematic evaluation (Dwyer, 1972a) seem to lend support to the hypothesis that visual testing may be a more reliable evaluation strategy than verbal-print tests as a predictor of student achievement of specific types of educational objectives. For example, in the heart studies on the drawing test students were required to draw a representative drawing of the heart and position the listed parts in their correct locations. The line drawing illustrations produced by students on this performance task most closely resembled the simple line drawing presentation (b&w and color). Students who received the simple line drawing presentations consistently achieved significantly higher scores on the drawing test than did students who received the more realistic type of visual presentations. The second most effective type of visualization in improving student achievement on the drawing test was the detailed line drawing presentation (b&w and color). Students appeared to be quite capable of absorbing the crucial cues from the detailed line drawing presentations and reconstructing the crucial information on the drawing test.

Figure 12-1 contains the type of illustration used in the identifica-

Figure 12-1. Drawing used in the identification test.

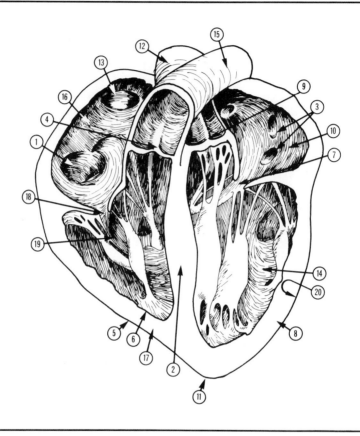

tion test and these drawings most closely resemble the detailed, shaded drawing presentation (b&w). The stimulus generalization hypothesis would contend then that students who received their instruction by means of the detailed, shaded drawing presentation would achieve significantly higher scores on this test since the visual used on the evaluation form represented the type of visualization students were exposed to in the instructional sequence. However, the detailed shaded drawing presentation (b&w) was not found to be the most efficient treatment in facilitating student achievement on any of the criterion measures. The continued inefficiency of this particular instructional presentation has been replicated in more than two dozen individual studies (Dwyer, 1972a). These findings are almost completely contrary to Lefkowith's work (1955b, p. 17) which contends, "Pictorial tests become more valid as their pictorial stimuli become iconic [more like the object they represent]."

It is also interesting to note that in the studies conducted by Dwyer, generally the objectives which were evaluated by means of the verbal-print format (terminology and comprehension) resulted in the occurrence of insignificant differences in student achievement between students who received their instruction without visualization (oral/verbal) and tested in the verbal-print format and those who received the differentially visualized treatments and were also evaluated via the verbal-print format. It is possible that differences in student achievement would have been detected for these educational objectives if visual test formats had been designed to assess student achievement.

DISCUSSION

Most of the research data available on visual testing indicates that there are no statistically significant differences in achievement scores between students who receive visualized instruction and are evaluated verbally (pencil-paper) and those who are evaluated visually. These results may be a function of how the visual materials are used in the instruction. If the illustrations are used to complement instruction, i.e., present redundant information visually, then visualization is just making sure that the oral/verbal script is conveying the message optimally. Under these circumstances the use of visualization may simply be providing an alternative iconic base from which students can comprehend complex content material. This line of reasoning seems to coincide with the verbal loop hypothesis (Glanzer & Clark, 1963b, 1964) which contends that a stimulus (object or illustration) viewed by the learner is translated into a series of words which are held in memory until they are needed by the learner in making a covert or overt response. In support of this particular position Travers & Alvarado (1970, pp. 62-63) make the point that ". . . information presented through pictures probably has to be coded into words if it is to be readily retained. This translation of visual information into a verbal code is necessary for the retention of precise information, for verbally coded information can be retained in great detail and in large quantity."

The results of preliminary research indicates that visual testing is a feasible, reliable, and valid way of measuring student achievement; however, it may be that visual testing will achieve its real potential when it is utilized to assess student achievement of specific educational objectives which have been taught visually. Presumably, visualization is used to assist in the conveyance of that content material which cannot be readily coded into words. If this is the case, then visual testing needs to be implemented in those situations in which typical paper-pencil tests are found to be invalid for assessing optimum student performance levels of specific types of educational tasks.

SUMMARY: MAIN IDEAS

A theoretical justification for visual testing appears to have its roots in the sign similarity hypothesis and the cue summation principle of learning.

Pictorial testing seems to have a number of significant advantages over verbal tests, equipment tests, and printed pictorial tests.

The strategy of implementing visualization both in the presentation and evaluation phases of instruction is an attempt to implement the stimulus generalization phenomena.

Proponents of the visual testing movement question the validity and reliability of verbal printed tests used to measure the instructional effects of visualization used in the teaching-learning process.

Most of the early research studies related to visual testing indicate that no significant differences occur in student performance as a result of their being evaluated visually rather than in the conventional verbal format.

Recent research focusing on the reliability, validity, and administration of visual tests has established that visual tests are indeed reliable, valid, and capable of being administered with a reasonable amount of success.

Very little effort has been expended in attempting to relate the advantages of visual testing to specific types of educational objectives.

REVIEW ACTIVITIES

1. Explain the rationale for visual testing.
2. Summarize the research findings related to visual testing.
3. Discuss the theoretical justification commonly cited in support of visual testing.
4. List the advantages and disadvantages of visual testing.
5. List the reasons why visual testing is not more widely used.

6. Construct a chart depicting the advantages that pictorial testing has over verbal testing, equipment testing, and printed pictorial testing.

RECOMMENDED READINGS

Fleming, M. L. & Sheikhian, M. 1972. Influence of pictorial attributes on recognition memory. *AV Commun. Rev. 20:* 423-441.

Goldstein, E. B. 1975. The perception of multiple images. *AV Commun. Rev. 23:* 34-68.

Levie, H. W. & Levie, D. 1975. Pictorial memory processes. *AV Commun. Rev. 23:* 81-97.

13

Directions for Research on Visualized Instruction

LEARNING OBJECTIVES

Upon completion of this chapter the student will be able to:

1. *Explain the basic objectives of the systematic program of evaluation conducted by the author and others and list examples.*
2. *Identify and discuss what is meant by the multivariate environment.*
3. *Describe in writing what is meant by the multidimensionality of both the dependent and independent variables in an instructional situation.*
4. *List several questions that need to be answered in order to develop situational guidelines for the selection and use of different types of visual stimuli.*
5. *List the kinds of questions that should be asked and answered prior to any experimental evaluation of visualized instruction.*
6. *Identify the procedural considerations which should be followed to implement a program of systematic evaluation of the instructional effectiveness of visualized instruction.*

ORIENTATION

Research on visualized instruction is just beginning to profit from the careful definition of learning criteria, rigidly controlled experimental conditions, and from the building of logical conceptual bridges to connect relevant variables. The experimental results ac-

242

cumulated in the systematic program of evaluation conducted by the author and others is considered to represent a departure from the fragmental research which in the past has failed to contribute to a cumulative analysis of the role of visual illustrations in the instructional process. The approach followed in the program of systematic evaluation, while analytic in tone, has been data-oriented and strictly descriptive. It is an attempt to construct experimental conditions based upon theoretical or logical propositions which dimensionalize the independent variables and propose logical relationships among different types of visual illustrations and their potential influences in effecting increased student achievement. Similiarly, it represents an effort to develop a collection of empirical facts in a systematic fashion and to order these discrete facts and propositions into a theoretical model which will approximate the complexity of the instructional process.

THE MULTIVARIATE ENVIRONMENT

Research on visualized instruction has progressed significantly since the early comparative-effectiveness studies in which single isolated variables were assessed to determine their potential influences on student achievement. At the present time there is no perfect formula for selecting the best type of visualization in all instructional circumstances. However, a sampling of the global variables have been identified which significantly influence the quantity and quality of learning that will occur from a visualized instructional presentation, e.g., type of testing format; type and method of cueing strategy employed; types of educational objective to be achieved; individual difference variables; method by which the instruction is presented to students (externally paced vs. self-paced). See Figure 13-1.

The data analysis from studies investigating the instructional effects of the cited variables substantiates the fact that the human being is a very complex organism and that the variables which influence learning are likewise extremely complex. Because so many variables are associated with the learning process and since most of these variables are continuous rather than discrete in nature, it is doubtful whether the development of a single learning theory to function as an effective predictor of visual learning will ever be possible.

In the typical instructional situation learning is a continuous process which is being influenced at any one time by a multitude of dimensional variables. Consequently, the process of synthesizing isolated bits and pieces of research evidence in order to construct a

Figure 13-1. Variables associated with visualized instruction.

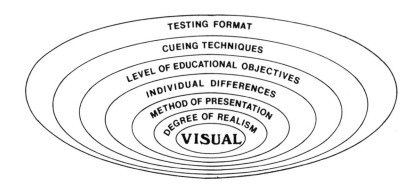

matrix of instructional variables and guidelines for the use of specific types of visualization seems insurmountable. To assess the instructional impact of variables in isolation does not appear to be logical since in combination some variables may be either more important or less important than others in producing optimal conditions which will maximize student achievement; some variables may also interact with others and cancel out their specific influences. It is also possible that specific individual difference variables will interact with specific types of stimuli characteristics in such a way as to make specific types of visual stimuli more or less effective in facilitating student achievement for particular types of educational objectives. In essence, we need to know when the effects of different variables summate to facilitate and extend student learning from specific types of visualized instruction, and also which variables interact to interfere with learning. The obvious multidimensionality of both the dependent and independent variables in the typical instructional situation demands that multivariate experimental designs be employed to answer questions basic to efficient and effective use of visual stimuli.

SITUATIONAL GUIDELINES

In acknowledging the complexity of the teaching-learning environment it seems apparent that it is going to be almost impossible to identify or construct a single theory for guiding the effective integration of visual stimuli into the instructional process. Probably the most that can be expected is the development of situational guidelines to govern the selection and use of different types of visual materials. Although there are limits in student differences beyond which a particular stimulus is not appropriate, usually a given type of visualization will be suitable across a wide range of individual difference variables.

If the ultimate objective of the research on visualized instruction is to produce meaningful educational insights, a sustained research effort focusing on the intricate interactions which exist among instructional variables appears to be mandatory. Following is a sampling of the types of questions which need to be answered to assist educators in the selection and use of different types of visual stimuli:

How are visual cues perceived, organized and processed?

What combinations of cueing strategies are most effective in facilitating student achievement of complex learning objectives?

What kinds of visuals used singly or in combinations are most effective in facilitating student achievement of different educational objectives?

What kinds of visual stimuli interact optimally with specific individual difference characteristics to improve learning?

How can visuals be best structured to facilitate retention and transfer of learning?

Under what conditions do visualized messages optimize information transmission?

What kinds of visuals increase and sustain attention and concentration?

For what types of objectives in an instructional sequence do we employ auditory stimuli and when do we employ visual stimuli?

How do we use combinations of different types of visuals and in what sequential configurations?

What types of visual configurations are necessary to effect optimum achievement of specific educational objectives?

IMPLEMENTING VISUALIZED INVESTIGATIONS

Acknowledging the many advantages associated with the use of multivariate designs and procedures in experimental investigations, answers to questions similar to the following should be prerequisite to any investigation:

1. What types of educational objectives are to be achieved by the students?
2. What individual difference characteristics appear to be logically related to student performance and which of these should be taken into consideration in a field testing program?
3. How is the visualized instruction to be presented to the students; that is, will the instruction be externally paced or self-paced?
4. What types of stimuli characteristics should the visuals contain?
5. What types of evaluation formats are to be employed?
6. What types of cueing techniques will be incorporated in the visualized instruction?
7. How is the visualization to be related to the subject content—redundant, related, etc.?

When questions of this type have been answered, it is possible to proceed toward the identification of the types of visual illustrations that would be most successful and efficient in facilitating student achievement of the learning objectives of the particular institution.

The following approach to the development of a tailor-made taxonomy of visual illustrations indigenous to a specific institution is from an article by Dwyer (1970e, pp. 290-291). This particular approach would necessarily be modified to the needs of the institution conducting the investigation. The proposed approach deals with externally paced instruction but could easily be adapted to apply to a self-paced instructional format. Adherence to the following procedure could well serve as an initial approach in a program of systematic evaluation designed to identify the types of visualization most effective in facilitating the objectives of the particular educational institution.

1. Initially the research should be limited to one content or learning area in which a particular instructional unit can be identified as having within it several different levels of learning tasks.
2. Criterion tests should be constructed to measure student achievement on the different learning tasks—reliability and validity should be established for each test. Several different testing formats should be explored, e.g., pencil-paper, oral, visual testing, etc.
3. The information in the instructional unit should be audiotaped (or preserved in some other way) in order to keep this portion of the instruction constant.
4. A sequence of different types of illustrations should be designed that presents as closely as possible visually the oral instruction that has been developed.
5. Multiple versions of the initial visual sequence should be designed. Each visual sequence should consist of a single type of visual illustration which might con-

ceivably be used to complement the oral instruction, and each sequence should differ only in the amount and kind of realistic detail in the illustrations.

6. Students to be involved in the research should be identified and randomly assigned to treatment groups.
7. Students receiving the audiotaped presentation without visuals should be considered the control group; students receiving the various visual sequences complementing their oral instruction should be the experimental groups.
8. All groups should receive a pretest to determine their present level of understanding of the type of information in the instructional unit.
9. Standardized tests (when available) should be used to measure the multidimensionality of select dependent and/or independent variables in the learning situation. These scores can then be utilized in multivariate experimental designs.
10. Each group should study their respective sequence of visual illustrations for an equal amount of time along with the oral instruction.
11. Immediately after receiving the instructional unit, the students should receive the criterion tests designed to measure their level of attainment.
12. The data obtained from the criterion tests, when subjected to the appropriate statistical techniques, should reveal the relative advantages and limitations of the various types of visual illustrations for promoting specific educational objectives under varying instructional circumstances.

SUMMARY: MAIN IDEAS

Research on visualized instruction is just beginning to profit from the careful definition of learning criteria, the rigidly controlled experimental conditions, and the building of logical conceptual bridges to connect relevant instructional variables.

To assess the instructional impact of variables in isolation does not appear to be logical since in combination some variables may be more or less effective than others in creating optimal learning conditions.

The multidimensionality of the dependent and independent variables in the typical instructional situations requires that multivariate experimental designs and procedures be implemented.

There are a number of questions which need to be answered about situational guidelines to assist educators in the selection and use of different types of visual stimuli.

REVIEW ACTIVITIES

1. Identify the characteristics prerequisite to the design and implementation of a systematic effort to investigate variables inherent in visualized instruction.
2. Discuss the complications associated with the development of a theory which would serve as a guide to the effective design and

use of visualized materials in the instructional process.
3. Explain what is meant by situational guidelines.
4. Generate a list of the types of questions which need to be answered if situational guidelines are to become a reality.
5. Design an empirical study which could realistically be conducted to answer one of the questions generated in the preceding activity. Construct a flow-chart illustrating the procedures and the sequence in which they are to be implemented.

RECOMMENDED READINGS

Glaser, R. 1966. Psychological bases for instructional design. *AV Commun. Rev. 14:* 433-449.

Gropper, G. L. 1976. A behavioral perspective on media selection. *AV Commun. Rev. 24:* 157-186.

Hartsell, H. C. & Margoles, R. A. 1967. Guidelines for the selection of instructional materials. *Audiovisual Instruction. 12:* 23-26.

Tosti, D. T. & Ball, J. R. 1969. A behavioral approach to instructional design and media selection. *AV Commun. Rev. 17:* 5-27.

AUTHOR INDEX

REFERENCES

Adams, J. A. & Chambers, R. W. 1962. Responses to simultaneous stimulus of two sense modalities. *J. Exp. Psychol. 63:* 198-206.

Adams, S., Rosemier, R. & Sleeman, P. 1965. Readable letter size and visibility for overhead projection transparencies. *AV Commun. Rev. 13:* 412-417.

Allen, D. I. 1970. Some effects of advance organizers and level of questions on the learning and retention of written social studies material. *J. Educ. Psychol. 61:* 333-3339.

Allen, W. H. 1952. Readability of instructional film commentary. *J. Appl. Psychol. 36:* 164-168.

———. 1960. Audio-visual communication. In C. W. Harris (ed.), *Encyclopedia of educational research.* New York: MacMillan 115-137.

———. 1975. Intellectual abilities and instructional media design. *AV Commun. Rev. 23:* 139-170.

Allen, W. H., Filep, R. F. & Cooney, S. M. 1967. *Visual and audio presentation of machine-programmed instruction.* USOE Final Report, Project No. 5-0724-02-12-1. Los Angeles: University of Southern California, Department of Cinema.

Allen, W. H., Cooney, S. M. & Weintraub, R. 1968. *Audio implementation of still and motion pictures.* HEW Final Report, Project No. 5-0741, Grant No. OE-7-14-1490-261. Los Angeles: University of Southern California, Department of Cinema.

Allison, R. B. 1960. *Learning parameters and human abilities.* Princeton University, Psychology Department, (multilith).

Allison, S. G. & Ash, P. 1951. *Relationship of aniety to learning from films.* Technical Report, SDC-269-7-24. Port Washington, N.Y.: Special Devices Center, Office of Naval Research.

Allport, G. W. & Odbert, H. S. 1936. Trait-names, a psycholexical study. *Psychol. Monog. 47:* 1.

Anderson, C. M. 1972. In search of a visual rhetoric for instructional television. *AV Commun. Rev. 20:* 43-63.

Anderson, N. S. & Fitts, P. M. 1958. Amount of information gained during brief exposures of numerals and colors. *J. Exp. Psychol. 55:* 247-254.

Anderson, R. C. 1967. Educational psychology. *Ann. Rev. Psychol. 18:* 103-164.

———. 1970. Control of student mediating processes during verbal learning and instruction. *Rev. Educ. Res. 40:* 349-369.

Anderson, R. C. & Faust, G. W. 1967. The effects of strong formal prompts in programmed instruction. *Amer. Educ. Res. J. 4:* 345-352.

Anderson, R. C., Kulhavy, R. W. & Andre, T. 1971. Feedback procedures in programmed instruction. *J. Educ. Psychol. 69:* 148-156.

Anderson, S. B., Ball, B. & Murphy, R. T. 1975. *Encyclopedia of educational evaluation.* Washington, D.C.: Jossey-Bass Publishers.

Arnheim, R. 1954. *Art and visual perception.* Los Angeles: University of California Press, Berkeley and Los Angeles.

———. 1969. *Visual thinking.* Berkeley and Los Angeles, University of California Press.

Arnold, T. A. & Dwyer, F. M. 1973. An investigation of the relationship between stimulus explicitness and entering behavior in facilitating student achievement. *J. Psychol. 84:* 129-132.

———. 1975a. Realism in visualized instruction. *Percept. & Motor Skills. 40:* 369-370.

———. 1975b. An empirical evaluation of the use of educational objectives as guidelines for the development of instructional units. *Calif. J. Educ. Res. 26:* 115-119.

———. 1976. An empirical analysis of the instructional effectiveness of stimulus explicitness in visualized instruction. *J. Exp. Educ. 44:* 11-16.

Arnoult, M. D. 1953. Transfer of predifferentiation training in multiple shape discrimination. *J. Exp. Psychol. 45:* 401-409.

Asch, S. E. 1971. Perceptual organization in learning. *Viewpoints,* Indiana University, Bloomington. Bulletin of the School of Education, *47:* 5-15.

Ash, P. & Carlton, B. 1951. *The value of note-taking during film instruction.* Technical Report, SDC-269-7-21. Port Washington, N.Y.: Special Devices Center, Office of Naval Research.

Ash, P. & Jaspen, N. 1953. *The effects of interactions of rate development, repetition, participation and room illumination on learning from a rear-projected film.* Technical Report, SDC-269-7-39. Port Washington, N.Y.: Special Devices Center, Office of Naval Research.

Asso, D. & Wyke, 1970. Visual discrimination and verbal comprehension of spatial relations by young children. *Brit. J. Psychol. 61:* 99-107.

Atkinson, J. W. & Reitman, W. R. 1956. Performance as a function of motive strength and expectency of goal attainment. *J. Abnorm. & Soc. Psychol. 53:* 361-366.

Attneave, F. 1954. Some informational aspects of visual perception. *Psychol. Rev. 61:* 183-193.

———. 1959. *Application of information theory to psychology.* New York: Holt.

———. 1971. Multistability in perception. *Scientific Amer. 225:* 62-71.

Ausubel, D. P. & Fitzgerald, D. 1962. Organizer, general background, and antecedent learning variables in sequential verbal learning. *J. Educ. Psychol. 53:* 243-259.

Ausubel, D. P. 1962. A subsumption theory of meaningful verbal learning and retention. *J. Gen. Psychol. 66:* 213-224.

———. 1968a. *Educational psychology; a cognitive view.* New York; Holt, Rinehart & Winston, Inc.

———. 1968b. *Educational psychology.* Holt, Rinehart & Winston, Inc.

Aylward, T. L. 1960. A study of the effects of production technique on a televised lecture. *Dissertation Abstr. 21:* 1660-1661.

Bahrick, H. P. & Bahrick, P. 1971. Independence of verbal and visual codes of the same stimuli. *J. Exp. Psychol. 91:* 344-346.

Bahrick, H. P. & Boucher, B. 1968. Retention of visual and verbal codes of the same stimuli. *J. Exp. Psychol. 78:* 417-442.

Baker, C. H. 1960. Observing behavior in a vigilance task. *Science. 132:* 674-675.

Baker, E. L. 1970. Value of pictorial embellishments in a tape-slide instructional program. *AV Commun. Rev. 13:* 397-404.

Baltes, P. & Wender, K. 1971. Age differences in pleasantness of visual patterns of different variability in late childhood and adolescence. *Child Develpm. 42:* 47-55.

Barnes, B. R. & Clawson, E. U. 1975. Do advance organizers facilitate learning? Recommendations for further research based on an analysis of thirty-two (32) studies. *Rev. Educ. Res. 45:* 637-659.

Bathurst, L. H. 1954. The comparative effectiveness of using a wall model, motion picture films, filmstrips, and the standard slide rule in teaching the operation of a slide rule. Doctoral dissertation, The Pennsylvania State University.

Beach, D. E. 1960. An analysis of the retention involved

in three methods of television news presentations. Masters thesis, Ohio University.

Belmont, J. M. 1972. Relations of age and intelligence to short-term color memory. *Child Develpm. 43:* 19-29.

Berliner, D. C. & Cahen, L. C. 1973. Trait-treatment interaction and learning. In F. N. Kerlinger (ed.), *Review of research in education.* Illinois: F. E. Peacock Publishers, Inc., pp. 58-94.

Berlyne, D. E. 1957. Conflict and information-theory variables as determinants of human perceptual curiosity. *J. Exp. Psychol. 53:* 399-404.

———— 1958a. Supplementary report: complexity and orienting responses with longer exposures. *J. Exp. Psychol. 56:* 183.

———— 1958b. The influence of complexity and novelty in visual figures on orienting responses. *J. Exp. Psychol. 55:* 289-296.

Berry, L. H. 1974. An exploratory study of the relative effective of realistic and non-realistic color in visual instructional materials. Doctoral dissertation, The Pennsylvania State University.

———— 1975. *An investigation of the effectiveness of realistic and non-realistic color in visualized instruction,* Paper presented at AECT National Convention, Dallas, Texas (ED 129 257).

———— 1976. *Interactive effects of color realism and learner I.Q. on visualized instruction.* Paper presented at AECT National Convention, Anaheim, California (ED 129 256).

———— 1977. *The effects of color realism on pictorial recognition memory.* Paper presented at AECT National Convention, Miami-Beach, Florida.

Birren, F. 1959. The effects of color on the human organism. *Amer. J. Occup. Ther. 13:* 125-129.

———— 1963. *Color—A Survey in Words and Pictures.* New Hyde Park: University Books, Inc.

Black, H. B. 1962. *Improving the programming of complex pictorial materials: discrimination learning as affected by prior exposure to an relevance of components of the figural discrimination.* NDEA Title VII Report, Project No. 688, U.S. Office of Education.

———— 1966. *Relevant and irrelevant pictorial color cues in discrimination learning.* HEW Final Report No. 7-24-0210-227, Office of Education, Educational Media Branch.

Blair, W. C. 1958. Measurement of observing responses in human monitoring. *Science. 128:* 348-350.

Bloom, B. S., Englehart, M. D., Furst, E. J., Hill, W. H. & Krathwohl, D. R. 1956. *A taxonomy of educational objectives: handbook I, the cognitive domain.* New York: Longmans, Green.

Boker, J. R. 1974. Immediate and delayed retention effects of interspersing questions in written instructional passages. *J. Educ. Psychol. 66:* 96-98.

Bourisseau, W., Davis, O. L., Jr., & Yamamoto, K. 1967. Sense-impression responses of Negro and white children to verbal and pictorial stimuli. *AV Commun. Rev. 15:* 259-268.

Bourne, L. E. & Restle, F. 1959. Mathematic theory of concept identification. *Psychol. Rev. 66:* 278-296.

Bourne, L. E. & Haygood, R. C. 1959. The role of stimulus redundancy in concept identification. *J. Exp. Psychol. 58:* 232-238.

———— 1961. Supplementary report: effect of redundant relevant information upon the identification of concepts. *J. Exp. Psychol. 3:* 259-260.

Bousfield, W. A., Esterson, J., & Whitmarsh, G. A. 1957. The effect of cocomitant colored and uncolored pictorial representations on the learning of stimulus words. *J. Appl. Psychol. 41:* 165-167.

Bracht, G. H. & Glass, G. V. 1968. The external validity of experiments. *Amer. Educ. Res. J. 5:* 437-474.

Bracht, G. H. 1969. The relationship of treatment tasks,

personological variables, and dependent variables to aptitude-treatment interactions. Doctoral dissertation, University of Colorado.

———— 1970. Experimental factors related to aptitude-treatment interactions. *Rev. Educ. Res. 40:* 627-645.

Brandt, H. F. 1953. The psychology of seeing motion pictures. In G. M. Elliott (ed.), *Film and education.* New York: Philosophical Library.

Bretz, R. 1970. *Color television in instruction.* Santa Monica, California: Rand Corporation.

———— 1971. *The selection of appropriate media for instruction: a guide for designers of Air Force technical programs.* Santa Monica, California, Communications Dept. Rand Report No. 601-PR.

Bricker, P. D. 1955. The identification of redundant stimulus patterns. *J. Exp. Psychol. 49:* 73-81.

Briggs, L. J. 1968a. *Sequencing of instruction in relation to hierarchies of competence.* Pittsburgh, Penna.: American Institutes for Research.

———— 1968b. Learner variables and educational media. *Rev. Educ. Res. 38:* 160-176.

Broadbent, D. E. 1956. Successive responses to simultaneous stimuli. *Quart. J. Exp. Psychol. 8:* 145-152.

———— 1957a. A mechanical model of human attention and immediate memory. *Psychol. Rev. 64:* 205-215.

———— 1957b. Immediate memory and simultaneous stimuli. Quart. *J. Exp. Psychol. 9:* 1-11.

———— 1958. *Perception and communication.* New York: Pergamon Press.

——— 1965. Information processing in the nervous system. *Science. 3695:* 457-462.

Brown, D. B., Brown, L. A., & Danielson, J. E. 1975. Instructional treatments, presenter types, and learner characteristics as significant variants in instructional television for adults. *J. Educ. Psychol. 67:* 391-404.

Brown, J. W. 1947. A comparison of verbal and projected verbal-pictorial tests as measures of the ability to apply science principles. Doctoral dissertation, The University of Chicago.

———— 1949. Visualized testing. *Educ. Screen. 28:* 116-117.

Brown, J. W., Lewis, R. B. & Harcleroad, F. F. 1973. *AV instruction: technology media and methods.* New York: McGraw-Hill.

Brown, L. T. & Gregory, L. P. 1968. Attentional response of humans and squirrel monkeys to visual patterns: final studies and resume. *Percept. & Motor Skills. 27:* 787-814.

Brown, L. 1969. The 3-D reconstruction of a 2-D visual display. *J. Genet. Psychol. 115:* 250-260.

Bruner, J. S., Postman, L. & Rodregues, R. 1951. Expectation and the perception of color. *Amer. J. Psychol. 64:* 216-227.

Bruner, J. S., Goodnow, J. J. & Austin, G. A. 1956. *A study of thinking.* New York: John Wiley.

Bruner, J. S. 1957. On perceptual readiness. *Psychol. Rev. 64:* 123-152.

———— 1960. *The Process of education.* Cambridge: Harvard University Press.

Buckland, P. R. 1967. The response in a linear program; its mode and importance. *Programmed Learning & Educ. Tech. 4:* 47-51.

Bulgarella, R. B. & Archer, E. J. 1962. Concept identification of auditory stimuli as a function of amount of relevant and irrelevant information. *J. Exp. Psychol. 63:* 254-257.

Burke Marketing Research, Inc. 1960. *Burke color study.* Cleveland: AVCO Broadcast Corporation.

Buswell, G. T. 1935. *How people look at pictures.* Chicago: University of Chicago Press.

Caban, J. G. 1971. Eye movement preferences and individual differences in learning from color and non-color pictures. Doctoral dissertation, University of Massachusetts.

Carpenter, C. R. 1949. *Progress Report No. 11-12.* Technical Report. Instructional Film Research Program, Port Washington, N.Y.: Special Devices Center, Office of Naval Research.

———— 1952. *Logistics of sound motion pictures for military training.* Technical Report, SCD 269-7-31. Port Washington, N.Y.: Special Devices Center, Office of Naval Research.

———— 1953. A theoretical orientation for instructional film research. *AV Commun. Rev. 1:* 38-52.

———— 1954. *Evaluation of the film: military police support in emergencies (riot control) TF19-1701.* Technical Report, SDC-269-7-52. Port Washington, N.Y.: Special Devices Center, Office of Naval Research.

Carpenter, C. R., Greenhill, L. P., Hittinger, W. F., McCoy, E. P., McIntyne, C. J., Murnin, J. A. & Watkins, P. W., 1954. The development of a sound motion picture proficiency test. *Pers. Psychol. 7:* 509-523.

Carpenter, C. R. & Greenhill, L. P. 1956. *Instructional film research reports,* Vol. II. Technical Report, SDC-269-7-61. Port Washington, N.Y.: Special Devices Center, Office of Naval Research.

———— 1958. *Instructional Television Research Report No. 2.* University Park, Pennsylvania: The Pennsylvania State University.

Carson, D. 1947. The American way of life as portrayed in filmstrips: an experiment in visual education. (Abstract). In F. Hoban & E. Van Ormer, *Instructional film research 1918-1950.* Technical Report, SDC-269-7-19. Port Washington, N.Y.: Special Devices Center, Office of Naval Research.

Carrol, J. B. 1963. A model of school learning. *Teachers Coll. Rec. 64:* 723-733.

Carterette, E. C. & Jones, M. H. 1967. Visual and auditory information processing in children and adults. *Science. 156:* 986-988.

Cattell, R. B. 1963. Theory of fluid and crystallized intelligence: a critical experiment. *J. Educ. Psychol. 54:* 1-22.

———— 1971. *Abilities their structure, growth, and action.* Houghton Mifflin Company, Boston.

Cermak, G. W. 1971. Short-term recognition memory for complex free-form figures. *Psychonomic Sci. 25:* 209-211.

Chan, A., & Travers, R. M. W. & Van Mondfrans, A. P. 1965. The effects of colored embellishment of a visual array on a simultaneously presented audio array. *AV Commun. Rev. 13:* 159-164.

———— Effect of colored embellishment of a visual array on a simultaneously presented audio array. *AV Commun. Rev. 13:* 159-164.

Chan, A. & Travers, R. M. W. 1966. The effect on retention of labeling visual displays. *Am. Educ. Res. J. 3:* 55-67.

Chen, Y. 1971. Visual discrimination of color normals and color deficients. *AV Commun. Rev. 19:* 417-431.

Cherry, C. E. 1953. Some experiments on the recognition of speech with one and two ears. *J. Acoust. Soc. of Amer. 25:* 975-979.

Christensen, C. M. & Stordahl, K. E. 1955. The effect of organizational aids on comprehension and retention. *J. Educ. Psychol. 46:* 65-74.

Christie, B., Delafield, G., Lucas, B., Winwood, M., & Gale, A. 1972. Differential effects of the number and the variety of display elements. *Canad. J. Psychol. 26:* 155-170.

Christner, C. A. & Ray, H. W. 1961. An evaluation of the effect of selected combinations on target and background coding on map-reading performance. *Human Factors. 3:* 131-146.

Chu, G. C. & Schramm, W. 1967. *Learning from television: what the research says.* Washington: National Association of Educational Broadcasters.

Clark, R. E. 1970. Predecisional information seeking as a function of interactions between subjective response uncertainty, dogmatism, and locus of control. Doctoral dissertation, Indiana University.

———— 1975. Constructing a taxonomy of media attributes for research purposes. *AV Commun. Rev. 23:* 197-215.

Clark, S. E. 1969. Retrieval of color information from perceptual memory. *J. Exp. Psychol. 82:* 263-266.

Cofer, C. N. 1959. A study of clustering in free recall based on synonyms. *J. Gen. Psychol. 60:* 3-10.

Coffing, D. G. 1971. Eye movement preferences as individual differences in learning. Doctoral dissertation, Stanford University.

Cogswell, J. F. 1952. *Effect of a stereoscopic sound motion picture on the learning of a perceptual-motor task.* Technical Report, SDC-269-7-32. Port Washington, N.Y.: Special Devices Center, Office of Naval Research.

———— 1953. A study of the effects of three-dimensional sound motion pictures on the learning of a perceptual-motor task: the assembly of a breech block of the 40mm anti-aircraft gun. Masters thesis, The Pennsylvania State University.

Cohen, B. H. 1963. An investigation of recording in free recall. *J. Exp. Psychol. 65:* 368-376.

Cole, M., Sharp, D. W., Glick, J. & Kessen, W. 1968. Conceptual and mnemonic factors in paired-associate learning. *J. Exp. Child Psychol. 6:* 120-130.

Collier, R. E. 1957. Factors related to children's expressed color preferences at selected grade levels. Doctoral dissertation, Syracuse University.

Collins, W. A. 1970. Learning of media content: a developmental study. *Child. Develpm. 41:* 1133-1142.

Conrad, R. 1964. Acoustic confusions in immediate memory. *Brit. J. Psychol. 55:* 75-84.

———— 1971. The chronology of the development of covert speech in children. *Developmental Psychol. 5:* 398-405.

Conway, J. K. 1967. Multiple-sensory modality and the problem of sign types. *AV Commun. Rev. 15:* 371-383.

Cook, J. O. & Spitzer, M. E. 1960. Supplementary report: prompting versus confirmation in paired-associate learning. *J. Exp. Psychol. 59:* 275-276.

Cooper, J. C. & Gaeth, J. H. 1967. Interactions of modality with age and with meaningfulness in verbal learning. *J. Educ. Psychol. 58:* 41-44.

Coppen, H. 1972. Film research in Great Britain: two studies. *Educ. Media International. 3:* 7-12.

Corballis, M. C. & Raeburn, B. J. 1970. Recall strategies in three-channel immediate memory. *Canad. J. Psychol. 24:* 109-116.

Corcoran D. W. J. 1967. Acoustic factors in proofreading. *Nature. 214:* 851-852.

Craig, G. O. 1956. A comparison between sound and silent films in teaching. *Brit. J. Educ. Psychol. 26:* 202-206.

Cronbach, L. J. & Snow, R. E. 1969. *Individual differences in learning ability as a function of instructional variables.* USOE Final Report, Contract No. OEC-4-6-061269-1217. Stanford: Stanford University, School of Education.

———— 1977. *Aptitudes and instructional methods.* New York: Irvington Press, Inc.

Cronbach, L. J. & Gleser, G. C. 1965. *Psychological tests and personnel decisions.* Urbana: University of Illinois Press.

Cronbach, L. J. 1967. How can instruction be adapted to individual differences? In R. M. Gagné (ed.), *Learning and individual differences.* Columbus, Ohio: Merrill Books.

Dale, E. 1946. *Audio-visual methods in teaching.* New York: Dryden Press.

———— 1954. Audio-visual methods in teaching. New

York: Holt.

Dalis, G. T. 1970. Effect of precise objectives upon student achievement in health education. *J. Exp. Educ. 39:* 20-23.

Davies, G. M. 1969. Recognition memory for pictured and named objects. *J. Exp. Child Psychol. 7:* 448-458.

Davis, J. A. 1965. Superimposition of supplemental information on an instructional film. *AV Commun. Rev. 13:* 275-288.

Davis, R. 1957. The human operator as a single channel information system. *J. Exp. Psychol. 9:* 110-129.

Davis, O. L., Jr. 1962. Textbooks and other printed materials. *Rev. Educ. Res. 22:* 127-140.

Day, H. 1965. Exploratory behavior as a function of individual differences and level of arousal. Doctoral dissertation, University of Toronto.

_____ 1966. Looking time as a function of stimulus variables and individual differences. *Percept. & Motor Skills, 22:* 423-428.

Day, W. F. & Beach, B. R. 1950. *A survey of the research literature comparing the visual and auditory presentation of information.* Air Force Technical Report 5921, Contract No. W33-039-AC-21269. Charlottesville: University of Virginia.

Deese, J. 1962. On the structure of associative meaning. *Psychol. Rev. 69:* 161-175.

Dember, W. N. & Earl, R. W. 1957. Analysis of exploratory, manipulatory, and curiosity behavior. *Psychol. Rev. 64:* 91-96.

_____ 1960. *Psychology of perception.* New York: Henry Holt & Company.

Devor, G. M. & Stern, C. 1971. Objects vs. pictures in the instruction of young children. *J. Sch. Psychol. 8:* 77-81.

Diamond, R. M. 1962. The effect of closed-circuit resource television upon achievement in the laboratory phase of a functional anatomy course: a comprehensive investigation of television as a magnification device during laboratory demonstrations. Doctoral dissertation, New York University.

Dilley, M., & Paivio, A. 1968. Pictures and words as stimulus and response items in paired associate learning of young children. *J. Exp. Child Psychol. 6:* 231-240.

Donahue, F. 1976. Effect of visualization in the learning and retention of German vocabulary at the college level. Doctoral dissertation, The Pennsylvania State University.

Dooley, R. P. & Harkins, L. E. 1970. Functional and attention-getting effects of color on graphic communications. *Percept. & Motor Skills. 31:* 851-854.

Doty, B. & Doty, L. A. 1964. Programmed instructional effectiveness in relation to certain student characteristics. *J. Educ. Psychol. 55:* 334-338.

DuBois, P. H. 1962. The design of correlational studies in training. In Robert Glaser (ed.), *Training research and education.* New York: John Wiley & Sons, pp. 63-86.

Dunathan, A. T. & Ten Brink, T. D. 1974. Visual mediators as aids to paired-associate learning. *AV Commun. Rev. 22:* 295-302.

Dwyer, F. M. 1967a. Adapting visual illustrations for effective learning. *Harvard Educ. Rev. 37:* 250-263.

_____ 1967b. The relative effectiveness of varied visual illustrations in complementing programmed instruction. *J. Exp. Educ. 36:* 34-42.

_____ 1967c. *A study of the relative effectiveness of varied visual illustrations.* USOE Final Report, Project No. 6-8840. University Park, The Pennsylvania State University, University Division of Instructional Services.

_____ 1968a. Effect of visual stimuli on varied learning objectives. *Percept. & Motor Skills. 27:* 1067-1070.

_____ 1968b. An experiment in visual learning at the eleventh-grade level. *J. Exp. Educ. 37:* 1-5.

_____ 1968c. When visuals are not the message. *Educ. Broadcast. Rev. 2:* 38-43.

_____ 1968d. The effectiveness of visual illustrations used to complement programmed instruction. *J. Psychol. 70:* 157-162.

_____ 1969a. An experiment in visual communication. *J. Res. Sci. Teach. 6:* 67-75.

_____ 1969b. The effect of stimulus variability on immediate and delayed retention. *J. Exp. Educ. 38:* 30-37.

_____ 1969c. An analysis of instructional effectiveness of visual illustrations presented via television. *J. Psychol. 72:* 61-64.

_____ 1969d. Motion as an instructional cue. *AV Commun. Rev. 3:* 20-21, 41-43.

_____ 1969e. The effect of varying the amount of realistic detail in visual illustrations designed to complement programmed instruction. *Programmed Learning & Educ. Tech. 6:* 147-153.

_____ 1969f. Student perception of the instructional value of visual illustration. *Med. & Biol. Ill. 19:* 42-45.

_____ 1970a. Effect of visual stimuli in complementing televised instruction. *Calif. J. Educ. Res. 21:* 43-47.

_____ 1970b. Exploratory studies in the effectiveness of visual illustrations. *AV Commun. Rev. 18:* 235-249.

_____ 1970c. The effect of image size on visual learning. *J. Exp. Educ. 39:* 36-41.

_____ 1970d. The effect of questions on visual learning. *Percept. & Motor Skills. 30:* 51-54.

_____ 1970e. Improving visuals for televised instruction. *Improving Coll. & Univ. Teach. 18:* 289-291.

_____ 1971a. Color as an instructional variable. *AV Commun. Rev. 19:* 399-416.

_____ 1971b. Visual learning: an analysis by sex and grade level. *Calif. J. Educ. Res. 22:* 170-176.

_____ 1971c. Student perceptions of the instructional effectiveness of black and white and colored illustrations. *J. Exp. Educ. 40:* 28-34.

_____ 1971d. Assessing students' perceptions of the instructional value of visual illustrations used to complement programmed instruction. *Programmed Learning & Educ. Tech. 8:* 73-80.

_____ 1971e. The effect of knowledge of objectives on visualized instruction. *J. Psychol. 77:* 219-221.

_____ 1971f. An experimental evaluation of the instructional effectiveness of black and white and colored illustrations. *Didakta Medica. 3&4:* 96-101.

_____ 1971g. Questions as advanced organizers in visualized instruction. *J. Psychol. 78:* 261-264.

_____ 1971h. Effect of questions on visualized instruction. *J. Psychol. 78:* 181-183.

_____ 1971j. Adapting varied visual illustrations for optimum teaching and learning. *Med. & Biol. Ill. 21:* 10-13.

_____ 1972a. *A guide for improving visualized instruction.* State College, Pennsylvania: Learning Services.

_____ 1972b. The effect of overt responses in improving visually programmed science instruction. *J. Res. Sci. Teach. 9:* 47-55.

_____ 1973a. Effect or oral cues on visualized instruction. *Percept. & Motor Skills. 37:* 843-846.

_____ 1973b. Effect of method in presenting visualized instruction. *AV Commun. Rev. 21:* 437-451.

_____ 1973c. The relative effectiveness of two methods of presenting visualized instruction. *J. Psychol. 85:* 297-300.

_____ 1974. The use of color in instructional visualization. *Didakta Medica* (Germany). *15:* 99-109.

_____ 1975. Effect of students' entering behavior on visualization. *J. Exp. Educ. 43:* 78-83.

_____ 1976a. The effect of IQ level on the instructional effectiveness of black-and-white and color illustrations. *AV Commun. Rev. 24:* 49-62.

_____ 1976b. Adapting media attributes for effective learning. *Educ. Tech. 16:* 7-13.

_____ 1977a. *Effect of method in cueing televised instruction.* Unpublished Research Report. University

Park, The Pennsylvania State University, University Division of Instructional Services.

―――― 1977b. *An investigation of the instructional effect of inductive vs. deductive sequencing of varied visual illustrations.* Unpublished Research Report. University Park. The Pennsylvania State University, University Division of Instructional Services.

―――― 1977c. *The effect of mental ability on students' ability to profit from visualized instruction.* Unpublished Research Report. University Park. The Pennsylvania State University, University Division of Instructional Services.

―――― 1977d. Considering the AV alternatives. *Sch. Shop. 36:* 19-21.

Dwyer, F. M. & Arnold, T. A. 1976. The instructional effect of verbal/visual feedback in visualized instruction. *J. Psychol. 94:* 39-41.

Ebel, R. L. 1951. Writing the test item. In E. I. Lindquist (ed), *Educational Measurement.* Washington, D.C.: American Council on Education, pp. 201-204.

Edling, J. V. 1968. Educational objectives and educational media. *Rev. Educ. Res. 38:* 177-194.

Elkind, D., Koegler, R. & Go, E., 1964. Studies in perceptual development: II. part-whole perception. *Child Develpm. 35:* 81-90.

Elliott, D. N. 1949. Characteristics and relationships of various criteria of teaching. Doctoral dissertation, Purdue University.

English, M. D. 1969. A comparison of the influences of colored as opposed to black and white instructional materials on the acquisition of learning. Doctoral dissertation, University of Wisconsin.

Enoch, J. M. 1959. Effect of the size of a complex display upon visual search. *J. Opt. Soc. Amer. 49:* 280-286.

Evans, R. I. 1964. An exploratory investigation of the psychological and educational impact of a filmed dialog with Carl Jung. *Conversations with Carl Jung and Reactions from Ernest Jones.* Princetown: D. VanNostrand, pp. 159-168.

Exner, J. E. 1959. The influence of color in projective testing. Doctoral dissertation, Cornell University.

Farley, F. H. & Grant, A. D. 1973. Arousal and reminiscence in learning from color and black-white audiovisual presentations. Paper presented at the AERA National Convention, New Orleans, Louisiana.

Faw, T. T. & Nunnally, J. C. 1967. The effects on eye movement of complexity, novelty, and affective tone. *Percept. & Psychophysics. 2:* 363-367.

Feigenbaum, E. A. & Simon, H. A. 1963. Brief notes on the EPAM theory of verbal learning. In C. N. Confer & B. S. Musgrave (eds.), *Verbal behavior and learning.* New York: McGraw-Hill.

Feldman, D. H. 1971. Map understanding as a possible crystalizer of cognitive structures. *Amer. Educ. Res. J. 8:* 485-503.

Feldman, S. C. 1961. Visual perception skills of children and their relation to reading. Doctoral dissertation, Columbia University.

Finn, J. D. 1953. Professionalizing the audio-visual field. *AV Commun. Rev. 1:* 6-17.

Fisher, M. & Ong, J. 1972. Effect of low illumination on galvanic skin response. *Amer. J. Optimetry & Archives of Amer. Acad. of Optometry. 49:* 503-507.

Fitts, P. M., Rappaport, M., Weinstein, M., Anderson, N. & Leonard, J. A. 1956. Stimulus correlates of visual pattern recognition: a probability approach. *J. Exp. Psychol. 5:* 1-11.

Fleming, M. L. 1970. Perceptual principles for the design of instructional materials. *Viewpoints.* Bloomington: Indiana University, Bulletin of the School of Education, pp. 69-200.

Fleming, M. L., & Sheikhian, M. 1972. Influence of pictorial attributes on recognition memory. *AV Commun. Rev. 20:* 423-442.

Fletcher, R. M. 1955. *Profile analysis and its effect on learning when used to shorten recorded film commentaries.* Technical Report, SCD-269-7-55. Port Washington, N.Y.: Special Devices Center, Office of Naval Research.

Fonesca, L. & Kearl, B. 1960. Comprehension of pictorial symbols: an experiment in rural Brazil. *Agric. Journalism Bull. 30:* 1-28.

Fowler, H. 1965. *Curiosity and exploratory behavior.* New York: MacMillan.

Fradkin, B. M. 1974. Effectiveness of multi-image presentation. *J. Educ. Tech. Sys. 2:* 201-216.

Franzwa, D. 1973. Influence of meaningfulness, picture detail, and presentation mode on visual retention. *AV Commun. Rev. 21:* 209-223.

Frase, L. T. 1967. Learning from prose material: length of passage, knowledge of results, and position of questions. *J. Educ. Psychol. 58:* 266-272.

―――― 1968a. Some data concerning the mathemagenic hypothesis. *Amer. Educ. Res. J. 5:* 181-190.

―――― 1968b. Effect of question location, pacing, and mode upon retention of prose material. *J. Educ. Psychol. 59:* 244-249.

Frederick, W. C., Blount, N. & Johnson, S. 1968. *A comparison of verbal statements, symbolic notation and figural representation of grammar concepts.* University of Wisconsin, Center for Cognitive Learning.

Freed, D. W. 1963. Variables in self-instruction materials designed to teach the operation of audio-visual equipment. Doctoral dissertation, The Pennsylvania State University.

Freeman, J. & Neidt, C. O. 1959. Effect of familiar background music upon film learning. *J. Educ. Res. 53:* 91-96.

French, J. E. 1952. Children's preferences for pictures of varied complexity of pictorial pattern. *Elem. Sch. J.* 90-95.

French, R. S. 1954. Pattern recognition in the presence of visual noise. *J. Exp. Psychol. 47:* 3-23.

Frick, F. C. 1953. Some perceptual problems from the point of view of information theory. In B. McMillian, et al., (eds.) *Current trends in information theory.* Pittsburgh, Pa.: University of Pittsburgh Press.

Fullerton, B. J. 1956. The comparative effect of color and black and white guidance films employed with and without "anticipatory" remarks upon acquisition and retention of factual information. Doctoral dissertation, University of Oklahoma.

Gagné, R. M. 1965. *The conditions of learning.* New York: Holt, Rinehart and Winston, Inc.

―――― 1967. Instruction and the conditions of learning. In L. Siegel (ed.), *Instruction—some contemporary viewpoints.* San Francisco, California: Chandler Publishing Company, pp. 291-313.

―――― 1970a. *The conditions of learning.* New York: Holt, Rinehart and Winston, Inc.

―――― 1970b. Learning theory, educational media, and individualized instruction. *Educ. Broadcast. Rev. 4:* 49-62.

Gagné, R. M. & Baker, K. E. 1950. Stimulus predifferentiation as a factor in transfer of training. *J. Exp. Psychol. 40:* 439-451.

Gagné, R. M. & Gropper, G. L. 1965. *Individual differences in learning from visual and verbal presentations.* Pittsburgh, Pa.: American Institutes for Research.

Galfo, A. 1970. Effects of certain audio and visual presentation sequences on pupil information acquisition. *J. Educ. Res. 64:* 172-176.

Gallup & Robinson, Inc. 1965. *Are color TV commercials worth the extra cost?* New York: Assoc. of National Advertisers.

Garner, W. R. 1962. *Uncertainty and structure as psychological concepts.* New York: Wiley.

Gerard, R. 1958. Color and emotional arousal. *Amer. Psychologist. 13:* 340.

Getzels, J. W. & Jackson, P. W. 1962. *Creativity and intelligence.* New York: John Wiley and Sons, Inc.

Gibson, J. J. 1947. *Motion picture testing and research.* Army Air Forces Psychology Program Research Report No. 7. Washington, D.C.: U.S. Government Printing Office.

―――― 1954. A theory of pictorial perception. *AV Commun. Rev. 2:* 2-23.

―――― 1966. *The senses considered as perceptual systems.* Boston: Houghton-Mifflin.

Gibson, E. J. 1969. *Principles of perceptual learning and development.* New York: Appleton Century-Crofts.

Gibson, E. J. & Yonas, A. 1966. A developmental study of visual search behavior. *Percept. & Psychophysics. 1:* 169-171.

Glaser, R. 1966. Psychological bases for instructional design. *AV Commun. Rev. 14:* 433-449.

Glasgow, M. W. 1961. *A study of the relative effectiveness of selected approaches to the in-service education of teachers in the utilization of in-school radio and television broadcasts.* NDEA Title Project No. 253. Washington, D.C.

Glanzer, M. & Clark, W. H. 1963a. Accuracy of perceptual recall: an analysis of organization. *J. Verb. Learn. & Verb. Behav. 1:* 289-299.

―――― 1963b. The verbal loop hypothesis: binary numbers. *J. Verb. Learn. & Verb. Behav. 2:* 301-309.

―――― 1964 The verbal loop hypothesis: conventional figures. *Amer. J. Psychol. 77:* 621-626.

Goldstein, E. B. 1975. The perception of multiple images. *AV Commun. Rev. 23:* 34-68.

Goldstein, K. 1942. Some experimental observations concerning the influence of color on the function of the organism. *Occup. Ther. 21:* 147-151.

Goodman, D. J. 1942. Comparative effectiveness of pictorial teaching aids. Doctoral dissertation, New York University.

Gorman, D. A. 1973. Effects of varying pictorial detail and presentation strategy on concept formation. *AV Commun. Rev. 21:* 337-350.

Green, B. F. & Anderson, L. K. 1956. Color coding in a visual search task. *J. Exp. Psychol. 51:* 19-24.

Greenhill, L. P. 1955a. *The recording of audience relations by infra-red photography.* Technical Report, SDC-269-7-56. Port Washington, N.Y.: Special Devices Center, Office of Naval Research.

―――― 1955b. *The evaluation of instructional films by a trained panel using a film analysis form.* Technical Report, SDC-269-7-57. Port Washington, N.Y.: Special Devices Center, Office of Naval Research.

Greenhill, L. P. & Kepler, L. F. 1955. *A study of the feasibility of local productions of minimum cost sound motion pictures.* Technical Report, SDC-269-7-48. Port Washington, N.Y.: Special Devices Center, Office of Naval Research.

Greenhill, L. P., Rich, O. S. & Carpenter, C. R. 1962. *The educational effectiveness, acceptability, and feasibility of the Ediophor large screen television projector.* University Park, The Pennsylvania State University, Division of Academic Research and Service.

Greenspoon, J. 1955. The reinforcing effect of two spoken sounds on the frequency of two responses. *Amer. J. Psychol. 68:* 490-516.

Grippin, P. C. 1973. Field independence and reflection-impulsivity as mediators of performance on a programmed learning task with and without strong prompts. In *Proceedings of the 81st Annual Convention of the American Psychological Association,* Montreal, Canada. *8:* 619-620.

Gropper, G. L. 1962. *Studies in Televised Instruction: The Role of Visuals in Verbal Learning.* Pittsburgh: Metropolitan Pittsburgh Educational Television Station and the American Institute for Research.

―――― 1963. Why is a picture worth a thousand words? *AV Commun. Rev. 11:* 75-95.

―――― 1966. Learning from visuals-some behavioral considerations. *AV Commun. Rev. 14:* 37-69.

Gross, L. S. 1969. A case for visual testing. *Educ./ Instructional Broadcast. 2:* 35-38.

Grosslight, J. H. & McIntyre, C. J. 1955. *Exploratory studies in the use of pictures and sound in teaching foreign language vocabulary.* Technical Report, SDC-269-7-53. Port Washington, D.C.: Special Devices Center, Office of Naval Research.

Grover, P. L. 1974. Effect of varied stimulus complexity and duration upon immediate recall of visual material in a serial learning task. *AV Commun. Rev. 22:* 439-452.

Guba, E., Wolf, W., Degroot, S., Knemeyer, M., Vanatta, R. & Light, L. 1964. Eye movements in TV viewing in children. *AV Commun. Rev. 12:* 386-401.

Guckin, J. P. 1966. A psycho-physical analysis of marginal linear perception and image resolution in eight millimeter and sixteen millimeter silent motion picture treatments with a junior high school population. Doctoral dissertation, The Pennsylvania State University.

Guilford, J. P. 1967. *The nature of human intelligence.* McGraw-Hill, New York.

Gulliksen, H. 1961. Measurement of learning and mental abilities. *Psychometrika. 26:* 93-107.

Hake, H. W., Rodwan, A. & Weintraub, D. 1966. Noise reduction in perception. In K. R. Hammond (ed.), *The psychology of Egon Brusswick.* New York: Holt, Reinhart and Winston, pp. 277-316.

Hale, G. A. & Morgan, J. S. 1973. Developmental trends in children's component selection. *J. Exp. Child. Psychol. 15:* 302-314.

Hale, G. A. & Taweel, S. S. 1974. Age difference in children's performance on measures of component selection and incidental learning. *J. Exp. Child. Psychol., 18:* 107-116.

Hall, K. R. L. 1950. The effect of names and titles upon the serial reproduction of pictorial and verbal material. *Brit. J. Psychol. 41:* 109-121.

Harby, S. F. 1952a. *Evaluation of procedure for using daylight projection of film loops in teaching skills.* Technical Report, SDC-269-7-25. Port Washington, N.Y.: Special Devices Center, Office of Naval Research.

―――― 1952b. *Comparison of mental practice and physical practice in the learning of physical skills.* Technical Report, SDC-269-7-27. Port Washington, N.Y.: Special Devices Center, Office of Naval Research.

Hare, R. D. 1972. Response requirements and directional fractionation of autonomic responses. *Psychophysiology. 9:* 429-427.

Harless, W. G., Parker, H. J., Lucas, N.C. & Nunnery, A. W. 1969. The total time hypothesis and computer assisted instruction. *Educ. Tech. 9:* 86-90.

Hartsell, H. C. & Margoles, R. A. 1967. Guidelines for the selection of instructional materials. *Audiovisual Instruction. 12:* 23-26.

Hartman, F. R. 1960. A review of research on learning from single and multiple channel communications and a proposed model with generalizations and implications for television communication. *Research on the Communication Process.* University Park, The Pennsylvania State University, Division of Academic Research and Service.

―――― 1961a. Recognition learning under multiple channel presentation and testing conditions. *AV Commun. Rev. 9:* 24-43.

―――― 1961b. Single and multiple channel communication: a review of research and a proposed model. *AV Commun. Rev. 9:* 235-262.

_____ 1963. A behavioristic approach to communication. *AV Commun. Rev. 11:* 155-190.

Haskell, R. W. 1971. Effect of certain individual learner personality differences on instructional methods. *AV Commun. Rev. 19:* 287-297.

Hebb, D. O. 1966. *A textbook of psychology.* Philadelphia: Saunders.

Heidgerken, L. E. 1948. An experimental study to measure the contributions of motion pictures and slide films to learning certain units in the course, introduction to nursing. Doctoral dissertation, Indiana University.

Heidt, E. U. 1977. Media and learner operations: the problem of a media taxonomy revisited. *Brit. J. Educ. Tech. 8:* 11-26.

Herman, L. M. 1965. Study of the single channel hypothesis and input regulation within a continuous, simultaneous task situation. *Quart. J. Exp. Psychol. 17:* 37-46.

Hernandez-Peon, R., Scherrer, H. & Jouvet, M. 1956. Modification of electrical activity in cochlear nucleus during "attention" in unanesthetized cats. *Science. 123:* 331-332.

Hernandez-Peon, R. 1961. Reticular mechanisms of sensory control. In W. A. Rosenblith (ed.) *Sensory communication.* New York: John Wiley & Sons, pp. 497-517.

Hershberger, W. 1964. Self-evaluation responding and typographical cueing: techniques for programming self-instructional reading materials. *J. Educ. Psychol. 55:* 288-296.

Hershenson, M., Munsinger, H. & Kessen, W. 1965. Preference for shapes of intermediate variability in newborn human. *Science. 147:* 630-631.

Hess, E. H. 1965. Attitude and pupil size. *Scientific Amer. 212:* 46-54.

Hewett, F. M. 1968. *The emotionally disturbed child.* Boston, Allyn and Bacon, Inc.

Hill, R. T. 1976. The development and implementation of a model for administering a visual test of achievement over broadcast television. Master thesis, The Pennsylvania State University.

Hinz, M. 1969. Effect of response mode on learning efficiency. *AV Commun. Rev. 17:* 77-83.

Hirsch, R. S. 1952. *The effects of knowledge of test results on learning of meaningful material.* Technical Report, SDC-269-7-30. Port Washington, N.Y.: Special Devices Center, Office of Naval Research.

Hoban, C. F. 1949. *Some aspects of learning from films.* Incidental Report No. 2. State College, Pa.: The Pennsylvania State College, Instructional Film Research Program.

_____ 1960. The usable residue of education film research. In Institute for Communication Research (eds.), *New teaching aids for the American classroom.* Stanford: Stanford University, pp. 99-115.

_____ 1961. Research on motion pictures and other media. In *New educational media.* University Park: The Pennsylvania State University, pp. 1-7.

Hoban, C. F. & Van Ormer, E. B. 1950a. *Instructional Film Research 1918-1950.* Technical Report No. SDC-269-7-19 Port Washington, N.Y.: Special Devices Center, Office of Naval Research.

_____ 1950b. *Practical principles governing the production and utilization of sound motion pictures.* State College, Pa.: The Pennsylvania State College, Instructional Film Research Program.

Hoban, T. 1965. Visual fixation response of infants to stimuli of varying complexity. *Child. Develpm. 37:* 629-638.

Hockberg, J. 1962. Psychophysics of pictorial perception. *AV Commun. Rev. 10:* 22-54.

Holland, J. G. 1957. Technique for behavioral analysis of human observing. *Science. 125:* 348-350.

Homer, R. B. 1946. The learning and retention of concepts IV. The influence of the complexity of the stimuli. *J. Exp. Psychol. 36:* 252-261.

Hopkins, K. D., Lefever, D. W. & Hopkins, B. R. 1967. TV vs. teacher administration of standardized tests: comparability of scores. *J. Educ. Meas. 4:* 35-40.

Hovland, C. I., Lumsdaine, A. A. & Sheffield, F. D. 1949. *Experiments on mass communication.* Princeton University Press.

Hsia, H. J. 1968a. On channel effectiveness. *AV Commun. Rev.* 16: 245-267.

_____ 1968b. Effects of noise and difficulty levels of input information in auditory, visual and audiovisual information processing. *Percept. & Motor Skills. 26:* 99-106.

_____ 1968c. Output, error, equivocation and recalled information in auditory, visual, and audiovisual information with constraint and noise. *J. Commun. 18:* 325-353.

_____ 1971. The information processing capacity of modality and channel performance. *AV Commun. Rev. 19:* 51-75.

Hull, C. L. 1951. *Essentials of Behavior.* New Haven: Yale University Press.

Hunt, E. B. 1962. *Concept learning.* New York: Wiley.

Hunt, D. E. 1975. Person-environment interaction: a challenge found wanting before it was tried. *Rev. Educ. Res. 2:* 209-230.

Hurst, P. M. 1955. *Relative effectiveness of verbal introductions to kinescope recordings and training films.* Technical Report, SDC-269-7-42. Port Washington, N.Y.: Special Devices Center, Office of Naval Research.

Ibison, R. A. 1952. Differential effects on the recall of textual materials associated with the inclusion of colored and uncolored illustrations. Doctoral dissertation, Indiana University.

Ingersoll, G. M. 1970. The effects of presentation modalities and modality preferences on learning and recall. Doctoral dissertation, The Pennsylvania State University.

Isaacs, D. 1969. The effect on learning of the color coding of pictorial stimuli. Doctoral dissertation, Indiana University.

Jacobson, H. 1950. The informational capacity of the human ear. *Science. 112:* 143-144.

_____ 1951. The information capacity of the human eye. *Science. 113:* 292-293.

Jakobson, R. 1967. About the relations between visual and auditory signs. In W. Walthen-Dunn (ed.), *Models for the perception of speech and visual form.* Cambridge, Mass.: MIT Press.

James, N. E. 1962. Personal preference for method as a factor in learning. *J. Educ. Psychol. 53:* 43-47.

Jaspen, N. 1950a. *Effects on training of experimental film variables, study I; verbalization, rate of development, nomenclature, errors "how-it-works", repetition.* Technical Report, SDC-269-7-17. Port Washington, N.Y.: Special Devices Center, Office of Naval Research.

_____ 1950b. *Effects on training of experimental film variables, study II: verbalization, "how-it-works", nomenclature, audience participation, and succinct treatment.* Technical Report, SDC-269-7-11. Port Washington, N.Y.: Special Devices Center, Office of Naval Research.

Jelden, D. L. 1971. *Predicting success in an individualized multi-media instructional program using variables of aptitude and personality.* Greeley: University of Northern Colorado (ED-056-460).

Jenkins, J. J. & Russell, W. A. 1952. Associative clustering during recall. *J. Abnorm. & Soc. Psychol. 47:* 818-821.

Jenkins, J. J., Mink, W. D. & Russell, W. A. 1958. Associative clustering as a function of verbal association strength. *Psychol. Rpt. 4:* 127-136.

Jenkins, J. R., Stack, W. B. & Deno, S. L. 1969. Children's recognition and recall of picture and word stimuli. *AV Commun. Rev. 17:* 265-271.

Jensen, A. R. 1968. Social class, race and genetics: implications for education. *Amer. Educ. Res. J. 5:* 1-42.

Johnson, R. B. 1968. The effect of prompting, practice and feedback in programmed videotape. *Amer. Educ. Res. J. 5:* 73-80.

Jones, J. K. 1965. Color as an aid to visual perception in early reading. *Brit. J. Educ. Psychol. 35:* 21-27.

Jones, M. R. 1962. Color coding. *Human factors. 6:* 355-365.

Kahneman, D. 1973. *Attention and effort.* Englewood Cliffs, New Jersey, Prentice-Hall, Inc.

Kale, S. V. & Grosslight, J. H. 1955. *Exploratory study in the use of pictures and sound for teaching foreign language vocabulary.* Technical Report, SDC-269-7-53. Port Washington, N.Y.: Special Devices Center, Office of Naval Research.

Kanner, J. H. & Rosenstein, A. J. 1960. Television in army training: color vs. black and white. *AV Commun. Rev. 8:* 243-252.

Kanner, J. H. 1961. Television and army training: color vs. black and white. *AV Commun. Rev. 9:* 44-49.

_____ 1968. *The instructional effectiveness of color in television: a review of the evidence.* Stanford: Stanford University, (ERIC, ED 015-675).

Kantor, B. R. 1960. Effectiveness of inserted questions in instructional films. *AV Commun. Rev. 8:* 104-108.

Kaplan, R. & Rothkopf, E. Z. 1974. Instructional objectives as directors to learners: effect of passage length and amount of objective-relevant content. *J. Educ. Psychol. 66:* 448-456.

Katzman, N. & Nyenhuis, J. 1972. Color vs. black and white effects on learning, opinion, and attention. *AV Commun. Rev. 20:* 16-28.

Kauffman, S. P. and Dwyer, F. M. 1974. Effectiveness of cartoons and photographs in in-service training. *Calif. J. Educ. Res. 4:* 197-204.

Keele, S. W. 1973. *Attention and human performance.* Pacific Palisades, Goodyear Publishing Company, Inc.

Kendall, K. 1952. Film production principles—the subject of research. *J. SMPTE. 58:* 428-444.

Kendler, H. H. 1966. Coding: associationistic or organizational. *J. Verbal Learn. Verbal Behav. 5:* 198-200.

Kennedy, L. D. 1971. Textbook usage in the intermediate-upper grades. *Reading Teach. 24:* 723-729.

Ketcham, C. H. & Heath, R. N. 1962. Teaching effectiveness of sound with pictures that do not embody the material being sought. *AV Commun. Rev. 10:* 89-93.

King, D. J. & Russell, G. W. 1966. A comparison of rate and meaningful learning of connected meaningful material. *J. Verb. Learn. Behav. 5:* 478-483.

Klausmeier, H. J. & Check, J. 1962. Retention and transfer in children of low, average, and high intelligence. *J. Educ. Res. 55:* 319-322.

Kleitman, N. 1945. The effect of motion pictures on body temperatures. *Science. 101:* 507-508.

Klemmer, E. T. 1956. Time sharing between auditory and visual channels. In G. Finch & F. Cameron (eds.), *Air Force engineering personnel and training.* Washington, D.C.: National Academy of Sciences, pp. 199-203.

_____ 1958. Time sharing between frequency coded auditory and visual channels. *J. Exp. Psychol. 55:* 229-235.

Knight, H. R. & Sassenrath, J. M. 1966. Relation of achievement motivation and test anxiety to performance in programmed instruction. *J. Educ. Psychol. 57:* 14-17.

Knowlton, J. Q. 1964. *A conceptual scheme for the audiovisual field.* Bloomington: Indiana University, Bulletin of the School of Education.

Koen, F. 1969. *Verbal and nonverbal mediators in recognition memory for complex visual stimuli.* Ann Arbor: University of Michigan, Center for Research on Language and Language Behavior.

Kopstein, F. F. & Roshal, S. M. 1954. Learning foreign vocabulary from pictures vs. words. *Amer. Psychologist. 9:* 407-408.

Koran, M. L., Snow, R. E. & McDonald, F. J. 1971. Teacher aptitude in observational learning of a teaching skill. *J. Educ. Psychol. 62:* 219-228.

Koran, M. L. & Koran, J. J. 1975. Interaction of learner aptitudes with question pacing in learning from prose. *J. Educ. Psychol. 67:* 76-82.

Koran, J. J., Koran, M. L. & Freeman, P. 1976. Acquisition of a concept: effects of mode of instruction and length of exposure to biology examples. *AV Commun. Rev. 24:* 357-366.

Kouwer, B. 1949. *Colors and their character.* The Hague, Martinue Nijhoff.

Krathwohl, D. R., Bloom, B. S. & Masia, B. 1964. *A taxonomy of educational objectives: handbook II, the effective domain.* New York: David MacKay.

Kropp, R. P., Nelson, W. H. & King, F. J. 1967. *Identification and definition of subject matter content variables related to human aptitudes.* USOE Cooperative Research Project No. 2914. Tallahassee, Florida State University.

Krumboltz, J. D. & Yabroff, W. W. 1965. The comparative effects of inductive deductive sequences in programmed instruction. *Amer. Edu. Res. J. 2:* 223-235.

Ksobiech, K. J. 1976. The importance of perceptual task and type of presentation in student response to instructional television. *AV Commun. Rev. 24:* 401-412.

Kumata, H. 1960. Two studies in classroom teaching. In W. Schramm (ed.), *The impact of educational television.* Urbana: University of Illinois Press, pp. 151-157.

Kurtz, A. K., Walter, J. S. & Brenner, H. 1950. *The effects of inserted questions and statements on film learning.* Technical Report, SDC-269-7-16. Port Washington, N.Y.: Special Devices Center, Office of Naval Research.

Lamberski, R. J. 1972. An exploratory investigation of the instructional effect of color and black and white cueing on immediate and delayed retention. Master thesis, The Pennsylvania State University.

Lantz, D. & Stefflre, V. 1964. Language and cognition revisited. *J. Abnorm. Soc. Psychol. 69:* 472-481.

Lathrop, C. W. & Norford, C. A. 1949. *Contributions of film introductions and film summaries to learning from instructional films.* Technical Report, SDC-269-7-8. Port Washington, N.Y.: Special Devices Center, Office of Naval Research.

Lathrop, C. W., Norford, C. A. & Greenhill, L. P. 1953. The contributions of film introductions and film summaries to learning from instructional films. *J. Educ. Psychol. 44:* 343-353.

Lefkowith, E. F. 1955a. The effect of pictorial stimuli similarity in teaching and testing. Doctoral dissertation, The Pennsylvania State University.

_____ 1955b. *The validity of pictorial tests and their interaction with audio-visual teaching methods.* Technical Report, SDC-269-7-49. Port Washington, N.Y.: Special Devices Center, Office of Naval Research.

Levie, W. H. & Dickie, K. E. 1973. The analysis and application of media. In Travers, R. M. W. (ed.), *Second handbook of research on teaching.* Chicago: Rand McNally.

Levie, W. H. & Levie, D. 1975. Pictorial memory processes. *AV Commun. Rev. 23:* 81-97.

Levin, J. R., Bender, B. G. & Lesgold, A. M. 1976. Pictures, repetition, and young children's oral prose learning. *AV Commun. Rev. 24:* 367-381.

Lindquist, E. F. 1953. *Design and analysis of experiments in psychology and education.* Boston: Houghton-Mifflin Company.

Lindsley, O. R. 1962. A behavioral measure of television viewing. *J. Advertising Res. 2:* 2-12.

Link, D. J. 1961. A comparison of the effects on learning of viewing films in color on a screen and in black and white over closed-circuit television. *Ontario J. Educ. Res. 3:* 111-115.

Livingstone, R. B. 1958. Central control of afferent activity. In H. H. Japser, et al. (ed.) *Reticular formation of the brain.* Boston: Little, Brown, pp. 177-185.

_____ 1959. Central control of receptors and sensory transmission systems. In M. J. Field, et al., (eds.), *Handbook of physiology.* Bethesda, Maryland: American Physiological Society, pp. 741-759.

_____ 1962. An adventure shared by psychology and neurophysiology. In S. Koch (ed.), *Psychology: a study of a science.* New York: McGraw-Hill, pp. 51-99.

Llewellyn-Thomas, E. 1963. Eye movement of a pilot during aircraft landings. *J. Aerospace Med. 34:* 424-426.

Lockhard, J. & Sidowski, J. B. 1961. Learning in fourth and sixth graders as a function of sensory mode of stimulus presentation and overt and covert practice. *J. Educ. Psychol. 52:* 262-265.

Long, A. L. 1945. The influence of color acquisition and retention as evidenced by the use of sound films. Doctoral dissertation, University of Colorado.

Lordahl, D. S. 1961. Concept identification using simultaneous auditory and visual signals. *J. Exp. Psychol. 62:* 283-290.

Loveless, N. E., Brebner, J. & Hamilton, P. 1970. Bisensory presentation of information. *Psychol. Bull. 73:* 161-199.

Lubin, A. 1961. The interpretation of significant interaction. *Educ. Psychol. Measmt. 21:* 807-817.

Lublin, S. C. 1965. Reinforcement schedules, scholastic aptitude, autonomy need, and achievement in a programmed course. *J. Educ. Psychol. 56:* 295-302.

Lumsdaine, A. A. & Sulzer, R. L. 1951. *The influence of simple animation techniques on the value of a training film.* Washington, U.S. Air Force Human Factors Research Lab. Report No. 24.

Lumsdaine, A. A., Sulzer, R. L. & Kopstein, F. F. 1953. The influence of simple animation techniques on the value of a training film. *AV Commun. Rev. 1:* 140-141.

_____ 1961. The effect of animation cues and repetition of examples on learning from an instructional film. In A. A. Lumsdaine (ed.), *Student response in programmed instruction.* Washington, D.C.: National Academy of Science and National Research Council.

Lumsdaine, A. A. & Gladstone, A. 1958. Overt practice and audiovisual embellishments. In M. A. May & A. A. Lumsdaine (eds.), *Learning from Films.* New Haven: Yale University Press, pp. 58-71.

Lumsdaine, A. A. & May, M. A. 1965. Mass communication and educational media. In P. R. Farnsworth (ed.), *Ann. Rev. Psychol. 16:* 475-534.

Lumsdaine, A. A. 1963. Instruments and media of instruction. In N. L. Gage (ed.), *Handbook of research on teaching.* Chicago: Rand-McNally pp. 583-682.

Luria, A. R. & Homskaya, E. D. 1970. Frontal lobes and the regulation of arousal processes. In D. I. Mostofsky (ed.) *Attention: contemporary theory and analysis.* New York: Appleton-Century Crofts.

Lynn, R. 1966. *Attention, arousal and the orientation reaction.* New York: Pergamon.

Maccoby, E. E. & Hagen, J. W. 1965. Effects of distraction upon central versus incidental recall: development trends. *J. Exp. Child Psychol. 2:* 280-289.

MacLean, W. P. 1930. A comparison of colored and uncolored pictures. *Educ. Screen. 9:* 196-199.

Mackworth, J. F. 1962. Presentation rate and immediate memory. *Canad. J. Psychol. 16:* 43-47.

Mackworth, N.H. & Morandi, A.J. 1967. The gaze selects informative details within pictures. *Percept. Psychophysics. 2:* 547-552.

Mackworth, N.H. & Bruner, J.T. 1970. How adults and children search and recognize pictures. *Human Develpm. 13:* 149-177.

MacLennan, D. W. & Reid, J. C. 1967. *Research in instructional television and film.* Washington, D. C.: U.S. Office of Education.

Macomber, F. G. & Siegel, L. 1957. A study in large group teaching procedures. *Educ. Res. 38:* 220-229.

Mager, R. F. 1962. *Preparing instructional objectives.* Palo Alto, California: Fearon Publishers.

Malter, M. S. 1948. Children's preferences for illustrative materials. *J. Educ. Res. 41:* 384-385.

Maltzman, I. & Raskin, D. C. 1966. Effects of individual differences in the orienting reflex on conditioning and complex processes. In P. Bakan (ed.), *Attention.* New York: Van Nostrand.

Marantz, S., & Dowaliby, F. 1973. Filmed versus lecture methods of instruction as related to imagability. Paper presented at the AERA National Convention, New Orleans, Louisiana.

Marshall, H. H. 1969. Learning as a function of task interest, reinforcement, and social class variables. *J. Educ. Psychol. 60:* 133-137.

May, M. A. & Lumsdaine, A. A. 1958. *Learning from films.* New Haven: Yale University Press.

McCluskey, F. D. & McCluskey, H. Y. 1924. Comparison of motion pictures, slides, sterographs and demonstrations as a means of teaching how to make a reed mat and a pasteboard box. In F. M. Freedman (ed.), *Visual Education.* Chicago: University of Chicago Press, pp. 310-334.

McCormick, E. J. 1957. *Human engineering.* New York: McGraw-Hill.

McCowan, A. C. 1940. A controlled experiment in visual education in general science. *Educ. Screen. 19:* 143-146.

McCoy, E. P. 1955. *An application of research findings to training film production.* Technical Report, SDC-269-7-44. Port Washington, N.Y.: Special Devices Center, Office of Naval Research.

McGeogh, J. A. & Irion, A. L. 1952. *The psychology of human learning.* New York: Longman, Green & Company.

McIntyre, C. J. 1954. *Training film evaluation—FB-254 cold weather uniforms: an evaluation of special effects and appeals.* Technical Report, SDC-269-7-51. Port Washington, N.Y.: Special Devices Center, Office of Naval Research.

McIntyre, C. J. & McCoy, E. P. 1954. *The application of sound motion pictures for recording billet analysis information.* Technical Report, SDC-269-7-41. Port Washington, N.Y.: Special Devices Center, Office of Naval Research.

McKeachie, W. J. 1967. Research in teaching: the gap between theory and practice. In B. Calvin & T. Lee (eds.), *Improving college teaching.* Washington, D.C.: American Council on Education.

McLuhan, M. 1960. *Report on understanding new media.* Toronto, Ontario: Project in Understanding New Media.

McNiven, M. 1955. *The effects on learning of the perceived usefulness of the material to be learned.* Technical Report, SDC-269-7-54. Port Washington, N.Y.: Special Devices Center, Office of Naval Research.

McTavish, C. L. 1949. *Effect of repetitive film showings on learning.* Technical Report, SDC-269-7-12. Port Washington, N.Y.: Special Devices Center, Office of

Naval Research.

Mechanic, A. 1965. An investigation of selectivity of incidental learners. *Proceedings* 73rd. Annual Convention of the APA, Washington, D. C.

Meldman, M. 1970. *Diseases of attention and perception.* New York: Pergamon.

Menne, J. M. & Menne, I. W. 1972. The relative efficiency of bimodal presentation as an aid to learning. *AV Commun. Rev. 20:* 170-180.

Mercer, J. 1952. *The relationship of optical effects of film literacy to learning from instructional films.* Technical Report, SDC-269-7-34. Port Washington, N.Y.: Special Devices Center, Office of Naval Research.

Merrill, M. D. 1973. Content and instructional analysis for cognitive transfer tasks. *AV Commun. Rev. 21:* 109-125.

Metcalf, R. M. 1967. *An exploratory analysis of projection variables (screen size, image size, image contrast) in terms of their effects on the speed and accuracy of discrimination.* Final Report USOE Title VII, Project No. 5-0422, Bloomington, Indiana: Indiana University, School of Education.

Michael, D. N. & Maccoby, N. 1953. Factors influencing verbal learning from films under conditions of audience participation. *J. Exp. Psychol. 46:* 411-418.

Milgram, N. A. 1967. Verbal context versus visual compound in paired-associate learning by children. *J. Exp. Child Psychol. 5:* 597-603.

Miller, E. E. 1971. *Comparison of pictorial techniques for guiding performance during training.* Alexandria, Virginia: HUMRO-Technical Report: 71-12.

Miller, G. A. 1956. The magical number seven, plus or minus two: some limitations on our capacity for processing information. *Psychol. Rev. 63:* 81-97.

Miller, G. A., Galanter, E. H. & Pribram, K. H. 1960. *Plans and structure of behavior.* New York: Holt.

Miller, N. E. (ed.) 1957. Graphic communication and the crisis in education. By Neal E. Miller in collaboration with William A. Allen, et al., *AV Commun. Rev. 5:* 1-120.

Miller, W. C. 1969. Film movement and effective response and the effect on learning and attitude formation. *AV Commun. Rev. 17:* 172-181.

Moore, D. M. & Sasse, E. B. 1971. Effect of size and type of still projected pictures on immediate recall of content. *AV Commun. Rev. 19:* 437-450.

Morris, C. W. 1946. Signs, languages and behavior. New York: Prentice-Hall.

Mowbray, G. H. 1952. Stimultenous vision and audition: the detection of elements missing from overlearned sequences. *J. Exp. Psychol. 44:* 292-300.

———— 1953. Simultaneous vision and audition: the comprehension of prose passages with varying levels of difficulty. *J. Exp. Psychol. 46:* 365-372.

———— 1954. The perception of short phrases presented simultaneously for visual and auditory perception. *Quart. J. Exp. Psychol. 6:* 86-92.

Mowrer, O. H. 1960. *Learning theory and behavior.* New York: Wiley.

Murnin, J. A., Hayes, W. & Harby, S. F. 1952. *Daylight projection of film loops as the teaching medium in perceptual-motor skill training.* Technical Report, SDC-269-7-26. Port Washington, N.Y.: Special Devices Center, Office of Naval Research.

Murnin, J. A., VanderMeer, A. W. & Vris, T. 1954. *Comparison of Training media; trainee manipulation and observation of functioning electrical systems versus trainee drawing of schematic electrical systems.* Technical Report, SDC-269-7-101. Port Washington, N.Y.: Special Devices Center, Office of Naval Research.

Murray, J. R. 1960. The comparative effectiveness of condensed visualized methods of teaching operation of the UM tape recorder and Victor 16mm projector. Doc-

toral dissertation, The Pennsylvania State University.

Nathan, P. E. & Wallace, W. G. 1965. An operant behavioral measure of TV commercial effectiveness. *J. Advert. Res. 5:* 13-20.

Neisser, U. 1964. Visual search. *Scientific Amer. 210:* 94-102.

Nelson, H. E. 1949. *The relative contributions to learning of video and audio elements in films.* Progress Report No. 13. State College: The Pennsylvania State College, Instructional Film Research Program.

Nelson, H. E. & Moll, K. R. 1950. *Comparison of the audio and video elements of instructional films.* Technical Report, SDC-269-7-18. Port Washington, N.Y.: Special Devices Center, Office of Naval Research.

Nelson, H. E. & VanderMeer, A. W. 1955. *The relative effectiveness of differing commentaries in an animated film on elementary meterology.* Technical Report, SDC-269-7-43. Port Washington, N.Y.: Special Devices Center, Office of Naval Research.

Neu, D. M. 1950. *The effect of attention gaining devices on film-mediated learning.* Technical Report, SDC-269-7-9. Port Washington, N.Y.: Special Devices Center, Office of Naval Research.

———— 1951. The effects of attention-gaining devices on film mediated learning. *J. Educ. Broadcast, 42:* 479-490. 490.

Niekamp, W. E. 1971. An exploratory analysis of selected factors of pictoral composition through the ocular photography of eye movements. Doctoral disseration, Indiana University.

Norberg, K. 1966. Visual perception theory and instructional communication. *AV Commun. Rev. 14:* 301-316.

Northrop, D. S. 1952. *Effects on learning of the prominance of organizational outlines in instructional films.* Technical Report, SDC-269-7-33. Port Washington, N.Y.: Special Devices Center, Office of Naval Research.

Nunnally, J. Faw, T. & Bashford, M. 1969. Effect of degrees of incongruity in visual fixations in children and adults. *J. Exp. Psychol. 81:* 360-364.

Okey, J. R. 1973. Developing and validating learning hierarchies. *AV Commun. Rev. 21:* 87-108.

Ortigiesen, L. 1954. The relative effectiveness of selected filmstrips and sound motion pictures in teaching soil conservations in ninth-grade social studies classes. Doctoral dissertation, University of Nebraska.

Osgood, C. E. 1953. *Method and theory in experimental psychology.* New York: Oxford University Press.

Osler, S. F. & Myrna, W. F. 1961. Concept attainment: the role of age and intelligence in concept attainment by induction. *J. Exp. Psychol. 62:* 1-8.

Otto, W. 1964. Hierarchical responses elicted by verbal and pictorial stimuli. *Amer. Educ. Res. J. 1:* 241-248.

Otto, W. & Askov, E. 1968. The role of color in learning and instruction. *J. Spec. Educ. 2:* 155-165.

Overing, R. L. R. & Travers, R. M. W. 1967. Variation in the amount of irrelevant cues in training and test conditions and the effect upon transfer. *J. Educ. Psychol. 58:* 62-68.

Paivio, A. & Csapo, K. 1969. Concrete-image and verbal memory codes. *J. Exp. Psychol. 80:* 279-285.

Paivio, A., Rogers, T. B. & Smythe, P. C. 1968. Why are pictures easier to recall than words? *Psychonomic Sci. 11:* 137-138.

Paivio, A. 1971. *Imagery and verbal processes.* New York: Holt, Rinehart and Winston.

Parkhurst, P. E. 1974. Assessing the effectiveness of self-paced visualized instruction; a multifactor analysis on five different educational tasks. Paper presented at AECT National Convention, Atlantic City, New Jersey.

———— 1975. Effect of students' I.Q. on performance in self-paced visualized instruction. Paper presented at

AECT National Convention, Dallas, Texas.

_____ 1976. Effect of students' level of reading comprehension and achievement with visualized instruction. Michigan State University, College of Osteopathic Medicine (Mimeographed).

Pearce, G. L. 1970. Alternate versions of overhead transparency projectuals designed to teach elementary statistical concepts. *AV Commun. Rev. 18:* 65-71.

Perrin, D. G. 1969. A theory of multiple-image communication. *AV Commun. Rev. 17:* 368-382.

Pessinger, G. 1969. Test administration by video tape. *Educ. Television. 1:* 19-20.

Peterson, J. C. & Hancock, R. R. 1974. Developing mathematical materials for the students cognitive style. Paper presented at AERA National Convention, New Orleans, Louisiana (ERIC ED 076-423).

_____ 1974. Developing mathematical materials for aptitude-treatment interaction. Paper presented at AERA National Convention, Chicago, Illinois.

Peterson, L. R. & Peterson, M. J. 1957. The role of context stimuli in verbal learning. *J. Exp. Psychol. 53:* 102-105.

Pollack, I. 1953. The information of elementary auditory displays. *J. Acoust. Soc. Amer. 25:* 765-769.

Postman, L. & Riley, D. A. 1957. A critique of Kohler's theory of association. *Psychol. Rev. 64:* 61-72.

Quastler, H. & Wulff, V. J. 1955. *Human performance in information transmission.* Control Systems Laboratory Report No. 62. University of Illinois.

Randhawa, B. S. 1971. Intellectual development and the ability to process visual and verbal information. *AV Commun. Rev. 19:* 298-312.

Rappaport, M. 1957. The role of redundancy in discrimination of visual forms. *J. Exp. Psychol. 53:* 3-10.

Reed, H. B. 1946. The learning and retention of concepts IV. The influence of the complexity of the stimuli. *J. Exp. Psychol. 36:* 252-261.

Reede, A. H. & Reede, R. K. 1963. *Televising instruction in elementary economics.* Industrial Research Bulletin No. 5 University Park, The Pennsylvania State University, College of Business Administration.

Reese, H. W. 1965. Imagery in pair-associated learning in children. *J. Exp. Child Psychol. 2:* 290-296.

Reich, C. & Meisner, A. 1976. A comparison of colour and black and white television as instructional media. *Brit. J. Educ. Tech. 7:* 24-35.

Reid, J. C. & MacLennan, D. W. 1967. *Research in instructional television and film.* Washington, D.C.: U.S. Office of Education. HEW, Bureau of Research.

Rhetts, J. E. 1974. Task learner and treatment variables in instructional design. *J. Educ. Psychol. 66:* 339-347.

Rimland, B. 1955. *Effectiveness of several methods of repetition of films.* Technical Report, SDC-269-7-45. Port Washington, N.Y.: Special Devices Center, Office of Naval Research.

Ripple, R. E., Millman, J. & Glock, M. D. 1969. Learner characteristics and instructional mode: a search for disordinal interactions. *J. Educ. Psychol. 60:* 113-120.

Rohwer, W. D., Lynch, S. Levine, J. R. & Suzuki, N. 1967. Pictorial and verbal factors in the efficient learning of paired associates. *J. Educ. Psychol. 58:* 278-284.

Rosemier, A. S. & Sleeman, P. 1965. Readable letter size and visibility for overhead projection transparencies. *AV Commun. Rev. 13:* 412-417.

Roshal, S. M. 1949. *Effects of learner representation in film-mediated perceptual motor learning.* Technical Report, SDC-269-7-5. Port Washington, N.Y.: Special Devices Center, Office of Naval Research.

Rosonke, R. J. 1974. A study of the effectiveness of three visual attention-directing devices on the recall of relevant information from line drawings. Doctoral dissertation, The University of Iowa.

_____ 1975. A study of the effectiveness of three visual attention-directing devices on the recall of relevant information from line drawings. Paper presented at AECT National Convention, Dallas, Texas.

Rothkopf, E. Z. 1965. Some theoretical and experimental approaches to problems in written instruction. In J. D. Krumboltz (ed.), *Learning and the educational process.* Chicago: Rand McNally, pp. 193-221.

Rothkopf, E. Z. & Bisbicos, E. 1967. Selective facilitative effects of interspersed questions on learning from written materials. *J. Educ. Psychol. 58:* 56-61.

Rothkopf, E. Z. 1971. Experiments on mathemagenic behavior and the technology of written instruction. In E. Z. Rothkopf and P. E. Johnson (ed.) *Verbal learning research and the technology of written instruction.* New York: Teachers College Press, 284-303.

Rudisill, M. 1952. Children's preferences for color versus other qualities in illustrations. *Elem. Sch. J. 52:* 444-451.

Rust, G. C. 1967. *A study to explore the effectiveness of color photographs in intrinsically programmed instructional materials.* Final Report, USOE. Bureau of Research, OEG-7-23-0970-1570. Carbondale, Southern Illinois University.

Ryan, T. A. & Schwartz, C. B. 1956. Speed of perception as a function of mode of representation. *Amer. J. Psychol. 39:* 60-69.

Salomon, G. & Sieber, J. E. 1970. Relative subjective response uncertainty as function of stimulus-task interaction. *Amer. Educ. Res. J. 7:* 337-350.

Salomon, G. & Cohen, A. 1976. The effects of TV formats on mental skills. Paper presented at the 8th Annual Conference on Visual Literacy. International Visual Literacy Association (IVLA), Nashville, Tennessee.

Salomon, G. 1972a. Can we affect cognitive skills through visual media? An hypothesis and initial findings. *AV Commun. Rev. 20:* 401-422.

_____ 1972b. Heuristic models for the generation of aptitude-treatment interaction hypothesis. *Rev. Educ. Res. 42:* 327-343.

_____ 1973. Cognitive effects of media: the case of Sesame Street in Israel. Address to the biannual meeting of the International Society for the Study of Behavioral Development, Ann Arbor.

Saltz, E. 1963. Compound stimuli in verbal learning: cognitive and sensory differentiation versus stimulus selection. *J. Exp. Psychol. 66:* 1-5.

Samuels, S. J. 1970. Effects of pictures on learning to read, comprehension and attitudes. *Rev. Educ. Res. 40:* 397-407.

Schaps, E., & Guest, L. 1968. Some pros and cons of color T.V. *J. Advert. Res. 8:* 28-39.

Schlater, R. 1970. Effect of speed of presentation on recall of television messages. *J. Broadcast. 14:* 207-214.

Scanlon, T. J. 1970s. Color television: new language? *Journ. Quart. 44:* 225-230.

_____ 1970b. Viewer perceptions on color, black and white, T.V.: an experiment. *Journ. Quart. 47:* 366-368.

Schramm, W. 1960. Television in the life of the child—implications for school. In Institute for Communication Research (eds.), *New teaching aids for the American classroom.* Stanford: Stanford University, pp. 50-70.

Schuyler, W. & Long, J. D. 1973. The effect of behavioral objectives on student achievement. *J. Exp. Educ. 42:* 40-41.

Schwartz, A. M. 1960. The effects of conditioning upon children's color choices and color usage. Doctoral dissertation, The Pennsylvania State University.

Senden, M. W. 1960. *Space and light.* Glencoe, Illinois: Free Press.

Senders, J. W. 1973. Visual scanning behavior. In National Academy of Services (eds.), *Visual search.* Washington, D.C., pp. 106-128.

Severin, W. J. 1967a. Cue summation in multiple channel communication. Doctoral dissertation, University of Wisconsin.

_____ 1967b. Another look at cue summation. *AV Commun. Rev. 15:* 233-245.

_____ 1967c. The effectiveness of relevant pictures in multiple-channel communications. *AV Commun. Rev. 15:* 386-401.

_____ 1967d. Relevant pictures in multi-channel communication. *Journ. Quart. 44:* 17-22.

Shannon, C. E. & Weaver, W. 1949. *The mathematical theory of communication,* Urbana, Illinois: University of Illinois Press.

Shapiro, K. R. 1975. An overview of problems encountered in aptitude treatment interaction (ATI) research for instruction. *AV Commun. Rev. 23:* 227-241.

Shavelson, R. J., Berliner, D. C., Ravitch, M. M. & Loeding, D. 1974. Effects of position and type of questions on learning from prose material: interaction of treatments with individual differences. *J. Educ. Psychol. 66:* 40-48.

Sheffield, F. D., Margolius, G. J. & Hoehn, A. J. 1961. Experiments on perceptual mediation in the learning of organizable sequences. In A. A. Lumsdaine (ed.), *Students responses in programmed instruction.* Washington, D.C: National Academy of Science, National Research Council.

Shepard, R. N. 1967. Recognition memory for words, sentences, and pictures. *J. Verb. Learn. Verb. Behav. 6:* 156-163.

Siegel, A. W. & Stevenson, H. W. 1966. Incidental learning: a developmental study. *Child. Develpmt. 37:* 811-817.

Silverman, R. E. 1958. *The comparative effectiveness of animated and static transparencies,* Technical Report, SDC-78-1. Port Washington, D.C.: Special Devices Center, Office of Naval Research.

Skinner, B. F. 1957. *Verbal behavior.* New York: Appleton.

_____ 1968. Teaching science in high school—what is wrong? *Science. 159:* 704-710.

Slattery, M. J. 1953. *An appraisal of the effectiveness of selected instructional sound motion pictures and silent filmstrips in elementary school instruction.* Washington: Catholic University Press.

Smith, K. R. & Van Ormer, E. B. 1949. *Learning theories and instructional film research.* Technical Report, SDC-269-7-6. Port Washington, N.Y.: Special Devices Center, Office of Naval Research.

Smith, B. O. 1964. *Education and the structure of knowledge.* Chicago: Rand McNally.

Smith, R. S. 1958. An investigation of the relationship between physiological and cognitive measures to the affective responses to color. Doctoral dissertation, University of Pennsylvania.

Smith, S. L. 1963. Color coding and visual separability in information displays. *J. Appl. Psychol. 47:* 358-364.

Smith, S. L. & Thomas, D. W. 1964. Color versus shape coding in information displays. *J. Appl. Psychol. 48:* 137-146.

Smith, S. L., Farquhar, B. B. & Thomas, D. W. 1965. Color coding in formatted displays. *J. Appl. Psychol. 49:* 393-398.

Smith, E. E. & Larson, D. E. 1970. The verbal loop hypothesis and the effects of similarity on recognition and communication in adults and children. *J. Verb. Learn. & Verb. Behav. 9:* 237-242.

Snow, R. E., Tiffin, J. & Seibert, W. 1965. Individual differences and instructional film effects. *J. Educ. Psychol. 56:* 315-326.

Snowberg, R. L. 1973. Bases for the selection of background colors for transparencies. *AV Commun. Rev. 21:* 191-209.

Solomon, R. L. & Howes, D. H. 1951. Word frequency, personal values, and visual duration thresholds. *Psychol Rev. 58:* 256-270.

Solley, C. M. & Murphy, G. 1960. *Development of the perceptual world.* New York: Basic Books.

Spangenberg, R. W. 1973. The motion variable in procedural learning. *AV Commun. Rev. 21:* 419-436.

Spaulding, S. 1955. Research on pictorial illustrations. *AV Commun. Rev. 3:* 35-45.

_____ 1956. Communication potential of pictorial illustrations. *AV Commun. Rev. 4:* 31-46.

Sperling, G. 1963. A model for visual memory tasks. *Human Factors. 5:* 19-31.

Sperling, G., Budiansky, J., Spivak, J. G. & Johnson, M. C. 1971. Extremely rapid visual search: the maximum rate of scanning letter for the presence of a numeral. *Science. 174:* 307-311.

Spitz, H. & Borland, M. D. 1967. Redundancy in line drawings of familiar objects: effects of age and intelligence. *Cognitive Psychol. 2:* 196-205.

Stallings, W. M. 1972. A comparison of television and audio presentations of the MLA French listening examination. *J. Educ. Res. 65:* 472-474.

Stake, R. 1958. Learning parameters, aptitudes and achievements. Princeton University Psychology Department. (multilith).

Stanley, J. C. 1960. Interactions of organisms with experimental variables as a key to the integration of organismic and variable-manipulating research. In Edith M. Huddleston (ed.), *Yearb. Nat. Counc. Measmt.* Washington, D.C.

Stevenson, A. H. & Lynn, D. B. 1971. Preference for high variability in young children. *Psychonomic Sci. 23:* 143-144.

Stevenson, H. W. & Siegel, A. 1969. Effects of instructions and age on retention of filmed content. *J. Educ. Psychol. 60:* 71-74.

Stickell, D. W. 1963. A critical review of the methodology and results of research comparing televised and face-to-face instruction. Doctoral dissertation, The Pennsylvania State University.

Stoker, H. W., Kropp, R. P. & Bashaw, W. L. 1968. *A comparison of scores obtained through normal and visual administrations of the occupational interest inventory* (ED 015837).

Stover, S. E. & Tear, D. G. 1953. *Evaluation of two kinescopes.* Technical Report, SDC-269-7-38. Port Washington, N.Y.: Special Devices Center, Office of Naval Research.

Strang, H. H. 1973. Pictoral and verbal media in self-instruction of procedural skills. *AV Commun. Rev. 21:* 225-232.

Symmes, D. & Eisengart, M. A. 1971. Evoked response correlates of meaningful visual stimuli in children. *Psychophysiology. 8:* 769-770.

Tallmadge, G. K. & Shearer, J. W. 1969. Relationship among learning styles, instructional methods, and the nature of learning experiences. *J. Educ. Psychol. 60:* 222-230.

_____ 1971. Interactive relationships among learner characteristics, types of learning, instructional methods, and subject matter variables. *J. Educ. Psychol. 62:* 31-38.

Tanner, J. & Dwyer, F. 1977. Students' perception of visual testing. *Percept. & Motor Skills. 45:* 744-746.

Ternes, W. & Yuille, J. C. 1972. Words and pictures in an STM task. *J. Exp. Psychol. 96:* 78-86.

Thalberg, S. P. 1964. An experimental investigation of the relative efficiency of the auditory and visual modes of presentation of verbal material. Doctoral dissertation, State University of Iowa.

Thalen, R. A. 1945. Testing by means of film slides with synchronized recorded sound. *Ed. Psychol. Measmt. 5:* 33-48.

Thomas, H. 1965. Visual-fixation responses of infants to stimuli of varying complexity. *Child. Develpm. 36:* 629-638.

Thompson, G. G. & Hunnicutt, C. W. 1944. The effect of

repeated praise or blame on the work achievement of "introverts" and "extroverts". *J. Educ. Psychol. 35:* 257-266.

Thurstone, L. L. 1941. A micro-film projector method for psychological tests. *Psychometrika. 6:* 235-248.

Tiemens, R. K. 1970. Some relationships of camera angle to communicator credibility. *J. Broadcast. 14:* 483-490.

Tobias, S. 1976. Achievement treatment interactions *Rev. Educ. Res. 46:* 61-74.

Torkelson, G. M. 1954. *The comparative effectiveness of a mockup, cutaway and projected charts in teaching nomenclature and function of the 40mm antiaircraft weapon and the Mark 13 type torpedo.* Technical Report, SDC-269-7-100. Port Washington, N.Y.: Special Devices Center, Office of Naval Research.

Tolliver, D. L. 1970. *A study of color in instructional materials and its effects upon learning.* USOE Final Report, Project No. 9E-101, Grant No. 5-9-245101-0061. Washington, D.C.: Bureau of Research.

Torrence, D. R. 1976. The television test of science processes. Doctoral dissertation, The Pennsylvania State University.

Travers, R. M. W. 1964. The transmission of information to human receivers. *AV Commun. Rev. 12:* 373-385.

——— 1967. *Research and theory related to audiovisual information transmission.* Revised Edition, Project No. 3-20-003. U.S. Department of Health, Education, and Welfare, Office of Education.

——— 1969. *A study of the advantages and disadvantages of using simplified visual presentations in instructional materials.* Final Report, Grant No. OEG-1-7-070144-5235. U.S. Department of Health, Education, and Welfare, Office of Education.

——— 1970. *Man's information system.* Scranton: Pa.: Chandler Publishing Company.

Travers, R. M. W. & Jester, R. E. 1964. Reference cited by Travers in Transmission of information to human receivers. *AV Commun. Rev. 12:* 373-385.

Travers, R. M. W., McCormick, M. C., Van Mondfrans, A. P. & Williams, F. E. 1964. *Research and theory related to audiovisual information transmission.* HEW Interim Report, Project No. 3-20-003. Salt Lake City: University of Utah, Bureau of Educational Research.

Travers, R. M. W., Chan, A. & Van Mondfrans, A. P. 1965. The effect of colored embellishments of a visual array on a simultaneously presented audio array. *AV Commun. Rev. 13:* 159-164.

Travers et al., 1966. *Studies related to the design of audiovisual teaching materials.* Final Report, Contract No. 3-20-003, U.S. Department of Health Education and Welfare, Office of Education.

Travers, R. M. W. & Alvarado, V. 1970. The design of pictures for teaching. *AV Commun. Rev. 18:* 47-64.

Treichler, D. G. 1967. Are you missing the boat in training aids? *Film & AV Commun. 1:* 14-16.

Tversky, B. 1969. Pictorial and verbal encoding in a short-term memory task. *Percept. & Psychophysics. 6:* 225-233.

——— 1973. Encoding processes in recognition and recall. *Cognitive Psychol. 5:* 275-287.

Twyford, L. 1951. *Film profiles.* Technical Report, SDC-269-7-23. Port Washington, N.Y.: Special Devices Center, Office of Naval Research.

Twyford, L. C., Church, J. G., McAshan, H. H. & Brown, R. M. 1964. *New media for improvement of science instruction.* The University of the State of New York, The State Education Department, Bureau of Classroom Communications.

Tyler, R. W. 1951. The functions of measurement in improving instruction. In E. F. Lindquist (ed.), *Educational measurement.* Washington, D.C.: American Council on Education. 47-67.

——— 1964. Some persistent questions on the defining of objectives. In C. M. Lindvall (ed.), *Defining edu-*

cational objectives. Pittsburgh: University of Pittsburgh Press, pp. 73-83.

Underwood, B. J. 1963. Stimulus selection in verbal learning. In C. Cofer (ed.), *Verbal behavior and learning: problems and processes.* New York: McGraw-Hill.

——— 1965. False recognition produced by implicit verbal responses. *J. Exp. Psychol. 70:* 122-129.

Unikel, I. & Harris, C. 1970. Experience and preference for complexity in children's choices. *Percept. & Motor Skills. 31:* 757-758.

Van Buskirk, W. L. 1932. An experimental study in vividness in learning and retention. *J. Exp. Psychol. 15:* 563-573.

Van De Riet, H. 1964. Effects of praise and reproof on paired-associated learning in educationally retarded children. *J. Educ. Psychol. 55:* 139-143.

VanderMeer, A. W. 1950a. *Relative Effectiveness of Instruction by Film Exclusively, Films plus Study Guides and Standard Lecture Methods.* Technical Report SDC-269-7-13. Port Washington, N.Y.: Special Devices Center, Office of Naval Research.

——— 1950b. Relative contributions to factual learning of the pictorial and verbal elements of a filmstrip. *Sch. Rev. 58:* 84-89.

——— 1951. *Effects of film-viewing practice on learning from instructional films.* Technical Report, SDC-269-7-20. Port Washington, N.Y.: Special Devices Center, Office of Naval Research.

——— 1952. *Relative effectiveness of color and black and white in instructional films.* Technical Report, SDC-269-7-28. Port Washington, N.Y.: Special Devices Center, Office of Naval Research.

——— 1953. *Training film evaluation: comparison between two films on personal hygiene: TF8-155 and TF8-1665.* Technical Report, SDC-7-50. Port Washington, N.Y.: Special Devices Center, Office of Naval Research.

——— 1954. Color versus black and white in instructional films. *AV Commun. Rev. 2:* 121-134.

VanderMeer, A. W. 1950a. *Relative effectiveness of instruction by film exclusively, films plus study guides and standard lecture methods.* Technical Report SDC-269-7-13. Port Washington, N.Y.: Special Devices Center, Office of Naval Research.

Van Mondfrans, A. P. & Travers, R. M. W. 1964. Learning of redundant material presented through two sensory modalities. *Percept. & Motor Skills. 19:* 743-751.

——— 1965. Paired-associate learning within and across sense modalities and involving simultaneous and sequential presentations. *Amer. Educ. Res. J. 2:* 89-99.

Van Mondfrans, A. P. 1964. An investigation of the interaction between the level of meaningfulness and redundancy in the content of the stimulus material, and the mode of presentation of the stimulus material. Masters thesis, University of Utah.

Vernon, M. D. 1946. Learning from graphical material. *Brit. J. Psychol. 36:* 145-148.

Vernon, P. E. 1969. *Intelligence and cultural environment.* London, Methuen.

Vestal, D. A. 1952. The relative effectiveness in the teaching of high school physics of two photographic techniques utilized by the sound motion picture. Doctoral dissertation, University of Nebraska.

Vincent, W. S., Ash, P. & Greenhill, L. P. 1949. *Relationship of length and fact frequency to effectiveness of instructional motion pictures.* Technical Report, SDC-269-7-7. Port Washington, N.Y.: Special Devices Center, Office of Naval Research.

Vitz, P. C. 1966. Preference for different amounts of visual complexity. *Behavioral Sci. 11:* 105-114.

Vollan, C. J. 1971. Effects of black and white, authentic and contrived color on children's perception of dynamic picture content. Doctoral disseration, University of Washington.

Vris, T. 1955. *A comparison of principles training and specific training using several types of training devices.* Technical Report, SDC-269-7-102. Port Washington, N.Y.: Special Devices Center, Office of Naval Research.

Vuke, G. J. 1962. *Effects of inserted questions in films on developing and understanding of controlled experimentation.* USOE Title VII, Project No. 657. Bloomington: Indiana University.

Wagner, R. W. 1955. The spectatory and the spectacle. *AV Commun. Rev. 3:* 294-300.

Walker, C. M. & Bourne, L. E. 1961. The identification of concepts as a function of amount of relevant and irrelevant information. *Amer. J. Psychol. 74:* 410-417.

Webb, W. B. & Walton, E. J. 1956. Comprehension by reading versus hearing. *J. Appl. Psychol. 40:* 237-240.

Weiss, W. & Margolius, G. 1954. The effect of context stimuli on learning and retention. *J. Exp. Psychol. 48:* 318-322.

Welford, A. T. 1968. *Fundamentals of skills.* London: Methuen.

Wells, R. F., Van Mondfrans, A. P., Postlethwait, S. N. & Butler, D. C. 1973. Effectiveness of three visual media and two study forms in teaching concepts involving time, space and motion. *AV Commun. Rev. 21:* 237-241.

Wendt, P. R. & Butts, G. K. 1962. Audiovisual materials. *Rev. Educ. Res. 32:* 141-155.

Wesley, B. H. & Barrow, L. C. 1959. Comparative teaching effectiveness of radio and television. *AV Commun. Rev. 32:* 289-295.

White, R. T. & Gagné, R. M. 1974. Past and future research on learning hierarchies. *Educ. Psychologist 11:* 19-28.

Wickelgren, W. A. 1965a. Acoustic similarity and retroactive interference in short-term memory. *J. Verb. Learn. & Verb. Behav. 4:* 53-62.

———— 1965b. Short term memory for phonemically similar lists. *Amer. J. Psychol. 78:* 567-574.

Wilkinson, G. L. 1976. Projection variables and performance. *AV Commun. Rev. 24:* 413-436.

Williams, D. C., Paul, J. & Ogilvie, J. C. 1957. Mass media, learning and retention. *Canad. J. Psychol. 11:* 157-163.

Williams, R. C. 1965. On the values of varying TV shots. *J. Broadcast. 9:* 33-43.

———— 1968. Film shots and expressed interest levels. *Speech Monogr. 35:* 166-169.

Williams, T. M. & Derks, P. L. 1963. Mode of presentation and the acquisition of paired associates that differ in pronouncibility and association value. *J. Verb. Learn. & Verb. Behav. 2:* 453-456.

Wise, H. A. 1939. *Motion pictures as an aid to teaching American History.* New Haven, Connecticut: Yale University Press.

Wittich, W. A. & Folkes, J. G. 1946. *Audiovisual paths to learning.* New York: Harper and Brothers.

Wittich, W. A. & Schuller, C. F. 1962. *Audiovisual material, their use and nature.* New York: Harper and Brothers.

Wohlwill, J. F. 1962. From perception to inference: a dimension of cognitive development. *Monogr. Soc. Res. Child Develpm. 27:* 87-107.

———— 1968. Amounts of stimulus exploration and preference as differential function of stimulus complexity. *Percept. & Psychol. Physics. 4:* 307-312.

Wolf, W. & Knemeyer, M. 1970. *A study of eye movement in television viewing.* USOE Final Report, Project No. 5-0427, Grant No. OEG-7-45-0430-234. Columbus: The Ohio State University, The Ohio State University Research Foundation.

Wolf, W. 1971. Perception of visual displays. *Viewpoints.* Bloomington: Indiana University, Bulletin of the School of Education, *47:* 112-140.

Woodworth R. S. & Schlosberg, H. 1954. *Experimental psychology,* New York: Holt, Rinehart & Winston, Inc.

Woodworth, R. S. 1958. *Dynamics of behavior.* New York: Holt, Rinehart & Winston, Inc.

Wyckoff, L. B. 1959. The role of observing responses in discrimination learning. *Psychol. Rev. 59:* 431-442.

Yarbus, A. L. 1967. *Eye movements and vision.* New York: Plenum Press.

Zukerman, J. V. 1949. *Commentary variations: level of verbalization, personal reference, and phase relations in instructional films on perceptual motor tasks.* Technical Report, SDC-269-7-4. Port Washington, N.Y.: Special Devices Center, Office of Naval Research.

Zuckerman, J. V. 1954. Predicting film learning by prelease testing. *AV Commun. Rev. 2:* 49-56.